# THE REAL
# KATE

# THE REAL
# KATE

*A Personal Biography of*

*Katharine Hepburn*

## CHARLOTTE CHANDLER

First published in Great Britain in 2010 by
JR Books, 10 Greenland Street, London NW1 0ND
www.jrbooks.com

*Designed by Jill Putorti*

ISBN 978-1-907532-01-6

1 3 5 7 9 10 8 6 4 2

Printed and bound by MPG Books, Bodmin, Cornwall

# Acknowledgments

## *With special appreciation*

Bob Bender, Ben Carbonetto, George Cukor, David Lean, Joseph Mankiewicz, Christopher Reeve, David Rosenthal, Liz Smith, and Dan Woodruff.

## *With appreciation*

Michael Accordino, Edward Albee, Angela Allen, Linda Ayton, Lucille Ball, Marcella Berger, Charles William Bush, Jack Cardiff, Fred Chase, George Christy, Gypsy da Silva, Mitch Douglas, Patty Doherty, Douglas Fairbanks, Jr., Marie Florio, Jane Fonda, Joan Fontaine, Joe Franklin, Steve Friedeman, Tom Gates, Bob Gazzale, Elliott Gould, Cary Grant, Tracey Guest, Guy Hamilton, Bob Hope, Anthony Hopkins, Peter Johnson, Van Johnson, Garson Kanin, Michael Kanin, Elia Kazan, Alexander Kordonsky, Karen Sharpe Kramer, Ted Landry, Jerome Lawrence, Johanna Li, Groucho Marx, Jackie Mavrovic, Jane Merrow, Walter Mirisch, Bill Molesky, Sheridan Morley, Paul Morrissey, Jeremiah Newton, Arthur Novell, Laurence Olivier, Dale Olson, Marvin Paige, Sidney Poitier, Jill Putorti, Luise Rainer, Ginger Rogers, George Rose, Robert Rosen, Marian Seldes, Daniel Selznick, Jeff Stafford, James Stewart, Kevin Thomas, Brian Ulicky, Billy Wilder, Billy Williams, Emlyn Williams, Tennessee Williams, Will Willoughby, and Robert Wise.

The American Film Institute, the Ben Carbonetto Photo Archives, the Mitch Douglas Archives, the Film Society of Lincoln Center, the Museum of Television and Radio, the New York Public Library for the Performing Arts, and UCLA Department of Theater, Film, and Television.

*To Kate*

# Contents

"Enjoy your success. When you're successful, eat it up. You never know when the famine is coming."

—KATHARINE HEPBURN

# THE REAL
# KATE

# 1

# Onliness

"'Onliness' is my word for what I call my philosophy of life," Katharine Hepburn told me. "It's a word I made up for myself when my teenage brother hanged himself.

"What I meant by it was that I wanted to be independent, to separate myself from all the others and never again to care so much about another person, so I would never feel the pain I felt when Tom left me.

"I was almost fourteen when Tom, my absolute hero—whom I loved and worshipped—had, what I call in my head, his 'accident.' I was the only one who believed it was an accident. I believed it because I couldn't bear to believe otherwise.

"I had a wonderfully warm feeling in my soul. I felt it so deeply that he would be there for me, that I could always count on him. It made me feel very secure. And then, suddenly, he wasn't there for me. He wasn't there for himself.

"If something had made him so unhappy that he no longer wanted to live, why hadn't he shared his trouble with me? I could have helped him. We were so close, how could I *not* have shared his pain? I couldn't bear it. I thought we were like twins, even though he was two years older. It was a nightmare that was real, and I was never going to wake up from it. I understood that now is forever.

"Tom was my best friend from the first moment I can remember. He never regarded me as the little sister he had to drag along. The opposite. At two, two and a half, I remember him holding my hand and showing me the ropes and how to swing on them, how to get along in life. When I was just barely walking, he was running with me. I wanted so to keep up with his long-legged strides. I wanted to run fast into life, not just to walk, and I wanted to run toward life with Tom.

"He had not yet had his sixteenth birthday. For the Easter school vacation, Tom and I were given a trip to visit a dear friend of Mother's who had been at Bryn Mawr with her. After we celebrated Easter with our family, we went to New York to stay with Aunt Mary Towle, who was a lawyer and had her own lovely little house in Greenwich Village. She wasn't really our aunt, but we'd always called her 'Auntie.' Whenever we visited her, it meant seeing many plays, seeing all the wondrous sights of New York City, and eating in lovely restaurants. We would dress up for our excursions.

"It was a darling house, not big. It was just right for Auntie Mary, who never married. She had her lovely room, and I stayed in the guest room. My brother had a cot in her attic, which was filled with trunks of books and everything she stored there. Sometimes girls have privileges, but I wouldn't have minded being in the attic. I'm sure Tom didn't. He was always protecting me, and being chivalrous."

Although Kate loved her visits to New York City, and so did Tom, she couldn't imagine herself living in New York. "Tom said he'd love to be right in New York City, especially in Greenwich Village, which we knew best."

Until then, their mother had always gone with them and stayed. "She enjoyed the visit with Auntie Mary and with Auntie Mary's law partner, Bertha, who had become a judge and was also a good friend of Mother's at Bryn Mawr. Auntie Bertha lived next door. This year, Mother had some other plan, and it was deemed we were old enough to make the short trip from Connecticut to Greenwich Village, where we would be chaperoned by Auntie Mary, who had known us since we were born. We'd been going to visit her at her Greenwich Village townhouse since before Tom and I could remember. We found the Village fascinating, walking around for hours. It was so different from where we lived.

"I don't know which one of us was more excited. It was a tie. I was always the more emotional one, jumping with glee. Tom was more composed, in a masculine, older-brother way. But I could tell how excited he was, because we had an almost telepathic bond between us.

"We went with Auntie Mary to see *A Connecticut Yankee in King Arthur's Court*. My brother was particularly taken by the show, and I enjoyed it, too, with my favorite companion, Tom. If he enjoyed something, I enjoyed it more because of that. I know he felt the same way about doing anything with me. Tom told me he liked our visit so much, he would be sorry to have it end. I knew I would be, too.

"The next day, our Uncle Floyd took us out sightseeing. He was my father's brother, and a bachelor. We had a wonderful time with him, as we always did. Uncle Floyd took the day off whenever we were in New York to show us all the sights and there were so many sights to see. Endless. Our uncle never ran out of places to show.

Tom had brought his banjo with him and that last night in New York, he played for us.

"The next morning, Auntie and I were eating breakfast and expecting Tom to come downstairs to join us. Auntie began putting some food together for a package Tom could take on the train because he was late and would be missing breakfast. Auntie was a lovely cook, and Tom and I enjoyed everything she fixed for us. Auntie took great pride in everything she prepared for us. She was not generally domestic, but she was so anxious that we should have a wonderful time.

"She said I should go upstairs and tell Tom that we were going to be late. Tom had bought our return tickets, and it was getting close to the time we had to be at the train station. Auntie said I'd better go up and wake my brother, or we'd miss our train. I knew he was packed, with his travel outfit neatly laid out for the trip.

"I went up. I knocked on the door. There was no answer. I knocked harder, calling, 'Tom, Tom.' Tom was not a heavy sleeper, and we were accustomed to getting up early. Tom told me that he had been waking up during the nights because what we were doing was so exciting and stimulating. I felt a little anxious.

"At first, I didn't see Tom. And then I saw him. He was there next to the bed.

"He was hanging from a rafter with a piece of material around his neck. His knees were bent and he had strangled.

"I took him down and put him on the bed. He felt very cold. I knew it was too late, but all I could think of was to run downstairs and out of the house to the nearby house where I'd seen a doctor's sign. The doctor wasn't in. It was no use. I ran next door to Auntie Bertha's house and I told her, 'Tom is dead!' She came back with me, and we told Auntie Mary. We called Mother and Father.

"Mother and Father arrived with Mother's close friend Jo Bennett. I felt numb. I don't remember too well what happened. People said I was amazingly calm. I was in shock. I stayed in shock for a long time. It was as if I couldn't feel anything when I cried. It seemed like the thing to do and what everyone expected of me. I found out that I could cry at will, anytime I chose, on less than a minute's notice. My crying on the outside wasn't real. What *was* real was I was crying on the inside. It was a chaotic time until I could make some kind of adjustment to the reality. But I never really did.

"There were police. There were some reporters. They all called it suicide. Such a terrible word.

"They talked about Tom's bent knees. The police said he had hanged himself, but he was too tall. Someone said, 'He would have had to bend his knees to finish the job.'"

Kate said that one night about a year before, her father had told the family at the dinner table about his undergraduate days, when his southern school, Randolph Macon, was playing a northern school. Some of the visiting northern players asked, only semiseriously, if they still lynched black men in the area.

"There happened to be a black man in the area who was known for his very special trick, Father told us. He was famous for being able to constrict the muscles in his neck so that he could fake being hanged. The southern students hired the man to perform his trick in a pretend stunt, a practical joke played on the northern team. The northerners fell for it. Then they were pretty surprised when the joke was on them, and they'd all been fooled."

Kate speculated that Tom remembered the story and was practicing this stunt. "One year later, seeing *A Connecticut Yankee in King Arthur's Court* during our New York visit might have overstimulated Tom's active imagination."

Kate wondered if Tom had experienced difficulty in sleeping, had awakened in the middle of the night in a strange place and in a makeshift sleeping situation, rather than in his own room, and had tried to do the trick. "There wasn't much he could do in the middle of the night without disturbing the household, and Tom was always considerate of everyone. So, it came to me that what he must have been doing was practicing the trick, so he could show our father and surprise him.

"I told Father, and it seemed to him to be a plausible possibility. Even though it meant that Father had played a sad part in it all, by telling the story of the prank, it was easier for him to face that than the alternative—his son a suicide.

"About a year later I overheard my father, in our house, talking with a friend of his, and the other doctor used the phrase 'adolescent insanity.' It was a serious, even grim, conversation. When I walked into the room, they stopped talking. That was unusual, because Father and Mother had always made a point of allowing us children to hear everything. They never stopped talking that way when we appeared. It was so unusual, it gave me pause. I wondered if they could have been talking about Tom.

"One of my most striking memories is of my mother's tears. I only saw my mother cry once in my life. I don't know if she *ever* cried, even when she was alone. Only she knew that. She was a stoic.

"We left New York and went on a boat to New Jersey to a crematorium. Mother was standing off to the side with her friend Jo. Father had his back to her. He was looking forward toward where we were going, not backward toward where we had been. Mother probably couldn't see me from where she was standing. There were wet tears on her cheeks.

"I didn't know what to do. I decided to do nothing. I didn't think she wanted me to know.

"I was sure she did not want Father to know. He didn't feel tears accomplished anything.

"We took the urn of Tom's ashes to the Cedar Hill Cemetery in

Hartford. As far as I know, my parents never went back. I never went there, but one day I'll live there next to Tom.

"My father believed that we had to put Tom's name out of our house and out of our minds and hearts so that his passing would not ruin our lives. He believed it would keep us from living lives of sadness. 'Depression is a contagious disease,' he would say.

"It was so much more terrible because we were not just told not to talk about Tom, but not to *think* about him. It was to be as if he'd never been part of our family.

"It was to be as if he had never lived. And so it was, I suppose, for everyone except me. It could never be like that for me. He had been a part of our family, and for me, he always would be, not just a part of our family, but a part of me.

"My father had said it, and no one, not even my mother, ever questioned my father's absolute authority.

"Because no one spoke Tom's name, I pledged to Tom and to myself that he would live in my heart and mind as long as I lived. I decided I had to live my life for two. It was the only way I could keep my brother alive. I decided I would share my life with my brother. The real date of his death would not be until the day *I* died.

"Tom had been born on November 8. I took that day as my birthday, in his memory. I discarded the day I was born, May 12. I decided that from then on that my birthday would be November 8, and so it's been. I told everyone and always wrote November 8. Some people thought I was lying about my birthday so I could be a few months younger.

"The sign for November 8 is Scorpio. When they heard about my November 8 birthday, people said, 'You're the perfect Scorpio.' Well, of course. Why not? I never said a word. Except I was a fake Scorpio. It was an adopted sign. I wasn't really that strong, but just as well not to tell anyone, and let them think what they wanted to. To tell you the truth, taking Tom's birthday for my own was comforting.

"Everyone in the world, our world, who knew Tom, felt he couldn't possibly have committed suicide. There was no reason. No one knew any reason. I don't know if knowing what happened would have made it easier for any of us. I only knew Tom and I could never do things together again.

"Practicing hanging yourself without killing yourself seemed kind of a silly thing to do, not to mention dangerous, especially if no one was around. But sometimes people do silly things. All of us, at some time or other, do silly things without weighing possible repercussions. I don't know if knowing any reason would have made any of the pain go away."

Kate's story about her brother followed a question George Cukor had asked as we sat in his living room. I was staying in the guest room in his Los Angeles house, and Kate was living in one of the cottages on his property. Kate trusted me because George trusted me, so I seemed part of the house.

"Tell me, my girl," Cukor had asked her, "who was the most important man in your life? Was it your father? Was it Spencer [Tracy]?"

"No and no," Kate had answered without hesitating. "Tom. My brother Tom was the most important man in my life. But he lived an incomplete life.

"I admired him so much. I was younger and a girl, but I was a more natural athlete. I think Tom was more intelligent than I was, but that wasn't what my father valued. He took our intelligence for granted."

Kate had been "going on," as George called it, "rhapsodizing about what a great man her father was." Cukor later commented to me that he never quite agreed with Kate's "obsessive fascination with her difficult-to-please father," who appeared to him to have been "rather a cold fish, a better doctor than a father. Just my opinion."

Cukor believed that Kate had been challenged by her father to succeed and to prove him wrong about her choice of a career as an actress. Cukor said he had rarely, if ever, heard her mention a brother named Tom.

"Tom was not exactly like our father," Kate continued. "He was a tall, handsome boy, intelligent, and a good athlete, but he lacked our father's perfect confidence. He didn't have Father's competitive spirit. I think Father would have liked to compete with every other man in the world. Tom only wanted to compete against himself.

"I was not able to believe he took his own life, deliberately planning it in advance. I can't believe he would have left without saying goodbye to me. Now I think that for my father there was not only sadness, but shame—that his eldest son would show that kind of weakness.

"After Tom was gone, I believe my personality changed. I went from being totally open to life, to being closed to life. You might say ingrown, sort of like a toenail can get when your shoe is too small. I didn't like meeting any new people.

"It was enough for me to have my family, who were used to me, and I was used to them. I remember we had an Irish seamstress who came on Thursdays, and I liked to be with her. She told me interesting stories, and I told her interesting stories. I didn't have much to tell at that point, but she always seemed fascinated. She had a very good disposition. She taught me how to sew on a button so it would never come off. She made me feel partly Irish.

" 'Just keep your head, Kath,' I would say to myself, if I found myself caring too much about anyone. In my head, I always called myself Kath. I didn't want to care for anyone except my family so deeply that I felt such pain. I was able to do that until Spence came along and took my breath away.

"When Tom died, it was so unexpected. Impossible to conceive of. Such a waste. He was gone from my life. He was gone from *his* life. Tom's death was never resolved. Worse, his *life* was never resolved."

"Have you ever thought about it, George," Kate said. "After all these years, it's almost as if you and I have been married."

"What do you mean, *almost*?" Cukor retorted.

Cukor lived in an Art Deco house on Cordell Drive in Los Angeles just outside Beverly Hills. The world-famous interiors were designed by a good friend of Cukor's, William Haines, who had been one of the most famous film actors of his time.

During the silent film era, Haines was a star who ranked almost with Rudolph Valentino. After retiring from films, he continued on in Hollywood as a popular interior decorator, with his initial launching by Joan Crawford and Cukor.

"Billy said to me," Cukor recalled as we sat in his living room, " 'What ideas do you have, George, about how you would like your house to look?'

"That was simple for me. I said, 'I want it to look like a Hollywood director's house.'

"That was all I said. It was all I needed to say. And this is the result." We were sitting in his suede-walled, oval living room, with its parquet floors and copper fireplace.

Kate had been renting a cottage on Cukor's property since Spencer Tracy had died. Before that, for the last five years of his life, mostly she had stayed with Tracy, who was renting the cottage. Whenever she felt like it, at least a few times a day, she used Cukor's kitchen, passing freely through his house. Over the years, she and Cukor had made ten films together, and they were extremely close friends.

Kate left us to go to the kitchen. "Those were Spencer's clothes she's wearing—the shirt, the sweater," Cukor said. "I don't know about the trousers."

Kate returned for something and heard what George was saying.

"The trousers, too," she said. "They're a bit baggy. I've thought of having them taken in, but I never get around to it. I wear them because it makes me feel close to Spence, and I don't like to waste good things, you know. I bought some of these things for him, and I think they suit me."

Kate left again. She returned with the report that she had checked the fridge and didn't find any butter for baking her brownies.

Cukor replied, "I'm sure Margaret [his cook] didn't leave us unbuttered." He turned to me and said, "I'm just a tourist in my own kitchen."

"There's some butter," Kate said, "but it's not in the glass butter dish, and I think it might be salted butter."

"Kate is the most eccentric person I know," Cukor said to me. "And the most eccentric thing about her is she thinks she's regular."

"I don't like to use salted butter in my brownies," she explained. "If I do use it, I have to adjust the proportions. You can always add salt. You can't take it away."

"I'm sure you're safe," Cukor reassured her. "Margaret is very European, and she always buys unsalted butter."

"I thought I might bake some brownies we could have for breakfast tomorrow," Kate said. "If you have some left from yesterday, we could finish them off now."

"We can't finish them off now," Cukor said, "because I've already finished them off. I told you not to leave them here. Now, I'll be wearing those brownies the rest of my life. I think you're in cahoots with my tailor to help him put his children through college."

"I'm really desperate for some chocolate, now," Kate said. "I must have some."

"The Cordell Drive cupboard is bare," George said. "If there were any chocolates, I've hidden them so well from myself, we'll never find them."

"I have some chocolates," I volunteered. "I've just come from Europe, and I have a big box of Teuscher Swiss chocolates I brought for George."

Cukor made a pouting face. "Are you going to open the chocolates you brought for me? This girl here [indicating Kate] can go through a pound of chocolates at a sitting, even if she's standing."

"The box I brought," I said, "is two kilos, over four pounds."

"Dark or light? Creams or nuts?" Cukor inquired.

"Every kind."

"All right," Cukor said in a mock huff. "Bring them on."

I went to the room where I was staying and I took the huge box of chocolates along with a small package in the shape of a Swiss blond paper doll wearing a pretty paper dress over the chocolates back to George and Kate. Kate immediately tore open, and *tore* is the correct word, the paper covering the box. She opened it, took two, and offered them to George. He looked at them and said, "I want to select my own."

"So, which ones do you want?" she asked.

He hesitated a moment, then said, "Those," indicating the two she had selected.

Kate picked up the paper doll package. She held it carefully and turned it around to examine it from all angles. She put it down.

"I never buy fancy boxes," she said. "You have to pay extra, and I'd rather invest my money in more chocolate. This one is adorable, though. Since you've already paid extra for it, are you planning to take the box away with you?" she asked me.

"No. I was just going to leave it for George."

"George doesn't play with dolls," she said, "and I like the flowers she's holding." It was a small bouquet of colored paper flowers. A few years later, when I visited her in New York, I saw the paper doll box in her kitchen. The chocolates were long gone, but the box had been given a full life.

Whitney, Cukor's yellow Labrador, had entered the room, aware of the chocolates, but more interested in Kate. When she rose to leave, he followed her. He had brought his leash with him.

"Whitney likes to walk with her," George told me. "He runs around the property here all day, but he's always ready for a walk with Kate."

Kate left, closely followed by Whitney and his wagging tail. Halfway through the door, she said, "George, do you really think you have enough butter for baking brownies for tomorrow?"

"I'll have to check with my accountant," he answered.


After she had gone, Cukor said to me, "You probably noticed the way she softened and changed when she said Spencer's name. Well, that's nothing compared to the way it was here when they were together. It was often just the three of us. Sometimes Ruth [Gordon] and Garson [Kanin] were here. Sometimes Joe Mankiewicz and Judy Garland, too. It was all very private, Kate giggling like a schoolgirl, simpering, blushing girlishly whenever Spencer just looked at her.

"A great deal of their romance was conducted here. I have a very romantic house. Their relationship was subtle and neither one would have committed any indiscretion or embarrassed anyone.

"But there is no doubt that with Spencer, our girl was a girl, not a woman. He brought out a side, an aspect of Kate that she enjoyed having brought out. That simple.

"She learned to cook the best steak anyone ever made. Steak was Spencer's favorite meal.

"There are some who would lean toward analysis. Kate would not have liked that. It's not my cup of tea. They might have said that she had missed that aspect of her girlhood and was enjoying it late. Or she had enjoyed her teenage years so much, her college days, that she was trying to relive the past. That wasn't so. I know because she told me she wasn't very happy then.

"She was just enjoying herself in a part for which life didn't seem to have cast her, but which she thoroughly enjoyed.

"She was recapturing the present."

# 2

# "Run on Your Toes"

"I was born into a world in which I was totally wanted, loved, treasured," Katharine Hepburn told me. "If you have that feeling, you start life blessed. Dear Stork.

"The most important choices in our lives aren't made by us at all. What counts most is our genes and our environment, especially our early environment—parents, home, all of which sets us within the bounds of our genes.

"I suppose you'd like to hear a bit about my background. Well, you have to hear it because you have to know where I came from and about my parents and my family to know me. I am so much a part of them that my background is really my foreground. My past, even perhaps before I can remember, is with me every day of my life. And that is the way I want it.

"There are people who don't remain close to their families because they say they can choose their friends, but they didn't choose their families.

"Well, if I could have chosen any family in all the world to belong to, I would have chosen mine. There aren't so many people who can say that.

"I've had every advantage. Isn't that ducky?"


"My father's father, Grandfather Hepburn, had a shaking head," Kate told me. "I got that gene, as you'll see from time to time. Or maybe you've already noticed. Don't let a few tremors startle you. I never know when they'll come or go.

"People have talked about my 'Parkinson's.' I've tried denying it because the truth is I don't have Parkinson's. It was something rare that ran in the family, but Grandfather Hepburn had the worst case. We were all used to it and didn't notice. Well, we didn't notice much. I've forgotten the name of it. Well, I don't give a damn what they call it. I call it a damned bother.

"Alfred Augustus Houghton, my mother's father, was left with a daughter when his young wife died. He had three more daughters with his second wife, Caroline Garlinghouse. The oldest one of them was my mother, Kit Houghton. She was a Katharine, too, though always called Kit.

"It was said in our family that Alfred didn't have much ambition because he always came to work late. I thought he might have come late because he had too much ambition and didn't think he could achieve his goal. I think it might be the same thing that Marilyn Monroe suffered from.

"They said he was suffering from depression. Well, I should think so! If he wasn't depressed, he would have *really* had to be crazy. I thought one reason he might have always come late was because he judged himself badly and was making sure everyone else would agree with him, and then he would get fired. I know what that feels like from my first years on the stage.

"He was visiting his rich older brother, Amory, in Corning, New York, when he left the house one day and shot himself in the head.

"Mother said that my grandmother had just found out that she had stomach cancer just after my grandfather committed suicide. I didn't say anything, but I wondered if maybe the doctors had found out and told my grandfather, and he couldn't face that ordeal again, a second young wife dying. My mother was sixteen when her mother died at the age of thirty-four."

Kate's father was born in Virginia, where he spent most of his childhood. His father's family had lost their money and land during the Civil War. His mother's family had been wealthy southerners, and they also had lost their land and money in the Civil War. Tom Hepburn particularly admired his mother and felt closest to her.

"My father was Thomas Norval Hepburn," Kate recounted. "His parents were members of prominent and well-to-do families in the South, both in lineage and money. Dad's mother's family was the more distinguished and by far the richer. Both families were equally poor after the Civil War. His mother's family seemed poorer because they'd had so much more to lose.

"His father, the Reverend Sewell Snowdon Hepburn, was a minister in the Episcopal Church. His father never earned enough to more than barely exist with their five children, of whom my father was the youngest. His parents believed in education and somehow, I can't imagine how, my father went to Randolph Macon College in Virginia. He not only got a bachelor's degree but he went on to graduate as a surgeon from Johns Hopkins University in Baltimore.

"Father was very attached to his mother, and I remember him occasionally mentioning that she was a Powell. He hoped as a boy that some day he would be able to restore her to the lofty heights from which the Civil War had removed her. It was a dream which was replaced by his dream of being a doctor, which was not the right career to choose if one aspired to making a fortune. It could, rather, provide a very comfortable life for his family.

"My maternal grandfather, Alfred Houghton, who was not a successful businessman, felt a sense of competition with his older brother, Amory, a sense of comparison. Uncle Amory had gone into glass in Corning, and he was a brilliant businessman. He was said to have the Midas touch.

"My mother, Katharine Martha Houghton, came from Buffalo, from a family of Houghtons, who originated from around Boston, and her mother and father were both dead by the time she was sixteen years old. Even more terrible, as I said, my grandfather had died by his own hand, taking his life, and they said there was no reason. But obviously there had to be a reason. It's just that it was *his* reason, and only he knew it, and he took it with him. That must have tortured my grandmother more than any reason could have.

"Because of what happened to my brother Tom, I identify. My grandmother found out she had cancer and not long to live. My father always said being happy or not being happy had so much to do with being well or sick, or with getting better if you were sick. My grandmother was desperately worried about her three young daughters who were going to be orphans.

"I wondered sometimes if the story about our grandfather who chose to end his life might have affected Tom. We never spoke of it.

"My mother had two younger sisters, and her mother had called her in before she died and said, 'I want you to get an education so that you will be able to have an independent point of view in life' which she certainly did have. She was a remarkable person with a great understanding of the terrors of people who didn't have enough money to swing it, or for women who were not protected by their family or a husband. She understood how important it is if you're lucky enough to get a start in life, and how hard it is if you don't get one. 'I want you to help your sisters go to college, too, to Bryn Mawr,' my grandmother told my mother.

"My mother graduated from Bryn Mawr in 1899. Can you imagine that? A different century. She studied history and political science. She went on to study chemistry and received her master's degree at Radcliffe in 1900.

"Her sister Edith, through my mother's brilliant plotting and planning as a teenager, was able to go there and graduate in 1901, followed by my mother's youngest sister, Marion, who graduated from Bryn Mawr in 1906.

"In 1904, Mother married my father, Dr. Thomas Hepburn.

"I asked Mother what it was like when Father courted her. She told me he didn't court her, that it was more she who courted him. She said she knew immediately when she met him, introduced by one of her sisters, that he was the one man in the world for her, and that it was she who pursued him."

"The Hartford I love so much exists in my mind," Kate sighed. "The Hartford of today is still a very nice place, but it's not the same place where I discovered life's adventures and fell in love with life. I love most the Hartford of my memories. There are more people and more cars and bigger buildings now. It was much cozier then, and it had so many more trees. I've always had a special love of trees.

"Father selected it as the place for his practice and for his home, where children could grow up with space, so I can't take any credit for where I was born, but if I'd had the choice, I would've chosen

Hartford at that time. It's a place that lives in my imagination more than in reality.

"I was born at 133 Hawthorne Street, in a big house that's gone. It was Victorian with black lace wooden trimming, three peaks, and it was on quite a large piece of property. It had woods on one side, and on the other side, some people we knew very well. They did all sorts of reform work with my parents.

"The family country home was, *is,* in Fenwick. Fenwick is a little sort of peninsula of land beyond Saybrook, and it has my memories stored there. It's home to me. It represents my security."

Katharine Houghton Hepburn was born in Hartford, Connecticut, on May 12, 1907. She was the second child, preceded by Tom two years earlier. After Kate, there were four other children.

"We were like three separate families of children because Dick and Bob followed Tom and me a few years after I was born, and several years later, my two younger sisters, Marion and Peg, were born. I felt more like their doting aunt."

Her father was a successful urologist and her mother an early advocate for family planning and women's rights, particularly women's suffrage. "I heard about birth control before I understood how sex was done, or could imagine why anyone would want to do it," Kate said.

"Father cared deeply about his work and took great pride in it. He and Mother were involved in every reform movement of the time, especially Mother. Family planning at a time when it wasn't mentioned at all. Women's suffrage, which was not yet the thing. All the fight against gonorrhea and syphilis Dad was occupied with, the early social hygiene movement, anything like that. Help the poor, help the blacks, help anyone who needed help and didn't get a square deal. Now a lot more people are interested in that, but in their day, it was rather rare.

"There were a lot of people around who thought these subjects were worse than unfashionable. My brother, Tom, and I were snubbed a lot when we were small children. There were other children who were instructed by their parents, 'Don't play with those Hepburn children because their parents are weird.' We didn't mind because we knew what our parents did was the right thing, helping people who needed help."

It was clear to Dr. Hepburn by the time his son was only four or five years old that bright as Tom was, he showed no special interest in medicine. When Dr. Hepburn took his son to the hospital where he operated, Tom watched his father's face attentively but not what his father was doing, never looking at the open wound. From that, Dr. Hepburn deduced that he might have to look to his little girl to follow in his footsteps.

When he was about five, Tom became ill with a high fever. His illness was diagnosed as rheumatic fever. People called this illness Saint Vitus' dance because of the convulsive movements with which the patient was afflicted. It was also called chorea.

The disease caused Tom to have a facial tic. After he recovered, the tic remained for some time, and Kate remembered other boys making fun of him. Tom did not want to go to school. "Father thought it was character-building for Tom to face the world with his tic, which gradually did fade away."

The illness took many months to totally wear off and, as happens, Tom was weakened by it. "Mother thought a tutor should be employed for Tom, and that I could study with him. I loved studying at home with Tom. Tom being the elder meant our studies were more advanced than what I would have been taught. What I liked most besides being with Tom was that I saved a lot of transportation time, which could be used for the outdoor sports I loved. It made all the difference in my diving."

Dr. Hepburn believed that as soon as Tom was well enough to get out of bed, he should follow an exercise program to facilitate his recovery. He strongly advocated the absolute minimum of bed rest, and believed bed rest had to be paid for later by prolonged incapacity. He also believed that a great deal of everything was "a matter of will." Kate remembered her father telling Tom that a greater effort of will might control the tic.

"Tom was barely six, and I knew he would have done anything in his power to please my father. But he was only a little boy, and he didn't have much power. What Father had in mind was that none of his family, himself included, should ever give in."

Dr. Hepburn thought Tom should have as much as possible of his exercise outdoors. He did not want his eldest child, his son, "lingering" in bed or using an illness as an excuse to avoid exercise, or for that matter, as a reason not to take the ice-cold baths that Dr. Hepburn took and believed were so "invigorating."

Young Tom Hepburn, who was his father's namesake, had a heavy burden to support on his young shoulders. What he knew above all at that early age, just shortly after he had entered school, was that his father was the absolute authority on everything, and that he wanted more than anything to please his father. Dr. Hepburn was interested in education or the lack of it, but he was even more interested in athletics and competitive sports. Tom's favorite playmate and co-conspirator was his little sister, Kathy, as Katharine Hepburn was then known by everyone.

Gradually, Tom recovered, but he was exhausted from his illness, and the slightest exertion called for an effort that would have brought tears to Kathy's eyes, if she hadn't known how her father felt about tears. He would say everyone in their family was too lucky to cry, and Kathy knew, even before she was four, that if she cried, she would lose her father's respect.

Dr. Hepburn had expectations for his firstborn son, going back to before that son was conceived. He wanted to register Tom for medical school even before he was born. He was certain that his wife's first child would be a boy. After that, he planned on having a large family, and he was perfectly happy that there would be several girls as well as boys. The first, however, he willed to be a boy.

"My father thought that being afraid was a weakness and some kind of disgrace. He seemed iron-willed, a person who was not only never afraid, but who scarcely understood what fear was, except intellectually.

"My father just didn't believe in fear. I don't know if he had any. If he did, he never showed it in front of us. Maybe he didn't have any, and that was why he never sympathized with people who had it.

"He didn't understand how they felt, and he believed that they could just get over it if they set their minds to doing so."

Kate said the first time she truly felt fear was that morning she found her brother hanged and realized he was dead.

"I've decided my father was wrong about fear. It isn't bad to feel fear. It can be very useful and save one from a bad situation or if you are already in one, it can make you more aware and even help you, but don't let fear control you.

"And that terrible partner of fear, panic. Panic destroys your rational ability.

"Father was demanding, but we didn't mind because we understood that whatever Father did and whatever he expected from us, it was for our own good, and he knew best. He never expected anything from us that he didn't do himself.

"Oh, those ice-cold baths!" Kate shivered. "One of the most vivid memories of my childhood. It was Father's idea, one of his most important health theories. It was a vital element in our well-being. As children, we all had to take them.

"Personally, I rather liked them. I still do it now, you know. I've always kept it up, cold baths. Even now, years after he died, I'm still doing it. Torture. Pure torture.

"I remember Spence thought it masochistic of me. Far from it. A nice cold bath brings back happy memories, and it's good for getting the adrenaline going.

"I never asked my brothers and sisters if they continued their icy soaks. I thought it too personal because I knew they would have told me the truth, and they might have been embarrassed if they hadn't continued Father's practice. But I did wonder if they did.

"Do you know what made the icy bath seem like a joy? An icy shower. My father preferred those. 'Invigorating,' he used to say. I can hear his voice now. Sometimes, he sang under the shower. He stayed longer than any of us could have, maybe than all of us could have, all put together. Then, Father would come strutting out, naked as the day he was born, and he would stride proudly past us. He saw nudity as nothing to be embarrassed by. I saw enough of my father and my brothers when I was a child to know all about naked men.

"Father did not like complainers or whiners. He would repeat that people who were as lucky as we were had no right to complain.

"When they were very little, I can remember one of my brothers or sisters angling for a little attention by saying they didn't feel well, a slightly exaggerated cold symptom perhaps. Well, that didn't get them anywhere with Father. They learned pretty quickly. All they could get out of Father was a cursory, 'Take an aspirin and go up to your room and rest. Don't stay here and depress the rest of us with your long face.' He would repeat, 'Depression is a contagious disease.' We all learned the lesson quickly. No rewards for whining or complaining.

"Whether Mother felt the same as Father, or whether she chose to be the way he wished her to be, we couldn't bury any tear-stained faces in her petticoats over a skinned knee or two of them. Skinned knees were taken for granted in the Hepburn household. They weren't even a badge of honor, just accepted as going with the territory, for my brothers Dick and Bob, and for my sisters Marion and Peggy, too."

"Something we children had was space and exercise," Kate said. "We had space for us and our imaginations, and we made up our own play, which was pretty physical. I was always running and jumping and looking for a spot outdoors where I could hang by my toes. I enjoyed being upside down. I haven't been upside down for quite a while now.

"Father particularly liked gymnastics, and I wanted to please him, so I became dedicated to gymnastics. I remember being up on the trapeze Father built in our yard. My view was usually from an upside-down position, and I never got dizzy, which was recognized in my family as a wonderful accomplishment. I never fell.

"I saw Father glowing over me, and I was only a little girl, so the thought I had was only a little thought, but I remember it well. Looking back, maybe it was a bigger thought than I understood.

"Father said something like I was a son any father would want. Tom was standing near, and I didn't know if he heard what Father said.

"I hoped my brother never felt slighted when Father praised me for my athletic ability. It may have been because I was a girl, and not so much was expected of me. My brother Tom was quite a good athlete, but I know he had to try much harder than I did.

"I was not allowed ever to say that I *hated* someone. When I was a little girl, I said that once about someone, I don't remember who it was or what it was about. What I do remember was that I was very agitated and emotional about it.

"Father admonished me. He said, 'Kath, you must not use that word.' I didn't usually question my father because I believed he was always right, but I was curious. 'Why?' I asked. I knew he didn't like the person I didn't like. He said, 'It's because your hating the person doesn't affect the other person at all. It only affects you. It's bad for your well-being, and it can make *you* sick. I say it to you because it's you I care about, Kath. Someday you won't even remember who the person was.' He was right. I don't."

"Fear is a striking emotion. Once you experience it intensely, I think it stays with you and you never forget it. A similar experience may give you well-remembered twinges many years later.

"I'll tell you the first twinge-of-fear experience I can remember. It was only a little fear, not like later with Tom, but it was the first time I'd felt that emotion at all. I think I was about three and a half at the time. What I most remember about it was I was more afraid of being afraid than I was of what I was going to do. It was something I wanted to do, but I didn't have any confidence that I could do it.

"The accomplishment was to ride a bicycle. I saw my parents riding their bicycles, and my brother Tom had his bicycle, too. It looked like a lot of fun. It meant freedom, too. I could go much farther than I could just on my feet. I looked forward to exploring on my own, or even better, with Tom.

"My father had the bicycle company build me a special bicycle. They didn't have little bicycles for children in those days. I had to be able to reach the pedals. I was tall for my age, but my legs barely reached them. They were growing all the time but not fast enough.

"How Mother felt about my learning to ride a bicycle at such a tender age, I don't know. Maybe she didn't really understand what Father had in mind. Even with this specially built bicycle, it was still a little big for me, because Father had taken into consideration I'd grow some while I used the bicycle.

"I'd been watching my legs grow, and I stretched a lot. Little did I know that Dad had already gone forward, and I was about to go forward, but not exactly in the way I'd imagined.

"We went to a park where there was a hill, maybe not as big a hill as it is in my memory, and he balanced me on the bicycle and gave me a push. I started rolling down the hill.

"He had a philosophy, you see. He believed people will do what they have to do. So he put me on the bicycle, gave me a push down the hill, and that's how I learned to ride a bicycle. My father was of the sink-or-swim school of learning.

"Way down there in the distance was a man, and he was watching me with great interest, and I was watching him with even greater interest. I was glued to the future, and my future was wherever the bicycle went. The bicycle was riding me right toward that man.

"At the bottom of the hill, he started to run for safety, and I went where the bicycle took me. I couldn't stop it. My father had neglected to explain the small detail of brakes. I ran into the man, and that did the job. I stopped. Just as well. I didn't know how to stop or even slow down.

"I landed on some grass unhurt. It was like being thrown by a horse. You're supposed to get back on the horse that threw you. Well, I couldn't wait to get back on that bicycle. But I couldn't do it by myself, and I had to wait for Father to come running down the hill and pick up my bicycle. I picked myself up. Happily, the man I hit wasn't hurt, either. Startled, I'm sure.

"The next time, I stayed on the bicycle, and I can count on my two hands the number of falls I've had after that. I loved riding the bicycle, even that first ride.

"I got a regular-size one as soon as my legs could reach the pedals. The bicycle offered a wonderful chance to see the world. There was a trolley car on Farmington Avenue and a certain amount of traffic, but it wasn't like today where you'd be dead in a block. I remember when someone told Mother, 'Kit, Kathy is on Farmington Avenue on her bicycle.' Mother said politely, 'Thank you. Thank you very much,' and she hung up. She didn't tell me not to do it, because my parents didn't believe in setting limitations for any of us. I rode all over the city on my bicycle. I don't know how Mother would have felt if she'd known how far I went. A city seen from a bicycle is an entirely different city. So you see, my parents' philosophy worked for us children. They were the right parents for us, and we all couldn't get over how lucky we were, and we've felt that way all our lives.

"Our back lawn was deep, and there was a park nearby. We had a raft on a pond, which wasn't exactly idyllic. What wasn't lovely were the rats by the pond, and that meant rats on the raft. Needless to say, we did our best to let the rats know they couldn't have a free ride, and they didn't get one. I wasn't a squeamish child.

"Mother admired Father's marvelous athletic ability, and she wasn't a bad athlete herself, if she'd been in any other family than ours. She had trouble keeping up, even with us children. I have to give it to her, she tried hard, and she was a big believer in lessons. I was always a big disbeliever in lessons. I thought they might cramp my style. I didn't want to learn anyone else's mistakes. I could invent enough of my own. I don't know if all the lessons did Mother any good. They didn't show much in her performing, I must say, but I think they showed in Mother's confidence, and they did keep her out on the court and on the course. When my younger brothers played with her, tennis or golf especially, I think they occasionally threw a game to make her feel better, but she never knew. I could never have done that. I always had to play to win.

"I could outrun anybody, and I was proud of that. I could out-climb anyone, boy or girl. We had a tree which I used to climb at the ripe old age of about three. I was a whiz at climbing and swinging, and it was quite a tall tree. I used to like to sit up on top of it. People would pass by and get all upset. They would tell Mother, 'Kathy is sitting on the top of the tree.' It made me feel I was on the top of the world. Mother said to people, 'Don't call to her,' or, 'Don't speak to her, because she doesn't realize it's dangerous.' I thought that was a wonderful comment. Isn't that just unique?"

"Everyone called me Kathy because I guess I looked like a Kathy more than like a Katharine or a Kate, or a Katie. I thought of myself as Kathy or Kath. Whenever I talked to myself in my head, it was that way. Even when I wanted everyone to call me Jimmy, to tell the truth, I never really thought of myself as Jimmy. Jimmy was for the others, not for the inner me.

"I didn't tell you, but I had a phase as a child when I wished I was a boy because I thought boys had all the fun. In those days, it seemed clear to me, at about seven, that it was a boy's world. Later, I realized you didn't have to be a boy to have all the fun. No complaints. I certainly had *my* share of fun and everything else.

"For a while in my childhood, I did wish I could be a boy, so I decided I wanted people to call me Jimmy. I just liked the name Jimmy. I told my family I wanted to be called Jimmy.

"I excelled at sports, and I liked to wear boy's clothing. Girl's clothes inhibited an active life in sports. I was never as comfortable in skirts. I wanted to compete with the boys. For the most part, I was better at swimming, diving, golf, tennis, acrobatics, et cetera, but it's harder for a filly to be taken seriously.

"I remember as clearly as if it were yesterday the evening at our dinner table when I announced that I thought it would be more fun to be a boy than a girl. I timed my message for the most dramatic moment. I waited for a pause in the conversation, and that could be quite a wait because we were a family of talkers.

"My moment came. I told my news. Then everyone went on talking as if I hadn't spoken. I assumed they hadn't understood the full significance of my words. I waited for another choice moment. Then, I repeated my announcement. I didn't get any more response than the first time. We weren't a family of listeners.

"I was surprised that my antics didn't attract more attention, and that may be why I became Jimmy.

"To be taken seriously, I realized it was a matter of action rather than of words. So, I cut off my hair. The next day, I appeared wearing some of the discarded clothes my brother had outgrown.

"I made my entrance exactly where my parents were standing. I posed. Then, I said, 'Now I'm Jimmy. Please call me Jimmy from now on.'

"I still didn't attract much attention, which I suppose must have been what I was trying to do. After a few days, as my father was leaving for the hospital, he glanced at me and said, 'That's not a very becoming hairstyle.'

"But I noticed he didn't say, 'That's not a very becoming hairstyle, Kathy.' Small victory.

"I didn't make much of an impression, even when I cut off just about all of my red hair. The most reaction I could get was when I finally asked Mother what she thought of my new hairstyle. She didn't even look, because I guess she'd already seen it. She said, 'It'll grow back.' Jimmy didn't get special attention, so that phase was temporary. My parents were pretty smart people.

"I think my parents were trying a bit of psychology on me. If your dog is about to get into a fight with another dog, sometimes you can stop the whole thing by appearing nonchalant and walking away. Since your dog is probably doing it for your benefit, if you aren't impressed, the other dog isn't of any more interest.

"Jimmy was a part I played. Jimmy the Menace. But Jimmy was not for me. I created Jimmy for the others. Inside I never felt like Jimmy. I was Kath. So Jimmy didn't last long and I put him away.

"There was another reason I wanted to be Jimmy. I never told this to anyone but Spence and his reaction was to laugh. Often, his reaction to me was to laugh. I asked him why he laughed at me. He said it was my Bryn Mawr accent, which made everything I said sound funny.

"When I was young, I would have told you I wasn't vain, and I believed it. What would have been true was, I wasn't *exceptionally* vain."

Young Kate had heard some girls whispering that Kathy Hepburn was "a funny-looking girl." She remembered saying to herself, "I don't care a bit what they think." But she did.

"I thought I wasn't pretty. When I compared myself to other girls—and you know we *all* do that—I didn't look like them. It struck me that I wasn't as pretty as the other girls.

"I told myself that I wasn't interested in boys, going back to before I attended Bryn Mawr. I told everyone else who was willing to listen—I bent a few ears, I'm sure. I wanted everyone to believe that I was *above* the silliness of the other girls whose lives were ring-centered, wedded to wedding. I felt somewhat superior because I wasn't affected by the epidemic of severe silliness.

"I can tell you now the real reason I remained apart from the girlish competition.

"I didn't think I could compete.

"My father had consciously and unconsciously drilled into me the idea that second-best doesn't exist.

"For my older brother, 'the best' was more clearly defined by athletic achievement, easy to measure. You win the race, your team gets the cup or the laurel wreath. Brilliance in school is measured in grades and place in class. You are valedictorian or you are not.

"But in the secret place in my heart, I knew very early what everyone prized most about a girl. Looks. The verdict is in very early.

"No one ever said to my mother about me, 'What a beautiful child you have.'

"I know now it was a reason I wanted to be a boy and preferred to be Jimmy. I preferred to compete as a boy on my athletic ability, rather than as a girl on my beauty.

"When I was in school, I didn't like being with so many girls. I had a few friends I liked who happened to be girls. That was fine. They were special. I didn't like them just because they were girls, but in spite of their being girls. Girls aren't good enough at sports the way I was, and they were usually afraid of getting hurt. They ducked when a ball came toward them so they wouldn't get hit in the face. Not me. I was fearless. I was something of an idiot.

"My father liked something about me from the first. My red hair. It was my mother who told me that. Well, I can't take any credit for it, but I was pleased. It was not the kind of thing my father would have said directly to me. I guess he would have thought it might have gone to my red head, if you'll pardon a bad joke.

"Officially, our family did not believe in or condone vanity, although, as I remember, all of us were somewhat vain, including Mother, and especially Father.

"I liked my red hair, too, even more when I understood it pleased him, which I was always trying to do. But it came with a price, a very delicate skin. I've had trouble with my skin all my life, a ton of freckles, and not just on my face. You should see the rest of me. No, you shouldn't.

"My skin was a special problem because the sports I loved were all played outdoors. And if you could play tennis indoors, that was not for me. I wasn't the parasol type. I couldn't give up tennis and golf. I made the choice to give up my face. At the time, I didn't understand the repercussions of the sun.

"On one occasion when I was very, *very* young, my father addressed me as 'Brick Top.' I'd noticed very early that the color of my hair resembled his. It made me feel I belonged to him even more, and I think it made me feel he belonged to me. I loved it when he called me 'Brick Top,' but he only called me that when I was very young. I spent years hoping he would call me that again. I hoped sometimes he thought of me that way.

"The next man to call me something like that, 'Red,' was Spence, many years later.

"I liked my birthday parties when I was little until I found out I was expected to give things instead of get them. That didn't seem right to me. Since then, I haven't cared about birthday parties. And now, I have another reason.

"I remember we did a play, *Beauty and the Beast*. Naturally, I was the beast. I liked to do plays in a tiny little theater with wooden figures that I could move around. I did plays that I'd make up. I loved making up the plays, so it's funny I never wanted to write plays, even to write a part for myself, or just lines. My desire to write just faded away. Too sedentary I guess.

"We went to public schools at first, and then, when I was about eleven or twelve, I went to a place called Oxford School, which was a private school. Then I was tutored for four years, which was heaven. I played a lot of golf. I was a very good golfer. I liked to play golf with a teacher, who was also very good. I usually won."

\*        \*        \*

On Saturday nights, the Hepburn children were taken to the movies, which at that time were silent with a musical accompaniment, usually an organ, sometimes with an orchestra, or just a solo piano. Sometimes sound effects were included. This was before the great movie palaces of the 1920s and 1930s had been built, so the theaters were vaudeville houses or converted legitimate stages, sometimes churches or storefronts made into makeshift film halls.

Mrs. Hepburn rarely went with them because, as the family knew, she found movies rather a waste of time, "silly." She thought the "flicks" were something temporary that people were certain to tire of quickly. She already had.

Although he didn't praise the movies, Dr. Hepburn almost never missed the Saturday night excursions. He claimed he did it for the children.

Of the three possible theaters in the Hartford area, the Empire, the Majestic, and the Strand, Dr. Hepburn preferred the Empire because there was parking space near it. The Empire was also the cinema that showed the westerns. Though he never said so, it was obvious that Dr. Hepburn liked westerns best, especially those starring the stony-faced William S. Hart.

"Dad would pile us into the car," Kate remembered, "and we were never late. We were as punctual as if we were going to surgery to perform an operation. There was another theater nearby that offered vaudeville performances along with the films, but Dad didn't like vaudeville. He said it bored him."

Kate loved the movies. She couldn't remember which was the first she ever saw, but she remembered that it was a western. Like her father, she particularly liked the westerns and western heroes like Hart, Tom Mix, and Bronco Billy Anderson.

"Growing up in Hartford, I wasn't a very discriminating moviegoer. I loved everything. In those days, I never saw a movie I didn't like. Later, I became more discriminating, I hope.

"Do you know *Manslaughter*? It was a silent film with Leatrice Joy that made a very great impression on me. Maybe there's a print around somewhere you could find. It's wonderful what they're doing now to locate films no one believed existed, and they're finding them in the strangest places.

"We didn't miss sound because we'd never known it. But I'll tell you something strange about the silent films and me. When I remember them, I think I heard them speak. I don't remember them as silent. Isn't that strange? When I think back to some of those wonderful silent films, I remember not only seeing them, but I remember *hearing* them.

"I can distinctly hear some of the lines being spoken in my memory when obviously they must have been titles on the screen. I was susceptible to the power of movies. Of course, I didn't know what they were going to mean in people's lives, not to mention in mine."


"Father often invited his colleagues to our family dinners, and they talked shop as if we weren't there. Since my father's 'shop' was a urologist's office, the subject matter was not what everyone would consider compatible with the delicious meal we would be eating. I remember one evening when Father was talking with a doctor friend about venereal diseases over a perfect roast that had been served with potatoes and peas and carrots.

"There was one story about venereal disease that haunted Father. It happened when he'd just begun his practice as a young doctor in Hartford.

"A man came to him and said that he wanted to have a very thorough examination. He was about to get married to the most wonderful girl in the world, but he couldn't marry her until Dr. Hepburn gave him a clean bill of health. His problem was that he had been 'consorting' with prostitutes, not known, of course, to his future bride.

"It had been his regular pursuit before he met his future wife. Even after he first met her, he confessed he had continued to patronize 'the ladies of the night' because, after all, his betrothed was a virgin, and he was not one to deflower her before their wedding. He said that he had not been with a prostitute for several months, not since he had proposed, and he had never had even the remotest sign of anything that could have been venereal disease. He asked my father to make the most thorough examination possible and to tell him the absolute truth, no matter what.

" 'If you do have it, what will you do?' my father asked his patient. The man answered without hesitation. 'I would immediately break off with my fiancée.' He said he might be too ashamed to confess the truth to the innocent girl, but he would certainly never marry her. He said he would *never* do anything to harm her physical well-being.

"Father was very thorough, and when he next met with his patient, he was relieved and happy to inform him that he was in perfect condition and that he could in good conscience go forward with his wedding.

"The patient was even more relieved and happy. He said, 'I'll never forget you, Dr. Hepburn.' Father said he didn't see him again for a few years when, by chance, he saw the man as each was walking in the street in Hartford. The man passed Dr. Hepburn without speaking. Dr. Hepburn thought he must not have recognized him without his white coat and out of the context of his office. And he knew he'd put on a little weight.

" 'Don't you remember me? I'm Dr. Hepburn.'

" 'I remember you,' the man said.

" 'Tell me,' Dr. Hepburn asked, 'did you marry, and are you happy?'

" 'Yes, I married, the only woman I shall ever love, the beautiful and innocent embodiment of all my dreams. But she's dead.

" 'We married, and I passed on to her my venereal disease. I am here, but she is gone—and I was responsible for her early death.'

"Father was horrified, not only because the woman had died, but it could mean that he had made a misdiagnosis. 'Am I guilty of a terrible error?' Father asked.

" 'No,' the man answered. 'I am.

" 'The last night before the wedding, some of my friends gave me a bachelor party. As my sort of going-away gift, they gave me a prostitute.'

"Mother patiently waited until the end of the story. Then, while the cook offered seconds of the meat, she passed around the peas, carrots, and potatoes.

"It never struck me as strange that venereal disease was tea talk or dinner discussion. My father's interest was not very popular in Hartford at that time. There were people who thought you could catch a venereal disease by talking about it. I didn't have anything else to compare it to. I only knew my home and my family. I never gave it a thought. If I'd been asked how I felt about it, I would've said, 'Isn't that what everyone does?'"

As a little girl, Kate marched in suffragette parades with her mother, but it was before she quite understood for what she was demonstrating. She enjoyed being there with her mother and the other ladies, who all seemed to know why they were there and were obviously passionate about the cause they were espousing.

"My mother was a dedicated feminist and advocate of women's rights. It led to a brick being thrown through the window of our

Hartford house. It was not popular at that time for a woman to be an outspoken advocate for women getting the vote.

"Father never objected to Mother's work. He picked up the brick, put up some cardboard, and we got a new window."

Kate never regarded herself as a feminist in the way her mother was. "I was selfishly pursuing my acting career, but in my later years, women are always telling me I've set an example and am a role model for women who want to be independent and to have the same opportunities as men. I lived my life selfishly, the way I wanted, but I hope my mother would feel that in my way I helped carry on her work.

"One of my earliest, most vivid memories is when we were walking in those parades, what are now called protests, demonstrations. I would be holding my mother's hand. I found it great fun. I was very proud to be 'protesting' with Mother. Often, I was the only child. Sometimes, Tom came with us, and he walked on the other side of Mother.

"Several women who were prominent in the suffragette movement came to our house to dinner. I didn't completely understand what they were saying, but I was excited by their energy and passion for it.

"I remember once when I was deeply engrossed in the sound of their voices, one of the women turned to me and said, in front of everyone, 'What are you thinking about all of this, Kathy?'

"I heard my name, and my cheeks grew warm. Mother, understanding as always, answered the question for me. 'She's thinking little girl thoughts,' she said.

"What I admired so much about my mother was she was always a lady, refined and polite. As we walked in the street, she would say hello to each woman she knew, even though the person had snubbed her the day before. And the next day, she would go about her business, holding my hand or without me, and the same women, I won't say 'ladies,' would snub her, us, and it wouldn't change the way she behaved at all. That was something I admired about my mother."

Her graceful mother was always perfectly attired, and Kate was, too, as they walked along the street. Kate heard the whispers that her mother was an activist for women's rights. Though she didn't quite understand what it meant, she knew it was something noble. The neighbors, however, had interpreted it as her mother's attack on home and family.

"She didn't let what they did change her. That would have been the terrible thing. I made up my mind that I was going to be just like my mother, that I was never going to let people who behaved badly toward me, change me. I don't know if I succeeded as well as my mother. Mostly, I didn't notice rudeness that much probably because I was so self-centered."

When women shunned their mother, the young Hepburns were not hurt. " 'Try not to hear and see bad things which can overwhelm you,' Mother said. 'If you think about it, you have given them the power to go on hurting you.' We understood and were immensely proud of our parents, who we knew were pioneers and rebels.

"The only aspect of it that worried Mother," Kate said, "was her concern that this perception of our family might hurt Father's practice as he was starting to build it." Kate remembered her mother admitting that to one of the suffragette leaders as they were having tea. "I was not asked to leave the table. To tell the truth, at that moment I was more involved with the freshly baked cookies than with the conversation."

"My mother was never a nag. I remember hearing other children's mothers always saying 'Don't.' 'Don't do this.' 'Don't do that.' Their lives were a series of unexamined limitations imposed by others who found it easy to just say 'Don't.' *Don't* wasn't in Mother's vocabulary.

"My mother's gift to us was she either didn't know *how* to nag or she didn't choose to. I believe she didn't choose to. She encouraged us to be open to life.

"We were a noisy bunch, really rowdy sometimes, but we were never told by Mother to make less noise. Our boisterousness was treated as a form of self-expression and a sign of our good health. It was a demonstration of our abundance of energy. The only time we might have a gentle 'hush' was when my father was home, but he wasn't home that much.

"I don't think it's good for children to have an egocentric mother, or an egocentric father, for that matter. But especially they shouldn't have an egocentric mother. The children should have the right to be the egomaniacs, at least for a while. A crying baby doesn't *think* about the others.

"You have to make sacrifices for children. Most of the sacrifices usually have to be made by the mother, who cannot put herself first. I had all the fun of being a mother to my younger brothers and sisters, without having to assume the total responsibility."


"I had an idyllic childhood. There was a clear demarcation between my extended childhood and the abrupt end of it, which happened all in one moment. It was that moment when I found my brother and understood he was dead, that his young life was over and we would never talk with each other again. It was so final.

"Tom's death was the end of my childhood," Kate said. "The death of my brother changed me forever.

"I'd led a rather sequestered life in the bosom of my family, which I feel kept me a child longer than I might have been. So when I came up against tragedy, I aged. I don't know if it showed outside, but it was certainly true inside.

"After what happened to Tom, I joined my parents as an adult in our house. I think they understood that. I felt I was an adult, even if I didn't look like one. I believe I was considered one by my family. To the outside world I was just rather a maladjusted type, but maladjustment didn't bother me.

"The way we lost Tom was so terrible and with a mystery about it that couldn't be explained. The pain of it didn't go away.

"I didn't want to go back to school. I didn't like the school anyway. It was a girls school. Too many girls.

"After the tragedy," Kate said, "I didn't know how I could face all those girls who thought pain was a skinned knee or a boy not asking you out for Saturday night. I knew they would all be asking me about what happened to my brother. I didn't understand it myself.

"The thought of repeating what happened to groups of two or three. Unbearable. Over and over. Then each one would say how sorry she was. It was like reliving Tom's death every time with each girl. They didn't understand. They couldn't be expected to understand. Tragedy hadn't touched their lives.

"I went back for a few weeks. I tried to stay as much by myself as possible. When someone asked me about Tom, I would say I wasn't ready, but would talk about it later. That didn't make me popular, but I wasn't popular anyway. It didn't make me any less popular.

"As soon as school finished in May, I told my parents I didn't want to go back to the school. They agreed that I could have tutors, and that turned out to be much better for me. I went by bicycle to the tutor. The tutoring I liked most was my golf lessons, and that was the subject I did best in."

"Mother talked a lot with me about Bryn Mawr. She could hardly wait to show it to me, so I would see it through her eyes. I guess none of us can ever exactly see anything through anyone else's eyes. She would have this dreamy look on her face when she talked about her college days. Mother, who wasn't an extremely emotional person, or tried not to be—I don't know which—looked as if those days at Bryn Mawr might have been the happiest days of her life."

Discussing her own time at Bryn Mawr, Kate told me, "It seemed to me that the other girls at school were always giggling. I don't know what they were giggling about. I didn't get close enough to find out what was the subject of their giggling. I didn't care. I didn't feel like giggling. I was never a giggler, anyway, but I was grieving and nobody could understand. How could they? I preferred to be alone. I preferred to go and get something in a restaurant, eat alone, and read my book rather than eat with everyone else in the dining hall. I was lucky I had an allowance, so I could go and eat on my own, in keeping with the increasingly antisocial tendencies I was developing.

"How could my mother's happiest days have happened before she had all of us, my brothers, sisters, before she knew my father? I understand better now. Before she went to Bryn Mawr, she'd had the death of her father by suicide, the death of her very young mother from stomach cancer, the responsibility of her two younger sisters and arranging for them to go to Bryn Mawr and fulfill her mother's dream. Then, those years at Bryn Mawr were Mother's, for herself.

"She was so anxious to bestow upon me the gift that was her dream. Then she did it, and it was somewhat wasted on a daughter who didn't love it the way she had. Me. It was more interesting to me that there was a very good golf course nearby. Dumb bunny me. Well, maybe I'm insulting bunnies. I've certainly had more advantages than they.

"My mother was a highbrow. There are those who affect being a highbrow, but Mother was a natural one. I sounded to many people like I was a highbrow, but the truth is I was a lowbrow with highbrow speech.

"Mother never showed any disappointment in my scholastic attainment. Though she never said it, I knew I would make her sad if I wanted to drop out or flunked out, so my goal was I had to graduate. It wasn't a lofty goal, but it was mine. If Mother was disappointed in any aspect of my sojourn at Bryn Mawr, it would have been—and I'm speculating because she never expressed this—that I didn't love Bryn Mawr and my years there the way she had.

"I didn't enjoy school, especially in the beginning. I knew my mother made friendships there that lasted her whole life. She had wanted desperately to go to school there, and she'd fought with her uncle to gain the opportunity for herself, and then for her two younger sisters. She looked back on those years as formative and joyful for her whole life. She'd looked forward to Bryn Mawr, and it didn't let her down for a minute.

"She told me it was more wonderful than she could have imagined. Attitude is so important. If you bring the right attitude with you, you may find what your optimism leads you to. If you have a bad attitude, you are pretty certain to prove your bad attitude correct because you aren't open to life."


Bryn Mawr College is located in Bryn Mawr, Pennsylvania, ten miles northwest of Philadelphia. Founded in 1885, it was the first women's higher education institution to offer graduate degrees. Bryn Mawr means "big hill" in Welsh.

"I spent my first two years of college in rather a throwaway of time," Kate remembered, "and they should have thrown me away. They almost did.

"I was not emotionally ready for Bryn Mawr. I was more tied to my family than I realized, and I wasn't used to the company of so many women. I didn't appreciate what the privilege of going to a wonderful school meant.

"No one owes it to you to make you happy. You owe it to yourself. No one owes it to you to motivate you, certainly not your teachers in school. The motivation has to be in you. The others have their own problems, sometimes much greater problems than you can imagine."


"I was never a girl who considered herself clever about men, because I wasn't," Kate told me. "I know I never considered that I needed to be, because one thing I knew was that I was not desirous of 'catching' one or of having one catch me. To the contrary.

"When I was in college, I was more concerned about not getting 'caught' myself. But I was in little danger. Not only was it not my wish to get married, but I was not threatened by courtship. All of the suitors were looking elsewhere. It wasn't what I *thought* I wanted, but not having the choice did ruffle my vanity a bit. It was only toward the end of my time at school, after I'd found the drama activities, that I began to have suitors. As I became active in theater there, I discovered what I wanted to do with my life.

"I admired my beautiful mother, mostly for her brilliance. I understood that she enjoyed her good looks and that my father appreciated her physically. I told her about my not being the belle of the ball, while at the same time making it perfectly clear that it wasn't what I aspired to. 'You're so lucky, Mother,' I said. 'Father immediately recognized your brilliance.'

" 'Oh, no, dear,' she said. 'It wasn't my mind which attracted your father to me. I think he just put up with it.'

"I was rather shocked, and especially when Mother admitted that *she* was the one who selected *him* and then made it clear to him that he would *not* be rejected. She told me, 'You will find this hard to imagine, but your father was rather shy in the days of our courtship.' It *was* difficult to imagine Father ever being shy, but I knew my mother only told me the truth."

"I admired my mother and worshipped my father. The approval I most wanted was from him. He was pleased by my athleticism when I was a child, although I can't remember him specifically expressing his pleasure. His way of complimenting me was to encourage me to do more, to try harder and do better.

"His way worked well for me. I don't know if it would have worked well with every child.

"My father always stressed the importance of attitude. He believed that attitude was, if not *all*-important, *extremely* important in everything in life, in life itself.

"He told me he had patients who were old, terribly ill, and for whom other doctors held out little hope, but who believed perfectly in him as their doctor and who were looking forward to life. They didn't want to let go of their hold on life, and Father said that helped him to pull them through. When someone came to him who didn't strongly believe in him as their doctor, he was handicapped."

I mentioned an interview I'd done with Dr. Denton Cooley, the famous Texas heart surgeon. He allowed me to watch him operate because he said to understand him, I had to know him doing what he did. "It's a terrible thing for a surgeon to have a patient who doesn't believe in him," he said.

Kate continued: "I'll never forget the time my father took me to surgery with him. I think it was a test to see if I was squeamish. I wasn't. But, oh, was I impressed!

"I was already impressed by Father at home, but there in the hospital he was saving lives, and that was what he did all day long, and night, too. If I could have been impressed by him more than I already was, that would have done it.

"I think he had another reason for taking me to the hospital besides to see if I passed the squeamishness test. He hoped I would want to become a doctor, and not just a doctor, but a surgeon. And you couldn't have a squeamish surgeon. But no matter how cut out I might have been for being a surgeon, if you'll pardon the pun, according to Father, I knew the truth. I didn't have the right attitude. I wanted something else, something he considered vain and foolish—to be an actress.

"For a long time, my father said he had hopes for me because I was a natural caregiver. I couldn't be a doctor because I had no inclination toward it. I couldn't keep my mind on what a doctor did. Imagine having a doctor who got bored while he was doing your operation. My father would have settled for me being a nurse, though it wouldn't have satisfied his dream of my being a great surgeon. But I only wanted to act the part of a doctor or a nurse in a play, and then to go on to the next role."

During her sophomore, junior, and senior years, Kate found the theater on campus and realized she loved being in the plays. "There was a special opportunity," she remembered, "for a girl who could play the male parts and didn't mind. Bryn Mawr was, after all, a girls school, and some of the best parts were for men."


"Mother believed tremendously in education. She wanted a good one, and Bryn Mawr represented the best education she felt a girl could have in her time. For Mother, Bryn Mawr meant independence. And Mother was extremely independent for her day. She believed a woman should be able to have a life outside her home, if she wanted, even if she married and had children. My father and she had six children to whom she was a marvelous mother.

"My parents both came from families that had come to America very early. Mother's family, like Father's, had lost their money, but they made more. They were involved with Corning Glass, and they were rich and well respected. We were the poor relations.

"I didn't think I looked very well when I was at Bryn Mawr, and for me, there was only one logical answer—to look worse. I didn't know if I could successfully achieve looking much better, but I was certain I could be successful at looking worse, and I managed it. One thing about the way I looked, like it or not—and I did, though not everyone did—I was too distinctive to carry a spear. I would be a leading lady, a star, or nothing.

"At Bryn Mawr, the most popular girls were blue-eyed blondes, cute, not too big, curvy. I didn't fit the cookie-cutter type. I was my own type, a wallflower. The other girls there had one major subject of conversation. Boys.

"Some of it was romantic, but mostly it was more pragmatic, getting a husband. All of the girls, it seemed, wanted to get married.

"A number of my classmates left, even during their first year, to elope. I couldn't understand their rush to give up their education.

"Your peers let you know right away where you stand among them. When I arrived on the campus, no one said hello to me. It was only later when I thought about it that I remembered I never said hello to anyone, either. I waited for them. How self-centered I was. Even more, how shy I was. I didn't smile. I frowned. People who know the public me find it difficult to believe how shy I was. But I was very thin-skinned. I needed a shell, and not an eggshell.

I remember late at night, the girls would talk about high romance with a generous dash of sex. It seemed to me all that talk about romance was a way of justifying what they wanted to do. They didn't have the advantage I had of knowing everything about hormones and how the body works. Mother knew it all from her education, work, and studies, and from her own personal experience, sex, babies, and a very active sex life with my father, which we children could regularly hear. Mother was more discreet in bed at night, although she told me she fully enjoyed sex with my father. Everyone in the house knew about how much Father enjoyed it, even when we didn't quite understand what 'it' was, or what was so enjoyable.

"At one point Father was worried about the marital future of his daughters. He felt that the independence he had encouraged might scare men away.

"Father said to me, 'You'll probably live a long life, a very long life, but you can't depend on it. So make every day count. Every day should have real satisfaction and some pleasure, too, but the satisfaction is more enduring.'

"Father looked very serious, and I could tell that what he was saying was important to him, and that meant it was important to me. I stored his words away under my red hair for the day when I would want to remember them.

"One day, Father said, 'You will have to choose well when you choose your career.' I know he hoped I would say I wanted to be a doctor, like him, a specialist in something, and I was flattered that he thought I *could* be a doctor. Even before I knew what I wanted, I knew one of the things I *didn't* want to do was to be a doctor. But I didn't open my mouth and played it smart.

"Father said, 'It's important to choose something that will last you through your life.'

"Mother apparently agreed with Father about acting. At that time, I believed she always agreed with him. If she hadn't, I felt she would have said something to give me some encouragement. Only later, I realized that Mother felt it was her place to always back up Father. She was a suffragette and a forward-thinking, independent woman everywhere but in our home.

"I knew what I wanted to do, and if that was a selfish thing to do, then, that's what I was, selfish. After my long career, I've heard from many strangers that I brought them a lot of pleasure. Well, it isn't like finding the cure for cancer, but I hope it's true, and it makes me feel good. I believe in the importance of people's state of mind. I think it plays a part in health. It was Father's theory.

"I hear Father's voice in my head, a tucked-away memory of my long-ago childhood, speaking words I always remember him saying to me:

" *'Kath, run on your toes!'*

"That was it. That was Father. That was what was important—to always run on your toes."

## 3

# "You Can't Ever Be That Young Again"

During her senior year at Bryn Mawr, Kate applied at a Baltimore theatrical stock company owned by Edwin H. Knopf, a member of the publishing family and later an M-G-M producer. She got a small part in an upcoming production, then more small parts. A stage manager told her she had talent but needed training as an actress. He advised that she apply to Frances Robinson-Duff, an acting teacher he knew in New York.

Over her family's objections, Kate commenced her voice studies with Robinson-Duff. Even though the Hepburn family considered being an actress "about like being a circus performer," her father paid for her studies.

She was in New York only a few weeks when Mr. Knopf, who

was moving to New York, offered her a part in a play, *The Big Pond*. She would also understudy the lead.

When the lead was fired just before the opening tryout night in Great Neck, Long Island, Kate went on in her place. Her performance was said to have begun well, but then deteriorated badly. She was fired. In the audience, however, was director-producer Arthur Hopkins, who liked what he'd seen.

He hired Kate for a role in his new Broadway play *These Days*, which closed after eight performances. She was immediately cast as the understudy to the lead, Hope Williams, in his next Broadway play, *Holiday*, by Philip Barry. The play was a great success and ten years later would be made into a Katharine Hepburn film, but Hope Williams never missed a performance. Shortly after *Holiday* opened, in December 1928, Kate married Ludlow Ogden Smith.

"In my senior year at Bryn Mawr," Kate told me, "I met Luddy. Full name, Ludlow Ogden Smith. He was a best friend of someone I knew who owned the property next door to Bryn Mawr. Luddy was eight years older than I.

"Luddy wasn't really rich-rich, but he wasn't poor. He never *had* to work, though he believed in doing so, and I never heard him mention money. His family lived on the Main Line in Philadelphia."

Smith was born on February 6, 1899. His Quaker family had arrived in America in the late seventeenth century, and they became doctors and lawyers. Smith himself served in France during World War I.

"He learned languages very easily," Kate remembered, "something to do with his musical ability, I think. His ability with languages was amazing. After the war, Luddy, as he was known to all, returned to France to study electrical engineering at the University of Grenoble. He loved airplanes the way I did, and the way so many of the men I cared about did, only his interest was very technical, their design and how they worked.

"Luddy spoke, as far as I could tell, perfect French, and French people responded to it that way. He moved to New York when I was there becoming an actress, I hoped. We'd have dinner with mutual friends, and Luddy would drive me back and forth for weekends at Fenwick. I liked Luddy, and I loved his car, not because it was the greatest car, but because it took me home to my family. My parents thought he was wonderful. Very quickly Luddy began mentioning the idea of our getting married. He said something about it every trip from New York to Connecticut, and every trip on the way back.

"I had the job as an understudy in *Holiday*, and I was thrilled. Grandfather Hepburn was visiting in Hartford, which made it convenient to get married at my home. So, even though I'd rather made up my mind I'd never marry, marrying Luddy was different, and my parents so loved him."

Smith was an amateur photographer, and Kate posed for him at his country cottage, where they were often alone, though nothing "intimate" had happened. "He told me he would like to take some pictures of me, which he often did, but this time, he wondered how I'd feel about posing seminude . . .

" 'Why do things halfway?' I answered boldly. I didn't have to be asked twice. I was very proud of my body and considered myself terribly attractive. My breasts were small, but very good ones. I was accustomed to nudity in our home, not just my father's, but everyone else, too, so taking naked pictures of me seemed great fun. And, after all, photography was an art and he was a very good amateur photographer. It was a perfect reason. Or excuse.

"When I saw the photos, I was thrilled. I was more beautiful without my clothes than with them. It struck me that someday I would be old and not look like that anymore, and it would be fun to look at the pictures and remember . . . But now that I'm old, I don't know where the pictures *are*. They probably don't exist anymore.

I have kind of an idea that Luddy destroyed them before he died. He wouldn't have wanted me to be embarrassed by them. He didn't understand. I wouldn't be embarrassed at all.

"I lost my virginity with the man who was to be my first husband, my only husband. He was my great friend before that occasion, after it, and for as long as he lived, which wasn't as long as it should have been.

"I don't think 'lost' is quite the right word. I gave it quite freely. It was such a big thing to Luddy, that he was the one. It wasn't such a big thing to me. It seemed like it was about time, anyway. Luddy was so surprised, almost overwhelmed.

"It wasn't a matter of great passion. Affection had much more to do with it. I hardly knew what I was doing. Hearing about it wasn't the same as doing it. Luddy knew more than I did. I didn't mind that. I was glad of it.

"It was the very best first experience anyone could ever have. I knew Luddy really loved me. He was in love with me, and he wanted to protect me and help in whatever I wanted. In my case, I was career-driven, and even when it was against his own personal interest, he wanted me to have what I wanted.

"He would have preferred that I marry him and become a real wife and mother. Not to be. Only the marriage was to be.

"I remember my first sexual experience in a fond way. It's not a strong memory, but then, it has been a long time. With Luddy there were no strong individual memories as much as one long memory of him. From the moment I met him until he departed this world, I felt loving gratitude to him.

"Sex with Luddy had been like my mother had explained it to me when she thought it was time I should know, not about the birds and the bees and how they did it, but about how people did it. I already had a good idea in my head, but from the head to the bed is quite a leap.

"What we had that night, he treated as totally preliminary to our marriage. For him, we were almost already married because of our bond and commitment.

"I didn't take the sexual act so big, either before or after. Before, I thought, oh well, what the hell, why not? Let's see what all the big fuss is about.

"It was very nice, and I could see it definitely had promise. After that, Luddy and I were sort of engaged, and then we got married, December 12, 1928, at my family home in Hartford. My grandfather, the minister who was visiting, performed the ceremony.

"My wedding dress was a Barbani of crushed white velvet with antique gold embroidery around the neck, a bit down the front and on the sleeves. It was so pretty," she sighed. She kept the dress all of her life.

"My parents couldn't have been more pleased. They thought Luddy was perfect. They were right. He *was* a perfect husband. It was just that I didn't want a husband. It was hard for poor Luddy to go against that.

"They loved Luddy as a member of the family. At one point, he actually became a blood relation. My sister was having twins, and suddenly she was in the hospital and very sick, and it turned out that it was Luddy who had her blood type, not one of us.

"That's how it was with Luddy. He was always there at the ready with his total support. Poor Luddy, who hated needles. But he gave freely, and my sister and the twins were fine.

"Luddy didn't say anything to the others, I don't think, but he told me he always felt a special connection to those babies.

"Luddy and I never talked about having children ourselves. I assumed that Luddy wanted some, someday, but he didn't express a desire to have children, so I accepted that it wasn't of primary interest to him. I didn't bring it up because I suppose I hadn't totally formulated my own thinking. If he'd said, 'Do you want to have children someday?' I probably would *not* have said, 'Never.' I certainly would have said, 'Not now. I want to have my career first.'

"But I hadn't really thought it out. I certainly wasn't thinking about having children. I was too busy thinking about my career. Of course, it wasn't clear that I *was* going to have a career. I hoped to have a stage career, but Hollywood was beyond my expectations at that moment. I hadn't been to Hollywood yet.

"Luddy understood. He wanted me to be happy, and he understood what acting meant to me.

"We left on December 15, [1928,] on our honeymoon for two weeks. We went on a ship called the *Bermuda, to* Bermuda."

On her return, Kate received a desperate call from Hopkins, who had formed a touring company of *Holiday*. He needed a replacement for the lead actress, who couldn't perform. "So I finally got to play Linda Seton onstage," she said. "Once."

In late 1929, Kate had a small role in the touring company of *Death Takes a Holiday*. Her next Broadway appearance, in 1930, was as an understudy to one of the supporting roles in Turgenev's *A Month in the Country* and that same year the lead in the short-lived *Art and Mrs. Bottle*, produced by Kenneth MacGowan. He was the former Baltimore stage manager who had advised her to go to New York.

Until 1932, Kate acted in summer stock and with touring companies. Then, she was cast in a supporting role in *The Warrior's Husband* by Julian Thompson on Broadway. One of the New York critics singled out her performance for praise.

In the audience was an ambitious young agent named Leland Hayward. He was so impressed with what he saw that he arranged a screen test for her at RKO in Hollywood. The studio was casting for a girl like her in an upcoming film with John Barrymore.

"After Luddy and I were married, we did what people who get married do, if they can afford it, and we could. We looked for a house. The obvious place seemed to be the Main Line in Philadelphia. I meant to be a good wife, or as good a wife as I could manage to be.

"We saw some lovely houses, but the life that went with them wasn't what I had in mind. Luddy's mother ordered calling cards for me, so I could arrange to drop in on other young matrons. It all sounded too boring to me.

"Dear Luddy understood me. We moved to New York City, where he had an apartment. He said we should find a house in New York City. Eventually, it was Luddy who spotted the house that was to become my home for the rest of my life. It was located in the area known as Turtle Bay. Luddy rented it, and several years later, after we were divorced, I bought it. By then, I knew, and Luddy had accepted, that I was right in saying that I wasn't meant for marriage.

"Even when I wasn't in the theater, I was thinking about it. Luddy was thinking about when I would be returning to him. I wasn't thinking all that much about him, being the self-centered thing I was.

"A background person who is a perfect confidant, who cares about you, and who has sense, is one of the most important assets a girl can have.

"He's not just a shoulder to lean on, but a whole person to lean on.

"I married mine, my shoulder to lean on. Our marriage didn't last, partly because I went off to California for my career. After about six years, we divorced, a Mexican divorce I obtained. But the friendship we had survived the marriage. Not a conventional marriage.

"I persuaded him to change his name to S. Ogden Ludlow because I didn't want to marry him and become Kate Smith. There already was a Kate Smith, who sang. She was stout and I was thin, but I said I didn't want any confusion. He did that for me. Then, I rarely used his name. I began my life as Katharine Hepburn and my career as Katharine Hepburn, and it stayed that way. I felt my name suited me. Luddy knew me as Kathy.

"When I married him, I wasn't certain about what I was doing, although I couldn't imagine that I would ever *like* anyone more than I liked him. I could imagine the possibility that I would love someone more or feel greater passion, but liking is very important.

"After we were divorced, I felt strange. In a way, I never really divorced him. It's so wonderful to have a person in your corner. He always felt I was right—even when I was wrong. I loved that. You have enough people in your life telling you what you're doing wrong."

In September 1934, after Kate and Luddy were divorced, a little more than two months later, he remarried.

"I had encouraged him not to wait. Why should he? He deserved a real marriage, a family, whatever he wanted. He deserved the best wife, and I wasn't the best wife.

"I was only happy for him. But, well, it did feel a little strange, the idea of Luddy being married to someone else. We'd talked about always being friends and how nothing could ever change that, but I knew his having a wife who wasn't me immediately changed that. For me, if not for him. I could have told Luddy anything. I didn't, but it was nice to know I could have. He would never have breached a confidence of mine. But with a wife, he might tell.

"After I married him, I learned more about myself. There were no surprises with Luddy. I knew him as well as I thought I did. I believed the best kind of marriage was one without surprises. Of course, that kind of marriage isn't full of excitement. Later, Spence was full of surprises. I didn't know myself as well as I thought I did. With Spence, I was always full of surprises, even for myself.

"I knew I'd never have a better husband. I was also certain I'd never have another husband.

"I felt my parents married Luddy, so it was terrible when I divorced him, because in a way I forced them to divorce Luddy. When I had told them I was going to marry Luddy, I felt my parents were finally proud of me for bringing such a perfect person into our family.

"They went on liking him, even after our divorce, after he had married someone else, but it couldn't be the same.

"I'd tried being married when I was very young with a dear, dear friend. That's the way it should be. I was a disaster as a wife. I didn't make a good try. I didn't even make a bad try. I was selfish and always put my career first. I was so selfish, I didn't even know I was being selfish. The marriage didn't survive, but the friendship truly survived, and that was what was so important.

"I've wondered if Luddy would have meant everything to me in those days when he did if my brother Tom had lived. Tom left a space in my life which needed filling. It was a bigger space than I realized.

"When we met, we were naive kids. Luddy loved Kathy. I became Katharine Hepburn, but for him, I was always Kathy. You can't ever be that young again."

# 4

# Flying Highest

"Money isn't everything, but it's a good bit," Kate told me. "It's lovely knowing you aren't going to starve.

"When I went to Hollywood, I felt very free. I wanted to succeed, but I knew if I didn't, I could always go back home. My family would scarcely know the difference, but *I* would have known the difference.

"It was my friend Laura Harding who delivered Leland Hayward to me. He was a part of her young, wealthy world, and he was there at Laura's coming-out party, one of five hundred at New York's Plaza Hotel. He dropped out of Princeton to go to Hollywood and become an agent. What a gift he was! I owe my career to dear Leland. We were to have a professional relationship that changed both our lives, and a personal one, an affair, the memory of which remained precious to both of us throughout our lives."

On July 3, 1932, Kate left for Hollywood on the *20th Century Limited*. Luddy saw her off at Croton-Harmon, thirty miles north of New York City. Kate would be traveling with Laura Harding, her closest friend, who was supposed to have boarded the train at Grand Central Terminal.

It was only after Kate was on the train, having boarded quickly, that she realized she'd forgotten to wave to him. "I'd rushed on the train and never looked back to wave to Luddy. I went to a window, and I saw him waving at the train, hoping he was waving to me. The part of the train where I was had already passed, so he never saw me wave back.

"Worse, I had the thought, what if Laura missed the train? What a time to think of that! I'd have to ride all the way to California alone. That didn't appeal at all to me.

"I should have gone to Grand Central Station so we could have boarded together. It hadn't occurred to me that anything could go wrong until it was too late to do anything about it. And if a photographer got a picture of me, so what? Isn't that what my going to Hollywood was all about, pictures? I'd never known Laura to be late or miss a train or anything, but it could happen.

"I suppose that's the way I've lived my life, depending on the good fortune that makes things go right, taking a lot of luck for granted, as just the way life was.

"I ran through the train, and there was the corridor, full of Vuitton luggage. I knew I'd found our drawing room and Laura."

Kate, who always loved fresh air, liked to go out on the observation platform of the train. That was what she was doing when suddenly she felt something sharp enter her eye. She hoped it would go as it had come, but it did not. "It stayed put," Kate remembered, and she realized she would need help when she reached Los Angeles.

"I've had this wonderful constitution all my life, and I've taken it for granted. Happy me. That was the best part of it all, taking it for granted.

"I hadn't thought then about how you have to be lucky every minute or, anyway, not unlucky.

"I tried rubbing my eye, opening it wide. Whatever I did seemed to make it worse. And my eye kept hurting more. I tried not to say anything about it to Laura, because I didn't want to upset her, especially since there was nothing she could do about it.

"If I complained out loud, I would be doing what my father considered being a 'whiner,' and the worst part of it would be, as I listened to myself complaining out loud, it would be reinforcing the pain for me. I hoped what had happened to my eye wouldn't interfere with my meetings in Hollywood.

"I tried to concentrate on my beautiful dress and accessories that I had purchased in New York City for the first impression I would make when I got off the train, but I felt that all they would see was my eye. It felt very big, as well as very sore.

"When I closed my eyes at night, it didn't help much. It still hurt. It seemed I didn't sleep at all, but I suppose I did. It certainly wasn't restful sleep.

"When we arrived in Pasadena, Leland Hayward was waiting for us with Myron Selznick, whom I hadn't met before. They were going to represent me. Myron Selznick was the brother of David 'O'Selznick,' but he didn't have the O. Later, it was explained to me the O wasn't part of their last name, but simply an initial David had chosen to add to his name. Well, why not? I'd chosen to be called Jimmy for a while, so I wasn't going to throw any stones.

"I was informed that we wouldn't be going first to my hotel and that only my baggage had that luxury. I was to be rushed immediately to RKO to meet George Cukor and David Selznick. They were waiting, and I gathered from Leland's tone that these were two men who weren't used to being kept waiting. I tried to tell Leland and Myron about my eye, but no one was listening.

"I took a screen test with my eye like that, and the only one who commiserated with me was John Barrymore. I would be working with him in my first film, *Bill of Divorcement*. What a wonderful actor and man! It was very exciting for me. He noticed my eye, and he spoke with me, considerately, away from any of the others. He said he often had problems with his eyes, and he offered me some of his eyedrops. I thanked him, but I told him I had something in my eye, and I knew it had to come out before I could feel better.

"Laura and I went out into the street and there was a man standing there. I asked him if he knew an eye doctor. He said he was a doctor, but not an eye doctor. He offered to take us to his office and see if he could help.

"In his office, when he looked at my eye, he said it wasn't something he was able to do, but he knew an eye doctor. He called her, and she waited for us. He drove us to her office.

"While she was doing what had to be done, I wasn't exactly in physical pain, although I had some unpleasant sensation of what was happening. I was pretending I wasn't a coward, that I was brave. I was petrified, but I remembered what my father had told me about the patient's fear getting in the way of the doctor's work. I certainly didn't want to get in the way. My father, who never seemed an overly emotional person, had said he would have preferred to work on marble statues. I set my mind to being a marble statue. After all, wasn't I an actress? Well, I wasn't *that* good an actress. I had painkillers, but I was all too awake and aware. I wondered why she hadn't sedated me completely, but I guess it enabled her to work more effectively on my eye.

"I didn't ask questions. I figured she knew what she was doing.

"She looked deep in concentration, but not too tense and worried, so I figured it must not seem as bad to her as it did to me. Well, we each had a different point of view. Bad pun.

"Worse than her digging about was the sound when she hit the metal pieces in my eye. There was that horrible word she used when she examined the metal in my eye, 'embedded.' I could hear the sound of her surgical implement hitting the metal. Uggh!"

Kate was shocked to learn that not one but three separate pieces of metal were embedded, which meant it would require three separate procedures, each to remove one piece of metal. She was advised that all of it should be removed at once, before it did irreparable damage to her eye. The word "irreparable" really alarmed her too.

The sound of the tapping on the metal inside her eye went on interminably, it seemed. It was the most horrible sound she had ever heard in her life. Near her ear, it was going on inside her in the most delicate part of her eye.

"When the first piece of metal was extracted," Kate said, "it was painful, but the worst agony was knowing the whole procedure had to happen twice more, and this time, both times, I knew what I was in for.

"When it was finished, I looked at the doctor's face. It's a good thing she hadn't looked that way when we started. She looked like she was going to pass out. I almost fainted myself—when it was over.

"She was saying something about how it was going to hurt when the painkiller wore off. Well, I knew that because the painkiller had been wearing off throughout the whole procedure.

"All I knew was I wanted to get out of there. I paid in cash. She said, 'Oh, you don't have to do that.' But I did. I had to close that door behind me, and leave that experience behind. I was able to, because the doctor had done a perfect job, as you can see, and more important, as *I* can see. My eye healed, and I never had any problem. But I didn't exactly totally forget the experience.

"I'd been thinking about how my career could have been ruined. I was worried about my career. I hadn't thought about how my *life* could have been ruined. I didn't have a very good brain.

"The kind doctor I'd met in the street, who had driven Laura and me, was still there waiting with Laura. He drove us to our hotel and left us there. Isn't it terrible? I don't remember his name. He and the lady eye doctor saved my career, and maybe my eye, and I've forgotten their names.

"When we got back to our hotel, we each had a chicken salad sandwich. Can you imagine? I remember that those sandwiches were chicken salad but I don't remember the doctors' names."

Leland Hayward was the son of U.S. Attorney Colonel William Hayward. He was a popular escort and date for all the young debutantes coming out in the New York City area. He followed his dream to go to Hollywood and become an agent and producer. He was five years older than Kate. His hobby was flying, preferably in an open cockpit.

Through their mutual friend Laura Harding's introduction, Hayward agreed to represent Kate. He had arranged to work with Myron Selznick, who had been working in London and who would bring Vivien Leigh to his older brother for *Gone With the Wind*.

*Bill of Divorcement* was Kate's first film, and it auspiciously launched her Hollywood career. She appeared with John Barrymore, who was near the end of his acting career. It was the beginning of her friendship, professional and personal, with director George Cukor. Kate, as it turned out, was of great importance in the early career of Leland Hayward.

As their professional relationship and their personal relationship grew, "Leland and I had a lovely affair," Kate said. "With Leland, there was nothing wrong, no obstacles to overcome. We were both free. We had a lovely time together. I hoped it would go on and on, just as it was. Nothing more. Leland was the most brilliant agent, especially for me because he had his heart so much in championing my career. I owe him a great deal.

"He said he wanted to make our relationship permanent, but I didn't know what to do about that. How could you say you would always feel the same way? I knew I didn't want to marry. I had decided that, and I had tried it, marriage to a wonderful man. But I didn't want to be a wife. I was married to my career.

"I heard scuttlebutt, whatever *that* is, that Leland was struck by the talent of actress Margaret Sullavan. Very struck. He married her.

"I was surprised. Very surprised. The word is really shocked. I'd thought it was just gossip about Margaret Sullavan. I'd said no to Leland several times. I suppose I was shocked that he had believed me. I'd spoken in a tone of certainty greater than anything I felt. I wondered if Leland was more in the mood to get married than he was in the mood to get married to me?

"I suppose my pride was hurt.

"Life is choices. I had made mine. He had made his. Mother asked me why I was so upset when I had told her that I wasn't considering saying yes to Leland.

"I didn't really have a good answer for her why I was so upset.

"We were 'perfectly' suited. I got up early. He got up late. He loved restaurants. I preferred to eat at home. We could be together without getting in each other's way. He went to sleep as I was getting up. I liked to eat a very early dinner, and he liked to eat a very late dinner. We didn't have to compromise at all. Compromise is very bad for relationships, especially love relationships. Nobody gets what he or she wants. Dinner at nine. I would have starved to death waiting and then eaten so much I couldn't go to sleep or had bad dreams. Meanwhile, Leland would have wondered what to do with the best part of the day, which for him was the last hours of the night going into the first hours of the morning. Neither one of us would have had what we wanted, and we would have resented it, and, at the same time, felt guilty because we were exacting a price from the other.

"So, I ate dinner at six, and he had drinks. Then, as I was preparing to go to bed, he left for a night of the high life. He was back before I woke up—except occasionally.

"I considered Leland one of the easiest-going people I ever met. That may have been because I didn't have expectations. He asked me to marry him several times. I don't mean he wanted me to marry him several times, I mean he asked me several times. I was definitely more in love with my career than with Leland.

"Back in Connecticut, I was going about Fenwick glum and sulking, and Mother said, 'You didn't say yes. You didn't want to marry him, so you have no cause to feel as you do, and I hope you've sent Leland a telegram or letter congratulating him and wishing him happiness. And that you meant it.' I knew she was right but still . . ."

Much later, Laura Harding heard that there had been gossip and innuendoes about her close friendship with Katharine Hepburn. There were those who whispered that Kate and Laura were more than just friends, that they were *too* close, that they were lovers.

When Kate heard the rumors, long before her friend did, she just laughed. Laura, however, was deeply troubled.

"Dear Laura was a great friend of mine. We were just girls when we met through mutual friends. She was a friend any girl would be lucky to have. She had it all herself—intelligence, looks, a wonderful personality, great riches. She lived at 955 Fifth Avenue in a six-story townhouse. When she came out at her debutante party for five hundred at the Plaza Hotel, her jewelry was pre-Confederate that had been passed on through her family. Her great-grandfather was Jay Cooke, the banker.

"But she was always looking out for me and encouraging me. She was generous with everything she had, and we shared our early lives. Those people who share your early life—memories, confidences, and secrets—they are irreplaceable.

"Laura also wanted to be an actress. She was very talented, and I'm sure she could have made it if she'd had more drive. She had so many interests, so Laura wasn't as dedicated as I was. I definitely was a simpler girl, more focused.

"Laura was *very* rich, and she showed me her world. It was fun.

"She had no reason to work for money, because she already had all the money in the world. She didn't stay with being an actress. I knew a lot of rich people, but Laura knew how to spend the money and how to live. I think there was another reason she didn't stick with acting. She wasn't accustomed to rejection. She couldn't understand it, and she couldn't accept it. She didn't see why she should.

"Even the most lauded actress has to accept a lot of rejection, not getting parts, bad reviews, shows that close, even getting fired, being at the mercy of others, that horrible waiting by the phone, and then, how short an actress's career can be. Laura tried for a while, watched my burgeoning career, and decided it wasn't a life she wanted—at least not enough.

"Even if you're born with a silver spoon in your mouth, as I was, or a jeweled platinum spoon like my friend Laura, when you become an actress, you're just a waif with a tin cup.

"I couldn't have made up a better best friend to have than Laura. She had a lot of backbone. So did I. But two backbones are better than one. And sometimes mine got tired.

"I'm pretty sure I would have gone to Hollywood even if Laura hadn't gone with me, but I'm not sure I would have stuck it out as long in the beginning, and had the career I did. Laura made me feel happier and more confident.

"She was an objective observer of my life in Hollywood and elsewhere, and that gave her a different perspective on what I was experiencing than my own. When you are involved in your own life, its ups and downs, and your own emotions are at play, you need someone standing back and watching who isn't so involved in your life as you are, who can explain your life to you."

Leland Hayward had only recently achieved his own celebrity status as "a gentleman agent" in Hollywood. Everyone noticed his Cartier silver propeller tie clasp, a discreet, but fine-quality sapphire in the center, the symbol of how much he loved to pilot his own airplane. People were amazed that he never lost the clasp, but actually he'd had a few dozen made. From the distance, you could see him coming in his yellow Rolls-Royce, and it was in that car that he delivered his new movie star, Kate, who had never made a film.

Cukor took charge of the Hepburn makeover, her haircut and her light pancake makeup to give the illusion of pale porcelain to her freckled complexion. Even Cukor was surprised when he saw her onscreen and noted "how she came alive for the camera."

He was even more surprised when he learned that Hayward had negotiated a salary for her of $1,500 a week, the same salary he was receiving. He decided Hayward was "a wizard with some special potion." John Barrymore had the great salary of $125,000 for the film.

As they worked together, Cukor knew that he and his young star had a bond that he felt would last throughout their lives, and that nothing would put it asunder. He wasn't quite correct, but he was right for decades.

## *A Bill of Divorcement (1932)*

Hilary Fairfield (John Barrymore), a shell-shock victim of the Great War, escapes from the asylum in which he has been confined for fifteen years. Although he believes himself cured, his disoriented behavior indicates otherwise.

Returning to his home, he finds his wife, Margaret (Billie Burke), has not only divorced him, but plans to marry another man. At first, Fairfield mistakes his grown daughter, Sydney (Katharine Hepburn), for his wife when she was young. He is shocked to realize how much time has passed since he was hospitalized.

Sydney is engaged to marry Kit Humphreys (David Manners), but meeting her father for the first time causes her to hesitate. Fairfield's behavior is erratic and unpredictable, indicating that he is not cured and may have to return to the asylum. She considers the possibility that insanity may run in her family and that she should not marry and have children.

During his lucid moments Fairfield sees that he is bringing nothing but unhappiness to his wife, who truly loves the new man in her life. He releases her to marry Gary Meredith (Paul Cavanagh). He cannot, however, release Sydney from the responsibility she has come to feel toward him. Not wishing to risk marriage nor wanting to send Fairfield back to the asylum, she breaks her engagement and commits herself to a life of caring for her father.

In *A Bill of Divorcement*, Cukor gave Laura Harding, who usually accompanied Kate, a part as an extra in the party scene. Harding said she could wear her own dress. "Chanel," Kate informed the director.

*A Bill of Divorcement* opened at Radio City Music Hall, and everyone involved enjoyed a great success. The reviews were laudatory for young Katharine Hepburn, who hadn't had that kind of immediate success on the stage. She loved California, "the smell of orange blossoms and the instant gratification of immediate success," but even so, she knew she could never stay there too long, away from her Connecticut home and her much-loved parents.

John Barrymore was the major star, and Billie Burke was a star, but Kate's role as the daughter was key. George Cukor remembered John Barrymore's words: "Our Miss Hepburn is a star and has stolen the picture."

When *Christopher Strong* was released in 1933, aviation was front-page news. Amelia Earhart had become an international star. "I would love to have played her in a film," Kate said. The physical resemblance between Kate and Earhart was striking.

"If I hadn't been an actress, I can't imagine what I would have been. Well, yes, I can. I would have liked being an aviator, like Amelia Earhart. But that isn't a career to last as long as mine did, especially if you have some bad luck, as she did. In that field, you don't get to have bad luck many times.

"Several of the men I was attracted to could fly a plane and were aviation enthusiasts. Leland, and Howard [Hughes] were dedicated fliers, and Luddy could have *built* a plane. Leland helped me 'fly my career.' Howard wore a little airplane on his jacket. He liked flying better than anything else in life. Howard's name was a synonym for flying. Obviously I was always attracted by flying and fliers."

# Christopher Strong (1933)

Lady Cynthia Darrington (Katharine Hepburn), a young aviatrix, meets Sir Christopher Strong (Colin Clive), a respected politician, at a social event in London, and they are instantly attracted to each other. In spite of Strong being married with a grown daughter and devoted to his career, and Cynthia being vehemently against any relationship that might hinder her ambitious career in the air, they become hopelessly involved. Neither has had an affair before, and they suffer pangs of guilt.

Finally, Strong can no longer endure his double life, and he accepts a temporary government appointment in New York, more to save his marriage than to advance his political career. Cynthia resigns herself to breaking off the affair because it has had an adverse effect on her aviation career. She passionately wishes to concentrate all her energies on flying.

They meet again in New York, and nothing has changed. Absence has only intensified their love for each other. They resume their affair, and Cynthia finds herself pregnant.

She accepts an opportunity to break the high-altitude record, saying goodbye to Strong as if for the last time. In the air, as she breaks the record, she takes off her oxygen mask. She loses consciousness, and the plane crashes.

The director, Dorothy Arzner, was one of the few women directors to work in Hollywood during the sound era. Before that time, during the silents, there had been several women directors.

While critics dismissed the picture, they noticed Katharine Hepburn, and already the studio was selling her as a star in what was only her second film.

In 1932, Douglas Fairbanks, Jr., received an offer to costar with "a new find" named Katharine Hepburn. She had achieved a modest success in supporting roles on Broadway. and she was about to be seen opposite John Barrymore in the film version of Clemence Dane's play *A Bill of Divorcement.*

"They showed me some photos of her, saying she had very unconventional looks," Fairbanks told me. "They said it rather apologetically, because she certainly didn't look like everyone else, or even *anyone* else. I thought she was beautiful. I hoped it wouldn't just be an example of those touched-up pictures the studio specialized in. I hoped she would look just like those pictures when I met her. Well, she didn't look *just* like them. She was even more beautiful.

"She was extremely attractive, not only in appearance, but in voice, diction, carriage, poise. When we met, she wasn't nervous at all. I was. I envied her self-confidence.

"The moment I met Kate, I fell madly in love with her. In those days, I fell madly in love rather easily. I found her adorable, and I adored her.

"There were some people who said she wasn't beautiful. Well, they needed vision tests and new glasses.

"In 1933, I worked with her on *Morning Glory*. Adolphe Menjou and I were with her in the film, and we were asked to help her out as much as we could. *She* won the Oscar.

"We were having a small affair, Kate and I. I call it small only in retrospect.

"At the time, it seemed very big to me. I was thrilled. It wasn't just sex, but I admired her intelligence, her sense of humor, and the way her mind worked. I liked the way she looked, too. Very natural beauty. And she was a wonderful athlete. I was quite athletic. We could swim together and play tennis.

"I hoped that our special friendship meant as much to her as it did to me, and that she was enjoying it as much as I was. I was given to what might have been considered an excess of verbal exuberance. Kate was restrained in speaking about our mutual affection, although she talked a great deal about everything else. She called me 'Dear,' and that was about it. But I could tell she liked me very much.

"One night, she suggested we go out to dinner a little earlier than usual. That was certainly fine with me. I was looking forward to after-dinner with Kate, even more than to dinner.

"She didn't eat very much, so then, neither did I. I hoped that her reason for eating lightly was the same as mine. At the end of dinner, she said she wasn't feeling well and thought she had a cold coming on. That was remarkable. She was never ill, and she never complained. She said she wanted to make it an early evening.

"I drove her home and believed I might be invited in for a nightcap, but she didn't even wait for me to get out and open the car door for her. A first.

"She opened it for herself and dashed out, calling back, 'I had a lovely time, Douglas, dear,' and she was gone.

"I just sat there, stunned. I was about to drive away when I saw down the block a man get out of his car and walk, very fast, toward the house where Kate was staying."

Fairbanks saw Kate open the door. In the light from the open door, he saw the man and recognized him as Leland Hayward. Hayward went in. The door closed behind him.

"Our affair, which turned out to be a small affair after all, ended that night, but the friendship lasted the rest of our lives.

"In later years, we both lived in New York. I would go over to her house to visit, but I never mentioned that night, and never the name of Leland Hayward."

"In *Morning Glory*," Kate told me, "I played a girl who gets a kick out of everything. There's a line in the film where a man tells me that. Well, it was true on the screen as well as in life. In *Morning Glory*, I play myself, only more so.

"I was desperate to get that part. Maybe some of my desperation to get it was not being wanted. It was made clear immediately I wasn't wanted. The front-runner was Constance Bennett. I wasn't even second choice.

"I know there are some who shrink away and accept their place when rejected. I never did that. At least not professionally.

"For me, it was like a red flag held up to a bull. I had to win, to get the part and to make them sorry they hadn't wanted me in the first place and have them be overjoyed by my brilliance. I wanted to hear them say, 'We should have known from the beginning. How could we not have seen her great talent?'

"Well, I got the part in *Morning Glory*. It was, as I remember, a seven-day film. Can you believe that? And I don't think doubling the days of shooting would have doubled its quality. We certainly couldn't have done it in half the time. Films could be made very quickly in those days."

*Morning Glory* was adapted for the screen by Zoë Akins from her own unperformed stage play. Previously, she had written the screenplay for *Christopher Strong*. In 1935, she won the Pulitzer Prize for drama for her play *The Old Maid*, based on a novella by Edith Wharton. *The Old Maid* was made into a movie starring Bette Davis in 1939. *Morning Glory* was remade in 1958 as *Stage Struck*, with Susan Strasberg and Henry Fonda.

# Morning Glory (1933)

Naïve young Eva Lovelace (Katharine Hepburn), convinced she is a great actress, comes to New York, determined to succeed on Broadway.

At the office of producer Louis Easton (Adolphe Menjou), Eva either charms or alienates everyone with her childlike directness. One of those alienated is Rita Vernon (Mary Duncan), the diva of Easton's shows. Easton himself finds Eva a bit peculiar, while playwright Joseph Sheridan (Douglas Fairbanks, Jr.) barely notices her. One of those who is charmed is veteran actor Robert Harley Hedges (C. Aubrey Smith), who cautions her not to be a morning glory, "a flower that fades before the sun is very high."

Eva gets a small part in Easton's new play, but it fails. While looking for another part, she runs into Hedges again. He notices that she hasn't eaten for a while and invites her to come with him to a party being given by Easton.

At the party, Eva drinks too much, then collapses after an impromptu performance of the balcony scene from *Romeo and Juliet* with Sheridan as Romeo. Easton tells Sheridan to take her into the bedroom.

Sheridan coaches her, using the part he has written for Rita Vernon in his new play as a practice piece. As he falls in love with Eva, Sheridan is asked by Easton to help him break off the affair that began between the producer and Eva after the party. Sheridan forgives Eva.

Just before opening night, Vernon confronts Easton and Sheridan with outrageous demands. Sheridan suggests Eva, who is familiar with the part, as her replacement.

She is a sensation, prompting Easton to say, "You don't belong to any man now. You belong to Broadway." Sharing Eva's success vicariously is her dresser, (Helen Ware) who was once an overnight sensation, "a morning glory."

Eva hopes that this is the beginning of her great career, rather than only a morning glory's brief appearance.

Kate remembered her favorite scene, "a great scene in the film which no one saw because it was cut out. It's my favorite, and it's Douglas's, too. It was from *Romeo and Juliet*. Douglas was Romeo and one guess who was Juliet.

"It was done like a dream. We were both very good, but Douglas was better than I. He looked more like Romeo than I looked like Juliet."

Decades afterwards, Douglas Fairbanks, Jr., showed me a publicity still of that deleted scene, saying with a laugh, "Look. I was more beautiful than she was."

I told Kate what he had said, and she agreed. "Oh, yes. That was true. He certainly was.

"I like the picture, but the most wonderful thing I got out of it was Douglas, a dear, dear friend throughout my life."

Fairbanks believed he might have received an Oscar nomination if the full *Romeo and Juliet* sequence had been left in. Kate did receive an Oscar for her performance.

"I never went to the Oscars when I was nominated," she said. "I always said I couldn't go because I didn't have anything to wear. It was a flippant answer. It was also the truth. I didn't care to have Oscar clothes in my wardrobe. Those fancy dresses use up so much space. But I could have afforded to buy a dress.

"In my more serious moments, I knew I didn't go because I didn't know I'd win and I've never been a good loser. After a while I said no to going so many times, it became a habit.

"When sometimes *Morning Glory* is shown somewhere, it surprises my fans, I suppose, to see me looking so young, and even what you might call pretty. Well, we're all young once. It always surprises even me to see myself so young. I've been middle-aged and old so long, nobody remembers that once upon a time, I was young. *I remember.*"

Fairbanks told me, "The original script for *Morning Glory*, included the fantasy dream sequence in which Miss Hepburn and I would play at least two scenes, and possibly a third, of the greatest scenes between Romeo and Juliet. That certainly intrigued and tempted me. It seemed a unique opportunity for me to play Romeo, a dream part, and I knew I had to hurry before I outgrew the part. I was in my early twenties, already a bit long-in-tooth for the teenage hero. Romeo was a teenager at the time of his tragic romance, and Juliet, too, a bit younger than Romeo. I hoped most people weren't aware of that and that Miss Hepburn, who was about my age, and I could carry it off.

"When I met Miss Hepburn, I was more than pleased. She came upon the scene from Broadway and then a wonderful first movie performance in *Bill of Divorcement* as John Barrymore's daughter, and she held her own with Barrymore. It was clear she had a brilliant future, and a brilliant present.

"I wasn't much of a judge of how fabulous Kate was as an artist, because my all-too-susceptible heart had been captivated by her. I fell in love with my Juliet, with Eva Lovelace, her character, who my character fell in love with in the film, and with Kate, the real-life, flesh-and-blood person.

"I had been warned that she was, in real life, a cool and very practical person, but I had not found her that way. In my arms, she seemed soft and vulnerable. As Juliet, she captured a fragile, vulnerable, innocent, yet deeply passionate quality. Since I'd been told that her looks were highly unconventional, but photogenic, I didn't know what to expect.

"When we met, she certainly was striking, and she didn't look like anyone else, so maybe that was what they meant by 'an unconventional type.'

"We had a lot in common. Underneath her exterior bravado, I felt that she was, as I was, basically shy. At the same time we were shy, we were also a bit arrogant because we had such great confidence in ourselves and our careers. We each knew we were going to make it. We both loved the theater, as well as making movies.

"She had her parents, who had done everything to make her feel secure and give her a good start in life. I had my mother, Anna Beth Sully, who had devoted herself to giving me a refined and sophisticated life, some of it in Paris, and I had my father's [Douglas Fairbanks, Sr.] brightly shining example in front of me. We both wanted our families, especially our fathers, to be proud of us. I also had as an inspiration my stepmother, Mary Pickford, who was endlessly kind to me. We both felt economically secure, though I probably felt more economically secure than I was. We were both educated, she, formally, Bryn Mawr, and I, informally, largely through travel and association with educated people. We were both energetic and extremely driven.

"Kate was always interesting. I was so fascinated. As we became more involved, I tried, I fear unsuccessfully, to express the depth of my feelings for her. I was an extreme romantic. Even in the midst of what we had together, I felt she kept her head and was more practical about it all.

"She was wonderful to play with in our Romeo and Juliet scenes. Every time I tried to work my thin frame into my tights, I wasn't certain I'd make it. I tried to stop eating much. Then, I tried to stop eating at all. Unfortunately, the more I tried to stop eating, the hungrier I felt and the more I thought about not eating, the more I ate and the tighter my tights got. I tried every position to enter them, including lying on the floor with my legs in the air. There was no lock on the door, and I got caught once. Someone opened the door, but I was too busy trying to extricate myself from one leg of the tights to see who it was. The person was too embarrassed by the sight to linger.

"For the part, as I remember, I wore one earring, and I had a wig. I scarcely looked in the mirror because I was afraid I would cry. I thought I looked little like Romeo and more like a transvestite.

"We did the scenes from *Romeo and Juliet* for small invited audiences, and we both felt we were 'of the theater.'"

Director Robert Wise told me about visiting his older brother, who was working at RKO, when he was a young man looking for a career. Wise was from the Midwest and had never seen anything like a motion picture lot.

"Actors and extras in every imaginable costume were walking between studio workers carrying sets and props from every epoch in history. Fantastic!

"In the middle of it all, shining like an angel, was this incredibly beautiful young woman dressed in an antebellum costume. She was Katharine Hepburn, between setups of *Little Women*. When I saw her shining presence, I *knew* I had to be a part of this world."

*Little Women* was one of the subjects RKO considered for Kate's second picture. Another was *Three Came Unarmed*, a story similar to Joan Crawford's 1929 *Untamed*. Both are stories of a young girl who has been reared out of civilization trying to make an adjustment to modern urban life. Instead of either of these, Kate did *Christopher Strong*. *Little Women* would not come until after *Morning Glory*. *Little Women* reunited Kate with her already favorite director, George Cukor.

"*Little Women* is one of the reasons I became known as a woman's director," Cukor told me. "And that, added to *The Women*, caused me to be hopelessly typecast. I've always insisted, to no avail, that

I am just as much a man's director, and there are a number of actors who would testify in my behalf, just as many as actresses. My personal preference is to be known simply as a director, but not as a simple director. I'm not a woman's director. I'm not a man's director. *I am a director.*"

Cukor felt that *Little Women* should be a period film, but RKO head David Selznick felt otherwise. He wanted to avoid the expenses of Civil War costumes and settings by updating the Louisa May Alcott novel. Subsequent events prove that Selznick, who produced *Gone With the Wind*, was not against Civil War settings, according to his son Daniel, only against the spending of a lot of money on a chancy project with a relatively unknown cast during the Great Depression.

Two scripts were prepared by the adaptors, Sarah Y. Mason and Victor Heerman, one placing the story in modern times, but Cukor was dissatisfied. He wanted the story filmed in its original settings, mid-nineteenth-century New England and New York City. After Selznick left RKO for M-G-M, Cukor got his way.

As it turned out, RKO's huge investment in Civil War costumes and settings paid off handsomely. The film established Katharine Hepburn as a major Hollywood star and enhanced the careers of everyone else involved, including Cukor. *Little Women* was a great success and has stood the test of time to become a classic.

"You know, it's a funny thing," Cukor told me, "I never read the novel. David kept importuning me to read it, but in those days, I was always so busy, I never had the time for more than just a few pages.

"I didn't really need to read it. It's a fairly simple story, and I got all I needed from reading all those drafts of the screenplay. But lately I've been thinking: maybe I ought to dig it out of my library and finish it in case somebody ever asks me a question about *Little Women*."

"There's one thing George and I agree on," Kate told me. "Actually, we agree on almost everything. I don't know anything we don't agree on. One thing we *really* agree on is, we love *Little Women*. We loved doing it. And we love the film we made.

"I was very good, and I owe everything to this man," she said, indicating Cukor, who was sitting in his living room with us. "He got all that out of me."

"I didn't *have* to direct her," Cukor said. "She directed herself."

Cukor called her Jo a few times during the conversation. "She is Jo. Of all of those characters she ever played, it is the one who is closest to Kate herself. Kate and Jo really are the same girl. There's no doubt that this girl put a lot of herself into Jo. Everything. Lines are important, but how they are delivered tells the tale. Expressions on her face, the way she moves . . ."

Director Paul Morrissey was a good friend of Cukor's, and he was frequently a dinner guest at Cukor's house, sometimes with Kate. He went on picnics with them. "Kate especially loved picnics," Morrissey told me. "I remember in the seventies, George said the character of Jo in *Little Women* was *exactly*, and he emphasized the word exactly, the character of Kate.

"He said he told her to play the character of Jo, you know that expression he always used, as 'full of beans.' George meant full of enthusiasm and energy and joy in life. Kate understood him perfectly."

## *Little Women (1933)*

Marmee March (Spring Byington) and her four daughters live out the Civil War in Concord, Massachusetts, while her husband (Samuel S. Hinds) serves in the Union army as a chaplain.

Josephine, "Jo" (Katharine Hepburn), hopes to be a writer and travel around the world. Her wealthy aunt (Edna May Oliver) has promised her a trip to Europe.

Amy (Joan Bennett) wants to be an artist, and Elizabeth, "Beth" (Jean Parker), a musician. Margaret, "Meg" (Frances Dee), wishes only to marry the man she loves and have children.

The Marches' wealthy neighbor, James Laurence (Henry Stephenson), offers Beth the use of his piano. His grandson "Laurie" (Douglass Montgomery) falls in love with Jo, but she wants only to remain best friends.

While helping her mother with charitable work, Beth contracts scarlet fever. At first, she seems to be recovering.

Jo leaves for New York, to pursue her writing ambitions. There, a Professor Bhaer (Paul Lukas), encourages her to write about what she knows. He falls in love with her, too.

Jo is upset by Laurie's failure to call when he passes through New York on his way to Europe. She is also hurt when her aunt chooses Amy instead of Jo as her companion for a European tour.

When Beth's condition worsens. Jo returns to Concord. Beth dies.

In Paris, Amy learns of Beth's death and feels a sense of sadness and guilt for not being by her sister's bedside at the end. Laurie, passing through Paris, comforts her.

Meg marries Laurie's tutor, John Brooke (John Davis Lodge). Amy and Laurie decide to marry and return from Europe. He hasn't forgiven Jo for rejecting him.

Professor Bhaer arrives at the March home with the news that Jo's novel has been accepted by a publisher. As he praises her book, he awkwardly tries to express his feeling for her. She understands. They enter the March home together.

Kate offered her opinion as to why Jo couldn't return Laurie's love. "It was because she loved the career to which she aspired more than she loved him. Though she didn't completely understand it herself, she really wasn't looking for marriage.

"Maybe that's how I felt about Howard [Hughes]."

Cukor especially liked directing "The Witch's Curse," the play scene that occurs in the film. "Very Cukor," he said, smiling. "That's 'cu' as in 'cucumber.'"

After making four pictures for RKO, Kate considered returning to the stage. She had been offered the lead in a Broadway play, *The Lake*. The play was by English writers Dorothy Massingham and Murray MacDonald, and was being produced and directed by Jed Harris, who had to his credit *The Front Page*, among other Broadway successes. Kate was impressed by the play and missed the live audiences of the theater. She also relished the thought of returning to Broadway as a star after having left as a supporting player in *The Warrior's Husband*.

RKO agreed to release her for the play if she would make one more film for them. The picture was *Spitfire* and was shot in one month.

## *Spitfire* (1934)

Trigger Hicks (Katharine Hepburn) is a peculiar young Ozark girl who lives in a mountain cabin. She frightens everyone in the town with her brash tomboy antics while at the same time fascinating them with wild claims of supernatural powers that cannot be substantiated. Half-believing her claims, townspeople have long ago learned to avoid her, but two engineers from a nearby dam find her rustic manner charming and disarming. One of them, John Stafford (Robert Young), wins her heart, then breaks it when she finds out he is married.

Confused and distraught, she impulsively kidnaps a baby who is dying. Under her untrained but caring treatment, the baby miraculously survives, and then appears to be thriving when returned to the parents. Back with them, the baby takes a turn for the worse and dies.

At first heralded as a savior and then as a devil, Trigger escapes a lynch mob with the help of the other dam engineer, George Fleetwood (Ralph Bellamy). Trigger is exiled from the town. As she leaves, she vows to return someday and take up residence in her mountain cabin because she is innocent of any wrongdoing.

While critics wrote negatively about *Spitfire*, they unanimously praised Katharine Hepburn's portrayal of an Ozark wild child, usually noting how wide a departure it was from her previous urbane roles and her own character as perceived by audiences.

In spite of mixed reviews, *The Lake* did reasonably well at the box office. This was not, however, what Kate had hoped for when she returned to Broadway. "I was hoping," she said, "to show everyone and be a sensation." Disappointed, she decided not to complete the six-month run.

Her agreement with Jed Harris being verbal, Kate could have walked away, but that was not her way. She asked Harris how much it would cost to compensate him for her leaving the play, which then closed early. She immediately accepted his estimate of $15,000 without any bargaining. "I suppose he was expecting me to bargain,"

Kate said, reviewing her business acumen of a half-century earlier. This wasn't important money to Kate, who had received almost that much for one day's overtime on *Spitfire*.

In early February of 1934, *The Lake* posted the banns, and Kate planned a European voyage. On the morning of her ship's sailing, she was informed that she had won the Best Actress Oscar for *Morning Glory*. On that note, she sailed off to Europe for a holiday. When she returned to New York, she bought the townhouse in Turtle Bay, which she and Luddy originally had rented. Until the end of her life, she lived there whenever she was in New York City, and she loved the house. When she died, she left it as part of her estate.

Kate returned to RKO in the summer of 1934, after a brief trip to Mexico to obtain her divorce from Luddy, and at RKO, she accepted the lead role in James M. Barrie's *The Little Minister*.

## The Little Minister (1934)

The townspeople of Thrums, Scotland, are impressed when their new minister, Gavin Dishart (John Beal) stands up to the town drunk and bully, Rob Dow (Alan Hale).

Dow is leader of the town weavers who threaten to rebel against Lord Rintoul (Frank Conroy), who has cut their earnings. These problems distract Rintoul from his intended betrothal to his ward, the Lady Babbie (Katharine Hepburn).

While out wandering, Gavin is tricked by a singing Gypsy girl into giving the signal for the weavers to attack the troops that have just arrived.

Gavin calms the mob, but he cannot answer Rintoul's question, "How did they know troops had been called in?"

When Gavin and Dr. McQueen (Donald Crisp) come to take an old woman (Mary Gordon) to the poorhouse, the Gypsy girl intervenes, promising to pay her rent. Then, she disappears.

She reappears as Lady Babbie, accepting the lord's marriage proposal.

Babbie meets Gavin as herself, not the Gypsy girl, and tells her story. As a child, she fell off her family's wagon in a Gypsy caravan. She was found by Lord Rintoul and became his ward.

Gavin and Babbie are seen kissing by Rob Dow, who tells the congregation, impatiently awaiting Gavin's arrival in church. The outraged elders decide to discharge their "little minister," as he is known. At his parsonage, they are calmed by his mother and defied by Babbie.

Outside the church, Gavin is accidentally stabbed by Rob Dow. Babbie's prayers move the elders, and they withdraw their plan to discharge him.

Babbie loves Gavin, and when Lord Rintoul comes for her, she informs him that she has chosen to marry Gavin. She gives up being lady of the manor to be the little minister's wife.

"Babbie really *is* a Gypsy, at heart," Kate said, "and she *wants* to be a Gypsy. Her idea of being a Gypsy is being free, without really understanding that the life she is choosing as the minister's wife is not that.

"Full of youthful energy, she is always running off to end scenes. Where will she run off to after they are married for a few years? What if there is a child?

"I don't think Babbie is going to be very content. She's carried away by drama and high romance. She likes to go against things for the sake of doing it.

"A line I remember is, 'A man's second childhood begins when he gets involved with a woman.' A man's *first* childhood begins with a woman, too, doesn't it?"

John Barrymore was supposed to play opposite Kate again in *Break of Hearts*, but he declined the part. He was replaced by Francis Lederer, who, after one week of shooting, was replaced by Charles Boyer.

## Break of Hearts (1935)

Constance Dane (Katharine Hepburn), an obscure composer, attracts the attention of the world-famous conductor Franz Roberti (Charles Boyer). While praising her musical talent, he leaves no doubt that he is even more impressed by her. After a short, passionate courtship in which Constance is swept off her feet by Roberti, they marry.

Their marital bliss does not last long, and Constance discovers that her attractive husband is seeing another woman. She leaves him, and then turns to another man for consolation. He is Johnny Lawrence (John Beal), quite a different type of man. He is dependable, not temperamental, and, for Constance, ultimately dull.

She goes back to Roberti, who has become an alcoholic in her absence. He is inspired by her compassion to try again with their marriage. To seal their renewed love, she plays a new composition for him that expresses their turbulent, but real, need for each other.

*Break of Hearts* was a critical and commercial failure for RKO. Most reviewers said that Katharine Hepburn deserved better material. One reviewer observed that only Mickey Mouse and Mae West had escaped some variation of this sentimental plot formula. After the disappointing box office of *Spitfire* and *The Little Minister*, the studio was desperately searching for something that might fulfill the promise of

*A Bill of Divorcement*, *Morning Glory*, and *Little Women*. Meanwhile, Kate was becoming homesick for her family and Fenwick.

When RKO producer Pandro S. Berman offered Kate Booth Tarkington's novel, *Alice Adams*, as her next film, she was delighted. She had already expressed an interest in Tarkington's *Seventeen*, and *Alice Adams* was also one of her favorite novels.

"Yes, Pandro and I really did flip a coin to choose the director of *Alice Adams*," Kate told me. "But the truth is, there were two coin tosses.

"We were trying to choose between Willie Wyler and George Stevens. Wyler had more experience and an outstanding track record, but he was under contract to Goldwyn, and would cost most of our minuscule budget. Stevens was already under contract to RKO, so he'd be cheaper, but we didn't know yet what a great director he was going to be.

"So, we flipped, and Wyler won. I said, 'Let's flip again.'

"We didn't bother to look at the second toss. We already knew we wanted Stevens. Maybe because it was such an American subject, and Wyler was European.

"I particularly liked my character in *Alice Adams*. It reminded me of the way small-minded people treated my mother, shunning her and us children, not because they thought we weren't good enough, but because they thought *we* thought that we were *too* good. Well, maybe we did, now that I look back.

"I volunteered to shop for Alice's dresses," Kate told me. "My offer was instantly accepted, and I was given a meager budget. I wasn't a bit daunted. I had more interest in dresses in those days.

"I picked up the required frocks that suited my character, Alice. It helped me to know her better, inside out, and I was able to come in under budget, except for one splurge which I was counting on. Ulterior motive.

"I'd seen a wonderful dress which was perfect for the party dress Alice would be wearing, and then, there was a special dividend. I'd been told that I could keep the wardrobe from the film when it wrapped. They would have had trouble finding anyone else with the figure for the dresses, and also probably nobody wanted them. But the party dress, that was something different. It was divine. But I was worried that they'd be angry because I spent much more on the dress than I was supposed to, so I modeled the dress for them and my theory was when they saw me in it, they would be overwhelmed, in spite of the price.

"Well, I was wrong. They didn't say anything about the price. They just said, 'Take it off!' They wanted me to take it off before I wrinkled it. It wasn't the price. They said the dress was too elegant. Alice would not only never have been able to afford it, she wouldn't have developed the taste to select it or to know where to find it. They told me I'd have to give it back and get another.

"I went out and got a lot of ribbons and made bows for the front and the back of the dress. Perfect bad taste. I was very careful not to sew the bows on too tightly and not to make holes in the material. They approved it and never knew it was the same dress."

## *Alice Adams (1935)*

Alice Adams (Katharine Hepburn) imagines herself as the belle of the ball, even though her father is a low-paid employee in the town's glue factory. Alice has wealthy friends, but she is not invited to any of their grand social events.

Arthur Russell (Fred MacMurray) is a town patrician who finds Alice attractive and amusing, and more. She invites him to her home to meet her family.

Alice hopes that her eccentric family will behave acceptably, but they carry unaccustomed social etiquette to ludicrous extremes. Dinner is served by an insolent, incompetent maid (Hattie McDaniel), hired for the occasion.

Mr. Adams (Fred Stone) has invented a new glue product he hopes will make him rich. His wife (Ann Shoemaker) wants him to go into business for himself, but he hopes his irascible boss, Mr. Lamb (Charley Grapewin) will want to become his partner in the business venture.

Alice's brother Walter (Frank Albertson) blurts out at the dinner table that he has embezzled money from Mr. Lamb. He intended returning the money, but now he doesn't have any to return.

Alice is embarrassed in front of her guest and fears she has lost Arthur's respect, but he is entertained by her family and does not blame her for their behavior.

Walter is able to return the money, Mr. Adams goes into business with Mr. Lamb, and Alice and Arthur appear to have a happy future ahead of them, together.

This ending was the second of two which were shot, and it was the one used for the final version of the film. In the first ending, Alice was seen ascending a staircase to a business school, waving goodbye to Arthur. This was the version first seen by a preview audience. The studio thought audiences expected a happier ending in which the couple wound up together, and that became the ending.

For a long time Kate felt she preferred the first ending. After some years, she came to like the happy ending, too.

*Alice Adams* was one of Katharine Hepburn's favorite films. She was nominated for a best-actress Academy Award, but lost to Bette Davis in *Dangerous*.

After dinner one night at George Cukor's house, I was sitting in the living room with him and Kate.

"George," Kate said, "do you remember *Sylvia Scarlett*, when you . . ."

"What do you mean, 'Do I remember *Sylvia Scarlett*?'" Cukor interrupted with mock indignation. "*Of course* I remember *Sylvia Scarlett*! How could I forget?"

"Well, then," Kate said, "do you remember the advice you gave me when we were doing it? I asked you, 'Am I getting it? Do you have any advice for me?' And do you remember what you said?"

"Well, no, not exactly. Give me a hint."

"You said, 'My advice to you is, 'Never whip a carousel horse.'"

Whenever Kate and Cukor reminisced about *Sylvia Scarlett,* he would call it "our love child." She would call it "our floperoo."

"No success that one," Cukor said. "But we were just a couple of kids then."

"Anyway, *you* were, George. You know, after *Sylvia Scarlett*, it's a wonder either one of us ever worked again."

"Our film *Sylvia Scarlett* was a terrible failure," Cukor said to me. "Terrible. We had gone into it with such high hopes. You really can't do anything without high hopes, which you need if you're ever going to have a success. What's remarkable is the high hopes you need to have a failure.

"For years and years, people have said, 'Why did you do it? Couldn't you see that it was going to be a failure?' Well, obviously not.

"No one sets out to make a failure. But you have to be prepared to fail or you can't ever try for success. The worst part about having a failure is if you let it change *you*. If it ruins your enthusiasm and wrecks your confidence, then you *are* lost."

"I sank some of my own money into *Sylvia Scarlett*," Kate said. "'Sank' is the right word. I could have dropped it into the ocean with bricks tied to it and had a better chance of seeing it again. Another example of why I let Father watch over my money and didn't even let him know I was contemplating investing in *Sylvia*. I always kept a little foolish money on the side. Foolish money is money I thought I could afford to be foolish with. It wasn't the money that was being foolish. It was I.

"The hard thing is to go on when you know yourself it isn't what you thought it was going to be. Not far into the film, George and I knew it wasn't going the way we dreamed, but we didn't say a word, even to each other, *especially* to each other.

"I didn't want to moan and bring down George's spirits, and he wanted to encourage me and pep me up. But we understood each other pretty well, and no one was fooling anyone. We hoped for the best, that it would turn around. I guess we hadn't judged it right at the beginning, so maybe we weren't going to be right at the middle, either.

"Do you hate your film that is a failure because it has publicly disgraced you, or do you love it better to make up for no one else loving it? Both.

"Actually, I never could hate *Sylvia Scarlett*. It was too much fun making it with George."

"Our girl here," Cukor said, indicating Kate, "was so successful when she was successful that it was quite easy to assume that people would come to see her no matter what the film.

"There was some miscalculation in our reasoning."

## Sylvia Scarlett (1936)

Widower Henry Scarlett (Edmund Gwenn) flees Marseilles for London with his daughter, Sylvia (Katharine Hepburn), to avoid arrest for petty theft. To confuse pursuers, she poses as Sylvester, a boy.

During the channel crossing, Henry tells a conniving cockney, Jimmy Monkley (Cary Grant), that he is smuggling valuable cloth into England. At customs, Jimmy denounces Henry.

Later, Jimmy admits to them that he is a diamond

smuggler who diverts attention from himself by exposing other smugglers. Penniless, they join him in crime.

Aided by Maudie Tilt (Dennie Moore), a lady's maid, they try, unsuccessfully, to rob a mansion. Henry falls for Maudie.

Finding crime unprofitable, they try show business. They buy a caravan and perform as clowns. At a beach resort, their act is stopped by a noisy group. When Sylvester upbraids their leader, Michael Fane (Brian Aherne), he invites them to his estate for a party. The wealthy artist is attracted to the cheeky boy.

A mysterious Russian woman named Lily (Natalie Paley) causes Michael to lose interest in Sylvester, who reacts jealously.

Later, Sylvester apologizes to Michael. She is in love with him.

The next day, Sylvia arrives at Michael's studio dressed as a beautiful girl. Though he is delighted, the arrival of Lily overshadows Sylvia, who leaves heartbroken.

Henry, after being distraught over Maudie, is found dead on a rocky beach. Lily attempts suicide over Michael, but is saved from drowning by Sylvia.

Leaving Lily in the caravan, Sylvia goes for Michael. When they return, Lily has left with Jimmy.

Michael and Sylvia catch up with them on the boat train to Paris. Michael and Sylvia realize that they don't want to leave each other, so at an unscheduled stop, they get off. They are seen leaving by Jimmy, who finds it hilarious as he listens to Lily's endless complaining.

"Before we did *Sylvia Scarlett*, George told me he was *terribly* impressed by Cary Grant. George used 'terribly' that way when he meant 'wonderfully.'

"He told me that I was going to like Cary. That was George's way, understatement. That was *some* understatement. Cary was so wonderful in our film that it makes *Sylvia Scarlett* still worth seeing today. But to see Cary, I'm sorry to say, you have to get me, too. That's not modesty on my part. It's truth."

Cary Grant told me, "I owe so much to George Cukor. I remember I was full of ideas for my character. Some directors would have thought I was a presumptuous upstart. Not Mr. Cukor. At that time, he was still 'Mr. Cukor' to me. I had a great feeling for my character. Mr. Cukor said, 'Go to it. Show us what you have in mind. Feel free. We'll try out your way and see how it works.' He used quite a few of my ideas for delivery and for movement. It helped me a lot to move as it came to me and to deliver the lines the way that suited my character and me."

Kate said, "Cary was very confident, never arrogant. He was at home in his own skin. That allowed him to get into all kinds of other skins for his parts.

"The preview of the film," Kate said, "was an utter disaster. We thought of our film as a comedy, but the audience apparently had missed that.

"What did I learn from *Sylvia Scarlett*? I learned what it's like to make a floperoo."

In recent years, *Sylvia Scarlett* has found a small but appreciative audience that considers it a comic masterpiece.


Kate met Howard Hughes in late summer of 1935 while shooting *Sylvia Scarlett*. "We shot a lot of *Sylvia Scarlett* out beyond Trancas Beach in California," Kate told me.

"George and I alternated with picnic lunches from our homes. Soup, hot or cold. Nice big salads. A hot main course, and the pièce

de résistance, vanilla or coffee ice cream with a choice of hot chocolate sauce or hot butterscotch.

"One day, a small plane landed in the field next to us. It landed
beautifully, but I was angry. It was obvious the pilot was good, but
I didn't think it was right to gamble with our lives. I wondered who
it was and why would anyone do such a crazy stunt. I said that to
Cary.

"Cary said, 'I know who that is. That's my good friend Howard
Hughes.'

"I wasn't dazzled as I suppose I was meant to be. It was too
obvious a maneuver, done for effect by a show-off. I preferred
something more subtle. But there was no doubt, Howard had a
lot of pizzazz.

"Cary said, 'Howard is here to meet you. He's been wanting to
meet you, and I told him I'd try.'

"Dashing? Fiddlesticks. It was plenty of nerve, I thought.

"Hughes joined us for lunch. I wasn't rude because of Cary, but
I was distinctly cool."

After lunch, he took off in his plane, and Kate went back to work.

"Cary asked me what I thought of Hughes, and I said, I loved
his leather flight jacket. Howard and Cary were great friends. That
always seemed strange to me then. They seemed an unlikely pair."

Grant and Hughes were actually a perfect match. They lived in
the same social world and in the film world. They both enjoyed and
were good at sports. Hughes had noticed Kate and wanted to meet
her. When Grant accepted the part in *Sylvia Scarlett*, Hughes asked
him to introduce him. Grant suggested that he "drop by" for lunch
on the set, and that's exactly what he did.

Howard Robard Hughes, Jr., was born in Houston, Texas, in
1905. His father owned the Hughes Tool Company. The company's
fortunes were based on his father's invention of an oil drilling tool,

which made him a millionaire. It was the young Hughes who multiplied the fortune many times over.

Both parents died while Howard was still in his teens. Before their deaths, he had described for them his ambitious dreams, of which they approved. They had instilled in him ambition and the faith in his ability to accomplish whatever he set out to do.

He told Kate a great sadness in his life was not being able to show his accomplishments to his parents. No one could understand this feeling better than Kate, who had always striven to win her parents' approval.

"Mine were very much alive," Kate said, "and I was certain they would be alive for a very long time." Still, Kate rather doubted that they would ever show great pride in her. It didn't seem it was in their nature. "Anyway, I don't think they were ashamed of me."

"I was happy to make *Mary of Scotland*," Kate said, "because it meant I would be working with John Ford, one of the truly great directors and one of the great people in my career. I considered him a genius, and he had a lot of sex appeal. For me, the genius part of him made him sexy. He was *very* Irish, and for some reason, men who are Irish have often appealed to me. He had a wonderful sense of humor. That was part of it. A big part of it was he liked me. I've never been attracted to a man who wasn't attracted to me. If they didn't have good taste, why would I be interested? It was nothing he said, but I felt it right away. He'd chosen me professionally because he would never have done anything that would have hurt his film. The moment I met him, I knew that he liked me, professionally and personally, too. He didn't try to keep it a secret.

"We never had a physical affair, because he had a wife of many years, and I liked her. He did, too. And he was a Catholic, and he and his wife were a couple.

"He said to me once it was a shame a man couldn't have two wives. Well, since I didn't want to be wife one or wife two, it wasn't a problem.

"I wish we could have worked together many times, and I wish we could have made a great film together. *Mary* wasn't a great film, but it was a good film, and we had a sort of affair of the minds. Ours was a special friendship, and it might have been more had the circumstances been right."

## Mary of Scotland (1936)

In 1561, Mary Stuart (Katharine Hepburn) returns to Scotland from France, where she had been married to the late French king. The return of Mary alarms Elizabeth Tudor (Florence Eldridge), who anticipates a Stuart claim to the throne of England.

In 1565, Mary weds her cousin, Henry Stuart, known as Lord Darnley (Douglas Walton), a Catholic nobleman considered a threat by the Protestants, who have recently come to power. A rebellion seems inevitable, but it is averted by Mary's protector, the Earl of Bothwell (Fredric March). Mary, however, comes to doubt the loyalty of the weak Darnley, who seems more intent on furthering his own political ambitions than on being loyal to her. In spite of her suspicions, she eventually has a son with him, the future King James I of England.

It is rumored that Mary's good friend, an Italian musician named David Rizzio (John Carradine), is having an affair with her. Rizzio is stabbed to death in her presence by a gang of Scottish noblemen accompanied by Darnley, who is only concerned with saving his own life. After Darnley is murdered, Mary weds Bothwell. It proves an unpopular move in terms of her destiny as queen, but she passionately loves Bothwell during their brief time together.

To save Mary's rule in Scotland, Bothwell agrees to leave the country. In his absence, the Scottish noblemen break their promise, and imprison Mary. She is rescued by supporters, who help her escape to England, where she naïvely believes Queen Elizabeth will shelter her and help restore her to power. Elizabeth feeling Mary is a threat to her own crown, imprisons Mary.

Mary remains incarcerated for eighteen years. After Bothwell dies, Elizabeth offers to release her if she will renounce her royal claims. Mary refuses, thinking of her son James's claim to the throne. She is condemned to death for treason and executed in 1586.

"I wanted to please him, and I wanted to do the best I could for the picture and for my part, so I learned to ride sidesaddle with a huge skirt and going fast.

"I was terrified, but I didn't want my director, whom I never called *Mr.* Ford, but sometimes Jack and sometimes Sean, to know my secret. It was like not having my father know that I was afraid.

"I always preferred a bicycle to a horse. I like to feel in control. Well, I practiced a lot, and gradually I started to feel pretty good about myself and the horse. I got the hang of it, and I started to feel pretty confident. 'Well, this isn't so hard after all,' I thought. That could have been the last thought I had.

"I was galloping along, heading straight for a tree branch that would have finished me off when I heard Jack scream:

" *'Duck!'*

"That was the most important word anyone ever said to me.

"Fortunately, Jack's voice was loud and clear and urgent, and I responded with perfect reflexes. Otherwise, I don't think we'd be sitting here and having this conversation today. I did the only thing there was to do. I ducked.

"I liked to call him Sean, his Irish name. It's a very masculine name, like him. He drank a lot and his pipe was part of him. It reminded me of the way Father's jacket smelled. He was one of the extraordinary people my career gave me the opportunity to meet and know.

*A Woman Rebels*, a women's rights drama set in Victorian England, was a subject that recalled for Kate her mother's dedication to winning the vote for women. The film introduced Van Heflin to the screen and to Katharine Hepburn, who chose him to play Macaulay Connor in the stage play of *The Philadelphia Story*. Later, he would win an Oscar, but not for the film version of the play, in which he was replaced by James Stewart.

## *A Woman Rebels (1936)*

Pamela Thistlewaite (Katharine Hepburn), an intelligent young woman who refuses to accept the strict rules for feminine behavior of the Victorian era, defies her conservative father, Judge Thistlewaite (Donald Crisp), in every way. She believes she is a liberated woman. Liberation, however, has its price. An affair with Gerald (Van Heflin), a charming but undependable young man, results in a child born out of wedlock. When Gerald refuses to accept responsibility for the child, Pamela asserts her independence as a woman in an even bolder manner by declining another man's offer of marriage because she is not in love with him. He is Thomas Lane (Herbert Marshall), who has always been in love with her.

Pamela wants a career for herself, and she achieves some fame and a certain amount of notoriety by becoming the editor of a crusading women's magazine. In the meantime, Thomas continues to pursue her. Finally, realizing that the values he offers are more enduring than those of fleeting passion and that he is willing to accept her for herself, she agrees to marry him.

*A Woman Rebels* was the second consecutive costume drama for Kate. Her next film, *Quality Street*, would also be a costume film. It was based on a play by James M. Barrie, author of *The Little Minister*.

Kate wanted to work with director George Stevens again. They had worked wonderfully well together while doing *Alice Adams*, and the picture was a success. Stevens, however, had his heart set on doing *Winterset*, but he couldn't say no to Kate. When *Quality Street* failed, Stevens accepted the blame, admitting that his mind was always on the big hit he thought he was missing, *Winterset*. "I felt guilty about not putting my heart into the film," Stevens confessed to Kate, but the bond between director and star held up.

## Quality Street (1937)

Phoebe Throssel (Katharine Hepburn) has just about given up hope that Dr. Valentine Brown (Franchot Tone) will ever propose to her. He has been courting her for a long time, but he only seems interested in her company for short periods of time, while she feels much more for him. When he marches away as a captain in the Napoleonic Wars without even mentioning the possibility of a wedding, she gives up entirely. Since no other suitors interest her, she accepts the fate of her older sister, Susan (Fay Bainter), imminent spinsterhood. She and Susan become schoolteachers.

After the battle of Trafalgar ends Napoleon's threat to Britain, Captain Brown marches back. Phoebe's hopes are rekindled and then doused when he fails to recognize her. She assumes this is because she has lost her bloom of youth, and determines to get revenge for all of the distress and humiliation she has suffered in her unsatisfying relationship with him.

To gain his attention, she disguises herself as a nonexistent niece of hers. As a flirtatious younger woman, she is able to win him back, if she wants him.

Far down in the credits was a very young Joan Fontaine. Over dinner at New York's Le Cirque she told her agent and friend, Milton Goldman, and me how important Katharine Hepburn had been in her career.

"At the crack of dawn, whenever we had an outdoor location for *Quality Street*, Miss Hepburn's wooden station wagon would come screeching onto the RKO Ranch, and she would emerge in her habitual slacks, her auburn hair flowing in the breeze. When we broke for lunch, she'd go back to her car and unload the wicker picnic baskets she'd brought for herself, the director, and certain fortunate members of the cast. Then they dined on the treats I think she must have prepared at home herself. When I got invited to join the select picnic group, I took it as an honor, which it was.

"I was described in the film as 'a silly goose,' to which Phoebe, Miss Hepburn's character, replies, 'That's what gentlemen prefer.' It was a tiny part, but everyone was wonderful to me, especially Miss Hepburn.

"She asked if I was English, and I am, but even British people don't notice that. She has a keen ear for that sort of thing. I told her I was trying to be an actress under a different name from my sister [Olivia de Havilland], who was doing quite well at Warners, while I wasn't having much success. She said she would talk to RKO about that, and I assumed she was just talking the way people do, or even joking. But, do you know, she wasn't. She was so powerful on the lot, people listened. Because of her, I got the lead in some B features. Then, I got my big break with Selznick and Mr. Hitchcock, when I became 'I' in *Rebecca*."

At the same time *Quality Street* was failing at the box office, Kate learned that Leland Hayward was marrying Margaret Sullavan. Kate sent the couple a congratulatory telegram, though without perfect enthusiasm. She could do so more sincerely, however, because someone else had entered her life.

RKO granted her request for taking time off to visit her family in the East. Finding suitable vehicles for her unique talent was proving difficult, as was her ability to carry routine material. She yearned to return to the Broadway stage where she had been more successful *after* she was a movie star.

While she was in New York, the Theatre Guild approached her with an attractive offer to star with Laurence Olivier in a new stage adaptation of Charlotte Bronte's *Jane Eyre*. They offered her $1,000 a week, but she held out for and got $1,500. Then Olivier became unavailable and was replaced by Dennis Hoey. Kate had accepted largely because she was thrilled by the idea of working with Olivier.

Instead of opening the play on Broadway after previews in New Haven, the Theatre Guild chose to preview it on a tour through Boston, Chicago, Cleveland, and Washington in order to work out "certain difficulties of staging." Sensing trouble, the *New York Times* took the unprecedented step of sending their foremost drama critic,

Brooks Atkinson, to review the Chicago production. He reported back that the show was, indeed, in trouble and that "Miss Hepburn is not yet the sort of trouping actress who can shape a full-length performance out of scrappy materials."

Knowing that Broadway's most influential critic was not likely to change his mind when the show reached New York, the Theatre Guild chose to settle for the tour only and to close in Washington.

The tour, however, was enormously successful, grossing close to $400,000. Katharine Hepburn was one reason for its success. The other was the new man in her life: Howard Hughes. He was seen accompanying her everywhere she went for practically the entire tour. They had met again in the fall of 1936, just after *Quality Street* wrapped.

"I was playing golf at the Bel Air Country Club. It was a lovely place to play, and they had a really good pro I enjoyed playing with. I didn't want instruction. Didn't need any. But I loved being out there with someone who was good enough.

"We were deep in our game when suddenly I heard the sound of a plane coming awfully close. I thought it was going to land on our heads, but it missed us and landed on the green in front of us. He made one of his typical on-a-dime landings, which I was to become very familiar with. I guessed what, or I should say, *who* it was. I only needed one guess.

"Howard.

"He got out of the small plane, and he was carrying his golf clubs. He joined us.

"The people at Bel Air were really angry, but they were appeased when he said he'd pay for everything. Howard believed he could buy anything. Well, just about.

"There wasn't enough room for him to take off. He had to have some aviation mechanics come with a truck and take the plane apart, take it away, and then have it put together again somewhere else.

"I said, 'Can I give you a ride?'

"He said, 'Yes. The Beverly Hills Hotel.'

"He asked me if I could have dinner with him the next week. I told him I'd be in Boston, where I would be doing *Jane Eyre*.

"He asked me where I would be staying in Boston.

"I said, 'The Ritz Hotel.'

"When I arrived in Boston, there were flowers from Howard, who had taken the largest suite at the Ritz. My room was so filled with flowers, there was hardly room for me. Howard asked me if I would have dinner with him. Surprise! I said yes.

"As we were finishing our ice cream, he asked me if I would have dinner again with him, the next night. You can guess my answer. And every night in Boston after that.

"So much for persistence in courtship."


By the time the Theatre Guild production reached Chicago, Katharine Hepburn and Howard Hughes were more than an item. They were front-page news.

Kate spent the rest of the summer in 1937 with her family at Fenwick, where Hughes would literally drop in.

"Howard would fly in to see me," Kate said, "flying his own plane. Usually he was alone. He was very dashing in those days—tall, slim, in his leather pilot's outfit. I would pretend to be blasé, relatively oblivious to the drama and the glamour of it. But I was definitely aware of who Howard was. He wasn't ordinary, and we didn't feel ordinary.

"Howard and I shared certain characteristics, which made it very easy for us to be compatible. We were both stay-at-homes. We were both very spoiled. We were so spoiled, we didn't even know it.

Each of us wanted his or her own way. As long as it suited the other person or didn't matter, it was fine. What we were was loners being together.

"My mother warned me that I had to be careful, that I might be arousing some neighbors' jealousy, envy among women who weren't being courted by rich aviators. I said, 'Too bad.' But I meant 'Too good.' It was certainly nothing that bothered me. Howard was more glamorous than Hollywood films, because his life and adventures were real.

"My parents were never fond of Howard, if the truth be told. They didn't express their opinions to me because it was felt I was an adult, in principle, anyway. I should make my own choices. But their attitude was clear, and Howard was aware of the way they felt. He was a very sensitive man. He did his best with my parents, for my sake, but I know he was never comfortable with them. Even if they had liked Howard more, I don't think Howard and my parents would ever have been great friends. At our house, he was always on the phone, and our phone was in the dining room.

"When I wasn't with Howard, I don't know if he was faithful to me. We certainly weren't married. We weren't engaged. We hadn't made any commitment for the future, although Howard had asked me to marry him a number of times. I never said yes. I never said no."

Hughes had been married to and divorced from the rich and socially prominent Ella Rice of Texas.

"I didn't think I had any right to ask him about what he did during all that time we were not together. I didn't expect him to be chaste during our separations. We hadn't exacted any promises from each other. I was only *slightly* curious about his escapades. I preferred he didn't tell me anything specific. He didn't tell me anything at all.

"If I had asked him, I don't know how he would have reacted. I think he would have been surprised. It would not have been what he would have expected of me. Maybe he would have thought I was joking and laughed. Maybe he would have been shocked.

"I think he would have answered me, and I think he would have told the truth.

"Howard was the best lover I ever had. No doubt about that. Our relationship was sexually charged.

"Howard was so right for me, in many ways. There were many reasons we were sexually a good fit. We had similar backgrounds. Having such similar backgrounds made us easy with each other. We weren't inhibited people. We certainly weren't inhibited about our bodies. And we had such tremendous energy that we could hardly contain it.

"We were young and healthy, and feeling our oats, or more specifically, as Father and Mother would have said, our hormones, and there was nothing to hold us back.

"I had been brought up to feel at perfect ease with nudity. Howard was not shy about sex. I think it was the only thing he wasn't shy about. He wasn't short of testosterone.

"He didn't like a fragile woman. I was practically a professional athlete.

"My experience with Luddy was a good beginning. With Howard, I found out that more was possible. My mother hadn't mentioned that. I don't know if she knew about *that* or not. Some things you have to find out for yourself. No inhibitions. No need to be embarrassed or to wonder about what the other person will think about you afterward. It was *our* moment. Our late twenties, early thirties. It was the right ages for passion."

"Luddy was the most perfect person to lose my virginity to. He was so impressed and thrilled by my gift. It meant everything to him. It meant a great deal less to me. Luddy was a considerate and gentle lover. He wanted to make me happy more than he wanted to please himself. Afterward, I figured I knew all there was to know about making love. It was nice, if I thought a bit overexaggerated in people's minds. I was able to put it into its proper perspective. Or so I thought. I've always been something of a know-it-all.

"With Howard, I learned about *making passion*. Passion and love are not the same thing, but they aren't unrelated. The first time, Howard was the shyest man I've ever been with. Then he got caught up in the thralls of our passion, and he was the least shy man I'd ever been with. I found out more about myself than I found out about Howard. It was very interesting to me, mysterious, surprising.

"Howard was a very sexually oriented person. I wasn't inhibited because he wasn't. It's important to have an uninhibited partner. Uninhibited passion is something special.

During the time of their romance, whenever Kate was preparing to work on a film in Hollywood, she stayed at Hughes's luxurious and spacious thirty-room mansion. Sometimes he was away. Sometimes he would fly back to join her.

They had separate suites of apartments. Kate lived in the one that had belonged to Hughes's wife. Separate chauffeurs were provided for the limousines.

There were separate staffs of servants so that a cook would always be available to prepare Kate's meals at the hours she preferred, and one for Hughes whenever he was in residence. Years later, Kate still remembered "how utterly delicious the meals were. The desserts were wonderful!"


"Once when I was searching for my character in a film, *Stage Door*," Kate said, "and I couldn't find her, I went to the director, and I asked him if he could give me a clue. Our director was Gregory La Cava. 'I am perplexed,' I said. 'Can you please tell me who I am?'

"Without hesitating a second, he said, 'You are a human question mark.' Isn't that a good phrase? It stayed in my head.

"I didn't ask him to explain. I didn't wish to appear stupid, and besides, I didn't think his explanation would be up to his statement. Overexplaining takes away the profundity.

"I've thought about it in terms of my professional self, who was *all* actress. The internal me was both more simple and more complex. I never believed in wasting my time investigating myself. I was not displeased by the way I had turned out."

## Stage Door (1937)

The Footlights Club is a boardinghouse for women who work or want to work on Broadway.

One of the girls, Jean Maitland (Ginger Rogers), gets a new roommate Terry Randall (Katharine Hepburn). Terry dresses stylishly with no concern for money. The other girls make fun of her finishing school manners.

One of those who doesn't resent Terry is Kay Hamilton (Andrea Leeds), a talented young actress who is starving in order to survive professionally. She desperately hopes to get the lead in Anthony Powell's new play, *Enchanted April*.

In the office of producer Powell (Adolphe Menjou), Terry witnesses Kay being casually rejected. When Terry upbraids Powell for not taking the hopes and dreams of these young actresses seriously, he vows never to cast Terry Randall in any show he produces.

Terry's wealthy father, Henry Sims (Samuel S. Hinds), tries to talk his daughter out of a stage career. She, however, is determined to try until she fails or succeeds.

Powell is approached by a man (Pierre Watkins) who represents an anonymous investor. He will finance the entire production of *Enchanted April* if Terry Randall plays the lead. Needing money, Powell accepts.

Terry is inexperienced and can only walk through the part, but Kay selflessly coaches Terry in the role she hoped would be hers. Then she commits suicide. Terry is blamed by the other girls.

Though nearly unable to go onstage opening night, Terry gives a performance that establishes her as a Broadway star. At her curtain call, she gives all credit to Kay, and her Footlights Club companions forgive her.

Terry's father, the secret backer of the show, was certain that she would fail if given the opportunity, and then she would give up her stage ambitions. Instead, he has a smash Broadway hit and a daughter who is a new star.

"The thinking of the character of my father in the film reminded me of my own father's attitude toward my intense pursuit of what seemed to him a silly goal. Unlike my father in the film, Father did not want to see me fail.

"I'm not a Method actress, but when that dear girl in the film commits suicide, I was moved, and I couldn't help but be thinking about Tom. I understood Kay's disappointment, but I never understood what disappointed Tom, or even if anything did."

During the filming of *Stage Door,* Kate became acquainted with Constance Collier, a member of the cast whose knowledge of stage and film acting was formidable. Always eager to improve her skills, Kate employed the veteran British actress as her drama coach from time to time until Collier's death in 1955.

"When Ginger Rogers was added to the cast," Kate said, "I was told there was gossip circulating about a rivalry between Ginger and me, about bad feelings because we'd both had relationships with Howard Hughes.

"It was also being said that Ginger was added to the cast to give it box office pop because I wasn't that kind of draw. I hoped that I was *my* kind of draw. Ginger and I didn't know each other all that well, but there was no bad feeling I ever noticed on her part, and I can guarantee there was none on mine.

"Though it wasn't my favorite film, I think Ginger must have only enhanced it. I don't think I ever saw the film when it was finished. I don't remember seeing it, and I don't even remember *not* seeing it.

"I never fussed a lot about my appearance before I went out in front of the camera. I wanted to look right for my character, even if that meant looking homelier than I was. I'm grateful that my looks suited so many parts.

"Ginger was quite the opposite of me. She always made a great fuss about her hair before she stepped into her scene. She would look in a mirror and then she would go back and look again.

"People said it was vanity. Fluffing up her hair, she'd get a side view, then she'd comb it, and look again. She explained, 'I *am* my hair.'

"I thought about it later and decided maybe it wasn't that Ginger was so vain as it was that she was insecure and felt dependent on her looks."

I spoke with Ginger Rogers about Katharine Hepburn years later. Rogers was in a wheelchair, and she was making a guest appearance at the 92nd Street Y in New York City because her publicist and friend, John Springer, had asked her to do it.

She said to me, "Don't mind this," indicating her chair. "I don't, so much. The worst thing about being in a wheelchair is the way people feel so sorry for you. I don't feel sorry for myself that way. I've had a wonderful life. I enjoyed it, every minute. I enjoyed even what I didn't enjoy. It's wonderful to be alive, and I'm planning to enjoy the rest of my life.

"I got fat because I don't get exercise anymore, and I don't want to give up eating. When you're a professional dancer, you get so much exercise, you can eat anything as often as you like.

"I'm leaving tomorrow, but I hope you'll write to me. If you do, I'll always answer." I did, and she did.

"When we were making *Stage Door*," Ginger Rogers continued, "the press built up a rivalry and competition between Katharine Hepburn and myself. Pretty silly stuff. We weren't girlfriends. We didn't know each other very well, unless sharing the same man at different times makes for a bond. I don't think so.

"I liked Howard Hughes and had good times with him. He was a better dancer than people knew, a good lead. We were close, but I wasn't in love with him, and he wasn't in love with me. Sometimes *not* being in love makes for a happier relationship.

"My mother didn't like him, and that mattered to me.

"Katharine Hepburn played such different types from me, almost opposites, and we were very different from each other. I'm very religious.

"I don't think any woman could have married Howard and held on to him unless she was willing to live with her eyes closed and had no pride."

As she wheeled herself away, she said, "Don't feel sorry for me. I'm dancing in my heart."


"In 1938 Hughes was the greatest hero in America," Kate recalled. "We had a lot of fun together, running away from the press, but I don't think either one of us would have liked it if no one noticed us."

Hughes taught Kate how to fly a plane. He told her she had good coordination, which was essential. Kate said to me, as she spoke about it, "Some teacher I had!

"I loved flying with Howard. We flew all over. I should say, Howard flew. I've flown myself and had zero fear. But with Howard, I had less than zero fear. I felt like a bird. We both felt like birds. Birds soaring. Eagles. What adrenaline! It was exhilarating.

"We'd land, and if we could, we'd find some secluded place where we could swim naked. I think we made a good-looking couple, naked and with our clothes on."

Kate especially loved Hughes's seaplane. He would land on the water in some isolated location, and she would take off all her clothes and dive from the wing into the water.

"We used to enjoy painting together. He asked me if I'd pose nude for him. I said, 'Sure, if you'll pose nude for *me*.' That ended the discussion."

Hughes made his round-the-world flight in 1938, and there was a ticker-tape parade in his honor. At that time, there was no greater celebrity in America. It was his moment, and he was sharing it with Katharine Hepburn.

The press and photographers gathered at Kate's New York City townhouse, hoping to get a picture of the lovers together. Howard and Kate met and stayed at Laura Harding's flat on East 52nd Street.

"We had a hideout meeting place, my friend Laura's place," Kate told me, "a few blocks from where I lived, which was right here, where we are now. [She was referring to her Turtle Bay townhouse.] Both Howard and I had ambivalent feelings toward publicity. We had the same feelings about the press. We didn't like tripping over them or being tripped up by them. The only thing worse for either of us, though we wouldn't have admitted it to each other, would have been being ignored by them."

Hughes was thirty-two, but he appeared boyish and shy. He was a year and a half older than Kate. "He had great confidence, despite being born in Humble, Texas," Kate said. "From Humble, but far from *humble*.

"I think Howard could understand me better than he could understand himself. Howard was the most purely passionate relationship of my life. Perhaps it was because it was a passionate age for me.

"I never liked a lot of mushy stuff. The words never seemed true if they came too easily. Howard wasn't one for a lot of excess words. He'd say, 'Will you marry me?' What more could he say?

"Howard thought it was funny to hear me use profanity or say something obscene. I didn't do it often, or I don't think he would have found it so charming. I suppose he enjoyed it because it was unexpected and shockingly against type for my public character and even for me, privately, except with Howard. Otherwise, I saved it for saying to Kath in my head. Nothing could shock Kath."

During the 1930s, because of the tense world situation, there was an especially patriotic spirit in the air in America. With his record-breaking round-the-world solo flight, Howard Hughes joined Charles Lindbergh, Wiley Post, Amelia Earhart, and other air pioneers as one of those who had helped establish the United States as the world leader in aviation.

"For Americans," Kate said, "he was the living personification of the American, though he was more reserved and modest about what he did than most people would be." Kate knew that Hughes's satisfaction was internal. He had shown *himself* that he could do it.

After Hughes had made his first round-the-world solo flight, he made another flight—for two. He took off with Kate from Westhampton, New York.

Kate understood that her greatest adventures would always be on-screen. Howard was a real-life hero. She risked only professional life and death, success or failure. "Howard put his *only* life on the line."

"Another dream of Hughes's was to become a motion picture producer." Not surprisingly, one of Hughes's first successes as a Hollywood producer was *Hell's Angels*, a film about flying.

"Howard spoke of my natural affinity for flying. Imagine hearing that from Howard. And he would never lie. At least, not where flying was concerned.

"It was fun, especially with Howard as my copilot.

"I could hardly wait to use my new skills in a picture. I wouldn't need a double and there wouldn't be any trickery."

Kate remembered newspapers speculating not on *whether* Hughes would marry Hepburn, only on *when*. "He was 'the King,' and I would be 'the Queen.'"

"I make an effort to get along with all of my costars, the director, everyone on the set," Cary Grant told me, "but I did not wish to establish a relationship with Baby." He was referring to the leopard in Howard Hawks's film *Bringing Up Baby*.

"I felt she might, at some moment, remember the call of her genes that told her she was a wild animal. Or she might like me too much and want to play. I hoped she'd had a good manicure, short claws, but I wasn't going to be the one to take a close look. Now, Kate was never as worried by Baby. She liked to pull her tail, fearless girl that she was, and Baby seemed to enjoy it. Kate didn't pull very hard."

"The way I saw my character, Susan," Kate said, "was, I did anything that came into my heart. There was a great deal of the way I see myself in Susan," Kate told me. I think of *Bringing Up Baby* as a farce of manners."

# Bringing Up Baby (1938)

Anthropologist David Huxley (Cary Grant) has almost reconstructed a brontosaurus skeleton. The missing bone will arrive the next day at Stuyvesant Museum of Natural History just as David is marrying his assistant, Alice Swallow (Virginia Walker).

That afternoon, David encounters Susan Vance (Katharine Hepburn), a peculiar young woman, first on the golf course, where he is soliciting an endowment for the museum, and then in a supper club, where negotiations are to continue. Unintentionally, she prevents him from meeting with the benefactor's lawyer (George Irving).

Next morning, after the bone arrives, Susan calls, desperate. Her brother has entrusted her with his pet leopard, Baby, and Susan is terrified. Believing she is in danger, David rushes to her apartment, carrying the bone along with him.

Susan is in no danger since Baby is quite tame. Susan persuades David to help her take Baby to her Aunt Elizabeth's home in Connecticut.

On the estate, Baby strays, making friends with Aunt Elizabeth's dog, George (Asta). George finds the bone and buries it.

David learns that Aunt Elizabeth (May Robson) is the museum benefactress. Susan introduces David as Mr. Bone.

David and Susan search for Baby. Thinking he has been captured by a touring circus, they release the wrong leopard from a cage in a passing truck.

David and Susan are jailed for disorderly conduct. Soon, they are joined by Aunt Elizabeth and a Major Applegate (Charles Ruggles). Learning that "Mr. Bone" is from Stuyvesant, Aunt Elizabeth decides not to go through with the endowment.

Back at the museum, David works on his incomplete brontosaurus, without the million-dollar bequest and unwed to Miss Swallow, who has rejected him.

Susan enters announcing *she* has her aunt's million dollars for the museum, and she has found the missing bone. When she climbs a rickety ladder to hand it to David, the entire skeleton collapses. David saves Susan as she is falling—for him.

"Kate and I spent a lot of time practicing together for the very tricky last scene," Grant remembered, "the great ending of the film, which was a lot easier for the writer to write than it was for us to do. Both Kate and I wanted to do the scene, but I voted for not doing it. I had experience in that kind of thing, but Kate had none, as far as I knew. She said, 'I could do that kind of thing when I was a child. My father strung up a trapeze for us, and I was *really* good.'

" 'Yes,' I said, 'but that was when you were a child.'

" 'You'll see,' she said, but still I was worried, more so because of the way it was set up. You see, she was supposed to grab on to me. If I had been grabbing her, I knew I would have no trouble holding on to her.

"It worked. It looked easy.

"I explained to her that she had to grab my wrists, which I had learned from someone in a circus. Not the hands. The wrists.

"I pulled her up, and it was delightfully easy. She was really light.

"I guess Howard Hawks the director, who hadn't shown any concern, may have had some. He looked quite happy when I *blithely* caught Kate. We didn't do any more takes. I asked her about it. I asked her if she'd been at all afraid.

" 'Oh, no.' She laughed. She looked innocently into my eyes. 'I trusted perfectly.' She said she knew I knew what I was doing.

"But the thing was, *she* was the one who had to do it just right. She really was a remarkable athlete, just as she had said. But you know, just the memory of that scene makes me shiver. If Kate had fallen, I'd never have forgiven myself. We were both crazy. *Bringing Up Baby* has always been called 'a screwball comedy.' Well, *we* were the two screwballs."

*Bringing Up Baby* lost money, "$365,000, give-or-take tens of thousands," Kate said.

In February 1938, the Independent Film Journal published an open letter to the Hollywood studios from the National Theatre Distributors of America. In it was a list of stars whom the writer of the letter, Harry Brandt, labeled as "box office poison." Kate was on the list, along with Bette Davis, Joan Crawford, Greta Garbo, and Marlene Dietrich. Brandt, who owned a chain of theaters in New York City, claimed that any one of these famous names was enough to keep audiences at home, that they were "box office poison." The Hollywood studios took this open letter quite seriously.

"Howard Hughes didn't talk a lot," Kate said. "Sometimes he felt he *had* to talk more when he was with strangers because if *he* didn't talk, *they* would talk, and he wouldn't hear them.

"With me, he could be quiet, but he did say some important words: 'Will you marry me?'

"He continued to ask me over a period of a few years. He was always very serious and very intense, and he chose romantic moments, but he never asked me when we were in bed. He said, 'Kate, never trust a man who asks you to marry him when he wants to go to bed with you. He'll say anything and then forget it just as easily.'

I appreciated Howard's advice, but I didn't need it. I wasn't looking for a husband—even Howard.

"Someone might say we were both cleanliness nuts. At the time we knew each other, it was within the bounds of reason, if a bit obsessive. I believe at that time, I was more obsessed than he. We each spent a lot of time washing our hands.

"We both firmly believed that a lot of germs were passed by not enough hand washing. I had my father's, the doctor's, firm belief in it to back me up. And the water should be hot enough, and the hands should be left under the water long enough.

"I think one of my most attractive features for Howard was my voice and diction. There were people who found my voice irritating. But Howard could hear me because I spoke so loudly and clearly.

"Howard never wanted to say 'What?' to people. He just pretended he heard them. What upset Howard most were people who mumbled. The mumblers were Howard's sworn enemies.

"Howard had everything. He was brilliant, athletic, daring, energetic, amusing, driven, fearless. Rich with a capital R.

"He was a wonderful lover. If I minded anything about it, it was that he was *too* good. Well practiced. Oh, well. There are worse things. He lived life to the fullest, like it could end at any time. And the way he lived, it could.

"In his teens, his hearing had begun to fail him. It had only begun, and it was not a real handicap—yet. The outside world grew fainter. It made him go more into himself. I don't know much about how deafness affects people, and Howard was never a complainer, but I think there were other problems, like ringing in his ears or hearing things, besides just not hearing well. He heard bits and pieces, which he had to put together. He still heard well enough to do editorial hearing. If you said something he wanted to hear, you could whisper into his ear. If he didn't want to accept what you were saying, shouting into a megaphone didn't help.

"The terrible accident he had may have caused his hearing to get worse. I think it did." On July 7, 1946, Hughes crashed in Beverly Hills while testing an experimental aircraft his company had been developing in secret. Hughes had insisted on being the test pilot himself.

"From then on, he was wrapped in a cocoon of pain. I don't think after that accident Howard ever had another moment without pain for the rest of his life. Any of us who has ever experienced excruciating pain can identify with somebody who never has it end.

"I thought I understood what pain was, but I didn't until I nearly lost my foot and experienced the inescapable pain that never went away, many years later, after my car accident. Like deafness, pain is isolating. I think Howard became addicted to painkillers.

Howard reached the point where he was trapped living only in his own mind. He had many early eccentricities. So did I. Howard was remembered at the end the way he was then, alone in his own strange world. In my mind, he lives at the height of his powers.

"I believe Howard's personality and his life were shaped by that deafness, which had begun to manifest itself long before I knew him. It was something gradual.

"As time passed, his hearing grew poorer. I tried to imagine what it was like for him. I had been lucky in life to be blessed by above-average hearing. I tried holding my hands over my ears to see what life would be like if I heard less well. I could still hear everything. What I wanted to experience was what Howard was enduring. I tried earplugs. I couldn't hear well when they were in. I could barely hear at all. It was terrible. I felt cut off. I felt isolated. I felt panic rising in me. But I knew I could take the earplugs out. So, I never could put myself into Howard's shoes.

"Howard was very intelligent, a genius. He had access to the best doctors in the world. So, very early, he knew that his future was threatened. I believe it was something hereditary. He never said anything about that.

"It may have influenced his desire to pack as much living into his early years as he possibly could. It may have made him more fearless. I was just as fearless as Howard.

"I knew nothing could happen to me. I knew it so perfectly, I didn't have to think about it. Stupid!

"Howard was fearless, in spite of, I think, being more aware of all of the dangers than anyone in the world. *That* is brave."


The disappointing public response to *Bringing Up Baby* caused RKO to rethink whatever ambitious plans they might have had for Katharine Hepburn, and they cast her in what they considered an audience-friendly vehicle: *Mother Carey's Chickens.* Kate rejected it and decided she had endured enough of Hollywood, to which she had never totally acclimated. Broadway was where she wanted to be, so she offered to buy out her RKO contract, and the studio readily agreed.

Before she left, however, there was one more film she wanted to make. It was actually the first film she had ever made. Her screen test was a scene from a successful play she had already done on stage: *Holiday* by Philip Barry.

A film had already been made of *Holiday*, in 1930 with Ann Harding, but Kate felt a sentimental attachment to the play and believed she could do it better. In those days, before television and video recordings, movies were generally forgotten by audiences as soon as they had left the theaters, especially early sound films.

Kate knew that Columbia owned the rights, so she offered to play Linda if they would remake the film. Her price, $175,000, was high for the studio, but they agreed to a one-picture deal. Part of their agreement was that George Cukor, the director of the screen test, would direct.

"I thought *Holiday* would have no part in my life," Kate said, "compared to all that work I'd done. How wrong can you be?

"When I did my screen test for *Bill of Divorcement*, I took a scene from *Holiday*. It won George Cukor and it won me my film debut in that wonderful part opposite the legendary John Barrymore and directed by George.

"When I was chosen to understudy Hope Williams in *Holiday* on Broadway, I was thrilled, at first. As time passed, I realized that Hope was a very healthy girl. It wasn't that I wished her anything bad. She was very talented and very nice. But I understood that being an understudy was almost worse than not being in the theater at all, if you understudied someone who never missed a performance.

"As we got close to the end of the run, and I'd given up hope where Hope was concerned, she said to me, 'Would you like me to stay home for a matinee performance so you can play the part once on Broadway?'

"I said, 'No, thank you.'

"It was really a very magnanimous gesture, and I think I wasn't very gracious in rejecting it. I don't remember exactly, so I hope I behaved better than I think I did. An excess of pride. It was what I suffered from.

"Through the years afterward, dear George said to me many times, 'Success can't be a favor, my girl.'"

## *Holiday* (1938)

Johnny Case (Cary Grant) has a special philosophy of life. He wants to earn enough money when he is young to retire very early while he can still enjoy his money. Then, he can go back to work in his old age, and he will have memories of good times and experiences he might not otherwise have had. "Retire young, work old" is his motto. "Then you'll know what you're working for."

Enjoying a financial windfall, Johnny takes a holiday at Lake Placid, where he meets Julia Seton (Doris Nolan), an attractive young woman who seems to agree with his unconventional ideas. Being an impulsive romantic, he falls in love with her and proposes, not realizing she is a member of one of New York's wealthiest families. She accepts.

When she takes him home to meet her family, he is surprised by their Manhattan mansion and opulent way of life.

Julia and her banker father (Henry Kolker) listen to his plan to retire in mid-life and inform him that they do not agree. Their strongly opposite views on what a husband is supposed to do threatened the couple's engagement plans.

Linda Seton (Katharine Hepburn), Julia's sister and the black sheep of the family, understands both sides of the argument and tries to reconcile them. Supporting her in these peacemaking efforts is her alcoholic brother, Ned (Lew Ayres), whose musical ambitions have been thwarted by his father's insistence that he work in the family bank.

Linda falls in love with Johnny, whose ideas are like hers. The engagement between Johnny and Julia is broken, and he leaves for his next "holiday," away from a conventional existence. Linda follows him.

*Holiday* was a commercial failure, attributed by some to Kate's "box office poison" status.

George Cukor was set to direct David Selznick's *Gone With the Wind*. Many believed that Katharine Hepburn was the leading candidate for the role of Scarlett O'Hara.

Bette Davis had been Kate's chief rival for the part, but she had been ruled out for, among other reasons, her *Jezebel* success.

Cukor said, "Selznick didn't like the idea of having Katharine Hepburn as his Scarlett. He had liked the idea of Bette Davis even less. Neither represented his dream. Then, he found Vivien Leigh. Gone with the part!

"Kate was certain she wouldn't be chosen by Selznick, so even before Vivien Leigh was selected, she said she didn't want the part."

" 'I wanted the part pretty much,' she told me, 'but I preferred to reject it rather than be rejected. I knew I wasn't beautiful enough. Come to think of it, I wasn't beautiful at all. I couldn't fill men's hearts with desire the way Scarlett was supposed to do.'"

After the commercial failure of *Holiday* and the mild disappointment of not getting Scarlett O'Hara, Kate returned to her parents' Fenwick home in Connecticut for an extended stay. There, she was hoping to revive her faltering screen career with a Broadway success when an unexpected natural catastrophe interrupted her reveries.

"I'm a very optimistic person," Kate said, "which is a happy-go-lucky way to be. I pretty much go forward on positive intuition, or on not thinking at all. I've never been one to stand still making possible scenarios.

"It's never seemed to me that pessimists have a good chance for success because they are stepping on their own hopes and dreams. Of course, there are some modest precautions anyone but a fool would take, and I never considered myself a fool. Before you dive, make sure there's water in the pool, although I'm sure I did make some risky moves, especially in sports, without understanding the extent of the danger. I always assumed foolishly that I might be slightly injured, sprain or break something, or even that I might kill myself. What I didn't consider was that I might have been permanently crippled, living the rest of my life in an impaired condition. I made it through without serious mishaps, so as it turned out, I'm glad I didn't know.

"My father believed in testing himself, and he thought nothing of testing us, of tying our sleds to his car when we were children, and we thought nothing of it, too, except we knew it was fun. We trusted Father perfectly in everything. He was *the doctor*. We knew that he had all of the answers, and all of the questions, too. He was our hero.

"Our mother never criticized him or disagreed with him. At least not in our presence. Their relationship seemed to us to be perfect romance, the dream relationship between a husband and wife.

"I never heard my father criticize her. He encouraged her to pursue interests outside our home that completed her. The only thing I found strange was after my mother's death, my father threw away a lot of pamphlets she had collected. I learned that he thought they were too far left to have other people find them and not understand.

"When a hurricane and floods took our beloved home, Fenwick, I called my father, who was in Hartford, as soon as I could, and his first words were, 'Is your mother safe?' She was.

"It was one of those unforgettable days in my life. It happened in 1938. I was at home. It was late September, so the summer people had boarded up, and I liked it that way. The water was considered too cold to swim. But not for me. I got up early so I wouldn't miss anything. I was generally alone at that time in the morning and I've always liked that. With few exceptions, I like eating breakfast alone.

"On the day of the hurricane, although I didn't know I would remember it all my life as 'the day of the hurricane,' I went for a swim. It seemed to be an especially beautiful day. One of those lovely cool breezes was blowing.

"The breeze was increasing when I went to play golf with a friend. Then, the most exciting thing happened, or so it seemed when it happened. But compared to what happened afterward, it wasn't so important.

"I got a hole in one! Imagine that!

"But before I could tell anyone, the wind was no longer a breeze. I couldn't remember it ever being like that. I could see the waves getting higher. We went there to swim and take advantage of those waves, and we stayed quite a while.

"I had a new car, a Lincoln, and I had a chauffeur. I was pretty successful. When we got home, I asked the chauffeur to put my car into the garage. Someone had come by to do some repairs, and when his car flew away, we knew this was no ordinary day.

"Then, the tide came across our lawn and a wing of our house broke off. Mother believed the house, a wooden house, built in 1870, was safe. But we decided we had to leave. Mother and I left by the window on the side of the house that looked safest. We found a rope and dropped out the window. My brother Dick was standing in water and caught us. The water wasn't normal at all, and we headed for high land. It was from there we watched our house sail away. As it sailed away, I forgot all about my hole in one. What's a hole in one compared to a hurricane? Anyway, I got a hole in one, and I know it.

"Our house got stuck before it floated away, and my brother recovered some of his papers from the second floor.

"We'd had the house twenty-five years, and it seemed like it had always been ours. We took shelter for the night in a nearby building, and at dawn I went out to see how badly damaged our house was.

"The problem was, we couldn't find our house.

"After it had sailed away, we began to dig. I spent days on my hands and knees, digging in the sand for a cup with a broken handle or a bent silver teaspoon, the bits and pieces of our life in the house. I especially hoped to find one of my mother's dear treasures, her tea service, the fragile china cups and cake plates, or more likely a silver cake fork, or a serving piece.

"Everyone else gave up, and they were leaving. 'You'll never find anything, Kath. There couldn't be anything worth saving buried under all that. You might as well give up.' But I was determined. I wasn't going to give up.

"Just then, I felt it. Something. It was still buried under sand, and every time I got hold of it, more sand moved over to cover it. I gave it a good pull and there it was, one of Mother's silver petit four dishes. I felt my heart beating faster. The dish was priceless to me. I couldn't wait to give it to her. And then I felt something else. It couldn't be, but it was. It was one of her teacups, and I carefully retrieved it, like in an archaeological dig. I couldn't believe it, but there was the handle. It was all in one piece. No chips. A miracle. I wasn't tired anymore.

"We children had always been very careful of Mother's dishes. We knew they meant so much to her. You could hold them up to the light and see right through them. That meant they were the best, but also the most fragile. Sometimes secretly, I wished she wouldn't use those wondrous dishes. I thought I would have died if I'd ever broken one. One day, I confided my worry to Mother.

"She said, 'Don't worry, Kath. I love you more than *any* dishes.' That made me happy, but no less worried.

"Some of my siblings returned to see about me, and when they saw what had transpired, they were quickly down on their hands and knees, engaged in a fervent treasure hunt.

"Well, you won't believe it, but we eventually found her set of dishes intact.

"There were two things we could do. We could sit there and cry and cry. That didn't seem a good choice. So, instead, we started drawing a plan for our new house, which we would be building on the same spot. We wanted it to be exactly the same as our house, but with a few touches, with a few improvements that would make a good thing out of a bad thing, for our trouble, inconveniences, and expense. It turned out my father had bought a lot of fire insurance because we lived in a big wooden house. He didn't have flood insurance.

"We rebuilt. Everyone was asked about little touches each of us would like. My father built up higher, about three feet higher, I think, but not as high as we should have. Our house never took off again, but it wasn't high enough that we didn't worry. We didn't worry much, however. We weren't a worrying family.

"When Father rebuilt the house, it was very similar. People called it identical, though it wasn't. There was a new cabinet for Mother's dishes and drawers for the silver. She used them for the rest of her life. The table was set for tea with those dishes when she died. After that, they stayed at Fenwick, and we all used them.

"It was a wonderful house, and we all enjoyed the new one more as it got a little worn and stopped looking so brand-new.

"We all loved it, but something I never told anyone was that I never felt about it the way I did about the old house. It didn't have the same memories. No matter how many years I lived there, it always seemed like a bit of a pretender.

"I slept with Howard Hughes to get *The Philadelphia Story*," Kate told me.

"Well, not exactly, but that's the way it worked out. We had a lot of fun. He was a brilliant man and going to bed with him was very pleasurable. But the pleasure of owning *The Philadelphia Story* lasted longer."

*The Philadelphia Story* opened on Broadway, March 28, 1939, produced by the Theatre Guild and featuring Katharine Hepburn.

It was a tremendous success with the opening night audience, with the audiences that followed as well as with the critics. The reviews emphasized the star, and Kate's reputation and morale soared.

"But I had trouble going on at eight P.M. and staying up much later," Kate told me. "I've always been completely a morning person. Starting at five A.M. didn't unhinge me. I often got up then, just from choice."

Kate gave a great deal of credit for the play's success to the marvelous cast that appeared with her. She raved over Joseph Cotten, saying he was one of the most unappreciated actors on Broadway. Cotten played C. K. Dexter Haven, Tracy Lord's ex-husband. Van Heflin was Macaulay Connor, the journalist, and his photographer assistant was Shirley Booth.

In Hollywood, there was studio interest in the play, particularly from Warners and M-G-M. Several actresses were considered for the lead—Ann Sheridan, Joan Crawford, Norma Shearer. One actress who was *not* considered was Katharine Hepburn. Kate told me she didn't think they even rejected her. "They just never even *thought* of me. I wasn't obvious enough, right up there on the stage, six nights a week and matinees."

The studios, producers, and agents met with a brick wall when they tried to negotiate for film rights. "I played Tracy Lord for a year on the stage, but no one made me any offers for a part in the Hollywood film. No one realized I owned it."

Howard Hughes, who was far wiser about business matters than Kate, advised her to buy the rights to *The Philadelphia Story*, and to do it quickly. "Buy it before it opens," he said. Kate readily acknowledged it as good advice; but she didn't feel she could raise $30,000 at that moment. She didn't want to go to her father because it would hurt her pride to have to ask him for the money, even though some of it was hers, earned by her. Kate always gave her father all of her money, and he invested it conservatively for her. She thought he wouldn't let her have it because it was far from Dr. Hepburn's idea of the proper way to invest money. She believed he would have thought it was throwing money away.

While Kate wondered what to do, Hughes, as always, was a man of action. He understood there was no time to be lost or Kate risked losing the part that had been tailor-made for her, and which he believed, as did she, was a part she *had* to have, a turning point in her career. There would be a lot of competition for such a great part.

So Hughes bought the film rights for *The Philadelphia Story* and gave them as a gift to Kate. She preferred this gift to any jewel he could possibly have given her, to any of those he already had given to her. Thirty thousand dollars was not a significant amount to Hughes, but even if it had been a great deal more, Kate knew money would not have deterred him.

"I'd acquired the film rights to *The Philadelphia Story*. Clever girl, me. Of course, it was really Howard who said to do it. He explained it to me. While I was thinking it made sense, he had the cash and acted fast. Generally, he didn't have to say anything more than once to me."

Joseph Mankiewicz told me, "Kate Hepburn was very fortunate to have Howard Hughes as her protector. I wouldn't have minded having a protector like that myself. He was her dedicated suitor. Personally, she was too thin for my taste."

Kate had the power, and no one would be able to acquire the film rights without her as the star. Also, she would have approval of the other actors and the director.

She favored Louis B. Mayer and M-G-M to do the film version. "He called me Katharine. I called him Mr. Mayer." Conveniently, Mayer made the best offer. Kate had told him that she didn't like to bargain, and that she wanted him to begin with his best offer.

Mayer offered her $175,000 for the rights and $75,000 to her for the starring role. Kate was especially gratified because she felt he genuinely wanted her as the star.

"It was just like everything I bought," she said. "Once I bought it, I never remembered what I paid for it. I just knew I owned it, and that was what was important. I could always call Howard and ask him what things cost. He might have thought I was a fool not to remember. Maybe he didn't remember, either, and would have to have someone look it up for him. I don't think Howard thought a lot about what things cost. He just knew what he wanted. That was one thing about Howard. He always knew what he wanted. The price of *Philadelphia Story* was small change in his world.

"I knew exactly who I wanted as director. Who else? George Cukor, of course. *A Bill of Divorcement, Little Women, Sylvia Scarlett, Holiday*, which was Phil Barry's play, too. I wouldn't have anyone else. Mr. Mayer felt just the way I did, about George being the perfect director.

"I knew which two actors I wanted, and they both had M-G-M contracts: Clark Gable and Spencer Tracy. Perfect, I thought. It turned out that they both had other commitments. I assumed that was true, but it might have been that one or both of them weren't enthusiastic about the parts. I had a perfect idea that was even better. Cary Grant. He should have been my first thought.

"Then Mr. Mayer suggested James Stewart, whom I'd admired so in *Mr. Smith Goes to Washington*. He said Stewart was very enthusiastic about the part and the play, and it turned out that it was true. I always loved enthusiastic people. A bit of enthusiasm never hurts, and more is even better. I asked which part he was enthusiastic about. He hadn't said. That was for the best.

"Cary was more difficult to deal with. It was better to offer him his choice. He chose to be the ex-husband." With Cary Grant in the part, the role was expanded. Tracy's brother was dropped entirely to allow for the expansion of Grant's part. In the play, it's Tracy's brother who arranges for the magazine to cover the wedding.

Philip Barry wrote the character of Tracy Lord based on the way he saw Katharine Hepburn. "Phil was a friend of mine," she said. "Wasn't I lucky?

"Tracy's voice is *my* voice! Don't you recognize me?

"Phil said the character wasn't *all* me. He said that there was another girl he knew, and that my part was a sort of a composite, even though *I* predominated.

"Well, I knew that was a lie. The part was *all* me, but Phil didn't want me to know that because he thought if there was something I didn't like about my character, I might get angry and say I wouldn't do it. No chance. I loved it. It was me, but Phil couldn't change his story.

"My having the name Tracy, that was just a lucky touch. I don't know why Phil chose that name. It predicted my future.

"Without *The Philadelphia Story* and Phil and Howard, my life would have been very different. It would have gone on, but maybe my career wouldn't have."

## The Philadelphia Story (1940)

In a brief silent opening, the marriage of Tracy Lord (Katharine Hepburn) and C. K. Dexter Haven (Cary Grant) is summarized and ended.

As she throws him out of her mansion in a prelude to divorce, she gleefully breaks one of his golf clubs in half. He retaliates by pushing her in the face, back through the front door, having briefly contemplated socking her instead. She lands on the carpeted floor with only her pride dented.

Two years later, Tracy is engaged to marry someone considered more stable, the politically ambitious George Kittredge (John Howard). Planning the ceremony, the Lords hope to keep the wedding as intimate as possible.

Sidney Kidd (Henry Daniell), publisher of *Spy* magazine, blackmails the Lord family into allowing one of his reporters, Macaulay "Mike" Connor (James Stewart), and a photographer, Liz Imbrie (Ruth Hussey), into the mansion to cover the event for a feature piece entitled "The Philadelphia Story." Their entrée is arranged by Dexter. The Lords have agreed to this unprecedented invasion of their privacy in exchange for Kidd not printing a scandalous story about their divorced father's romantic involvement with a dancer.

Dexter is far from unwelcome in the Lord household. Both Tracy's mother (Mary Nash) and her little sister, Dinah (Virginia Weidler), welcome Dexter's temporary return with open arms, but dislike the intrusion of *Spy*.

Tracy, however, is intrigued by Mike after she reads some of his short stories. Although their backgrounds are different, she finds she has more in common with him than she has with the stiff, mirthless George. Both of them, however, are preferable to Dexter, whom she appears to loathe. Dexter considers her "a spoiled prig."

In spite of Mike's distaste for her world and his own romance with Liz, he becomes infatuated with Tracy, and he is encouraged in this by Dexter, who doesn't approve of George at all. Dexter still loves Tracy, and she loves him, though she denies it, even to herself.

Just before the wedding, George learns that his bride to be and Mike may have spent a drunken night together. He demands an explanation or he threatens to call off the wedding. Tracy is relieved to be rid of him. Mike offers to take his place as groom, but Tracy rejects his offer and chooses to remarry Dexter.

"Tracy didn't really want to be in an ivory tower," Kate said. "I understood my character quite well because it was exactly how both Katharine Hepburn and Kathy felt."

Kate had the opportunity to display her aquatic skills when her character dives into the pool. She was proud of that dive. "It was a very good dive in only one take."

*The Philadelphia Story* was filmed in eight weeks. Producer Joseph Mankiewicz told me about the parts of C. K. Dexter Haven and Tracy Lord's brother being combined.

"L. B. Mayer loved the play but demanded that Kate have two leading men. I agreed with him. It would have placed me in a difficult position *not* to agree with him, but in this instance, I thought he was quite right. Kate's last picture, *Holiday*, had been a flop, and it was by Barry, too. Our thinking was that even if she still was 'box office poison,' a couple of male stars might be the perfect solution. But the part of the ex-husband was too small, so it was my idea to combine him with the play's character of Tracy's brother.

"It worked. The picture was a smash hit that won two Oscars out of eight nominations. Kate was nominated for Best Actress. James Stewart won an Oscar for Best Actor and Donald Ogden Stewart for Best Screenplay.

"Some people said that Stewart won because he had deserved to win the year before for *Mr. Smith Goes to Washington*. Well, I thought his performance in *The Philadelphia Story* was wonderful and that he *deserved* his Oscar."

Mankiewicz said he had received a call from Stewart just after the actor received the *Philadelphia Story* script. Everything was great except that he didn't want to play the fiancé. He loved the part of the reporter, and that was the part he hoped he could have. He started to present his reasons why he was better suited to the part of the reporter, but Mankiewicz cut him off.

"You've got it," Mankiewicz said.

"Don't you have to ask anyone else?" Stewart said. "You can just do it all by yourself?"

"Yes, Jim. I can because that's the part we had you down for."

"I'll tell you the experience I had that I always think of when I think about Katharine Hepburn," James Stewart told me. "It happened while we were filming *Philadelphia Story*. I'd always liked to fly. I liked it a lot, and Kate knew I did. She asked if she could fly with me. She told me that she'd flown a lot with Howard Hughes. I knew that. Everybody knew that. I said I'd be pleased to have her along, and I meant it.

"But it turned out she was a backseat flier, like there are backseat drivers, only I'd never flown with a backseat flier before. I hope I never do again.

" 'Yak, yak, yak. She never stopped. And she didn't just ask questions. She asked the kind of questions which required answers from me. I couldn't just shrug them off with a yup or a headshake no. They were pretty complicated questions. She knew a lot about planes. I didn't think these were things she needed to know and surely not at that moment. I thought she could wait to get better informed until we were standing on terra firma. I couldn't be rude and say, 'Keep quiet,' even 'Please keep quiet.' I thought of pretending to be hard of hearing, but that didn't do the job. She just shouted, and could she ever shout, with that great voice and diction, but it wasn't any fun on a small plane.

"I envied Cary being able to give her a pretty good push in that first scene of *Philadelphia Story*. Of course, I'd never have done it, but there was a certain point where I couldn't help feeling that way, especially when I was landing the plane.

"Once we were standing outside the plane, Kate smiled that wonderful smile of hers at me, and she said, 'Oh, that was wonderful. I enjoyed it so much. Thank you. Let's do it very soon again.'

"I think I turned white. I began thinking about future excuses to get me out of it. I didn't want any bad feeling to wreck our big love scene. Besides, I liked her, only I thought it probably would be better if I didn't offer her a ride home, but I had to.

"All I can say is Hughes must have been made of iron, or something stronger."

"On *Philadelphia Story*," Stewart told me, "George Cukor encouraged us to ad-lib whenever we got inspired, and I'm really proud of one ad-lib I contributed.

"I had what seemed like this perfect moment for me to have some hiccoughs. I didn't even tell George Cukor what I was going to do. I wasn't sure myself how I would do it or that it would turn out right. But I felt I couldn't telegraph hiccoughs and have people waiting for it. That would spoil all the spontaneity of an ad-libbed hiccough. It was the sort of thing I didn't even practice at home more than a couple times. I was worried about getting a stagey hiccough. It's not wise to fine-tune a hiccough.

"It was a scene with Cary Grant. Well, I did it. I hiccoughed. He wasn't expecting it, but his reaction was perfect. He ad-libbed an 'Excuse me.' I hiccoughed again. He never stopped his performance, and it was a great take. After it was all over, Cary expressed his respect for my hiccoughs.

"I think our friendship after that was founded on a hiccough.

"I wouldn't have tried it with just any director, but George was always open to suggestions. He'd say, 'Let's try it.' There were people who said he was a woman's director, implying that he was better for actresses and more generous to them than he was with actors. Not so. He helped me a lot. I think he helped me more than he did Kate, but I needed it more. I'd say he was 'an actor's director.' He came from a Broadway stage background, and he always thought about how to help the actor. Then he'd take you aside, so you were never embarrassed in front of everyone else. It was yours and his business and no one else's."

"Owning *The Philadelphia Story*," Kate told me, "was one of the best things that ever happened to me. I think I made a little money, too. It was life-changing, what it did for my career. Howard knew best."

The film opened at New York City's Radio City Music Hall after Christmas 1940, and broke the previous attendance records established by *Snow White and the Seven Dwarfs*. It closed only because another film was booked, Alfred Hitchcock's *Rebecca*.

"When my affair with Howard Hughes ended," Kate said, "he believed I wasn't going to marry him because finally he believed *I* believed I wasn't.

"Looking back, I'm not sure *why* I didn't marry him. I said no the first time without giving much thought to it, and I guess it got to be like that, a habit, especially if you assume the offer will be made again. And so it was, for a few years.

"Well, one day, or rather one night, Howard asked me to marry him, and I, having come to take for granted one of the most brilliant, exciting, bravest, kindest, most attractive men in the world, who cared about me, said no without any serious thought. I didn't know it was the last time he would ask me to marry him, that he finally got tired of hearing me say no.

"I knew for sure just after the hurricane when his plane landed and someone else stepped out. I thought it would be Howard, but it wasn't. He didn't fly in himself. He had sent someone else to deliver the bottled water. At first I thought he didn't come himself because he sensed my parents wouldn't welcome his arrival at that moment, which was true.

"At that moment, I wanted Howard more than bottled water. I understood Howard didn't care about how much a bottle of water cost brought in that way. I knew he never gave that kind of money any thought, but he valued his time. He said he knew how much money he had, but he didn't know how much time he had. The way he lived his life, he could say that again. No scaredy-cat he. He wrote his own life insurance policy.

"At first, I was glad to see the water, but when I thought about it, it was like those bottles you find that have a message in them. As the pilot gave us our water, I understood that Howard and me, as it had been, was over. Our love affair had turned into a friendship.

"We remained friends over the years, keeping in touch by phone. He always began every conversation with me by asking me how I was and wanting to hear how everything was going for me. 'How are you' wasn't the usual polite opening. He wanted to know everything I wanted to tell. He cared. He was a totally magnanimous person.

"Several years after our intense friendship was no longer intense, he called me and said the regular, 'How are you? How is everything? Is there anything I can do for you?'

"Well, it so happened there was. I said, 'Yes I'm about to be house hunting in Los Angeles.'

" 'I've got the answer,' he said, 'a lovely house RKO owns. You can use that one as long as you want, and it's rent-free.'

"Howard was the owner of RKO at that time. He said, 'Rent-free and you can come to the warehouse and select from everything the studio owns, anything you want for the house. It's already well furnished, but help yourself to anything you like at the warehouse.

There are some nice things there. They have a lot of pretty vases for your flowers. And I'll be the first to send you flowers.'

"I caught my breath. That could mean a florist shop emptied and on my doorstep, or knowing Howard, probably all assimilated and arranged in Lalique vases. Howard's generosity was awesome.

"When I arrived in California, I couldn't resist going immediately to the RKO warehouse to see what was there. In one of the dim, object-filled rooms, I saw the tall, lanky figure I knew so well, a little stooped, but still handsome. We were both a little shy.

"He said, 'It's good to see you, Kath. You're looking swell. Beautiful.' Not great dialogue, but I was pleased. Howard never said what he didn't mean. I have to admit I felt some old feelings I'd had, palpitations.

"When I left, I said I'd be back to select some things, another day.

"He said, 'Another day. Fine.'

"I never knew how Howard could have known just when I would be there. It was the last time we saw each other.

"He was one of the few people I told about Spencer, from the beginning. I didn't really think about it. Trusting him came naturally. Howard would not have known how to betray anyone, especially me. I would never have insulted him by saying, 'It's a secret. Please don't tell anyone.' If there was anything Howard understood it was privacy and secrecy. Howard was the living embodiment of discretion.

"I have great memories of Howard. He was almost fearless. I say 'almost fearless' because I never saw him show any sign of fear. But that doesn't mean that deep down, inside where no one could see, he didn't have a little wellspring of fear. It might have been so deep and secret, he didn't even know about it himself. If he did have fear, and he had to because he was not stupid, then he was even braver than we know. He was able to go out and act fearlessly.

"When he asked me to marry him, I knew it couldn't work. Each of us loved our work better than we could love each other. Perhaps love wasn't the right word. But we did feel a great bond, and it lasted through the years.

"He was considered very eccentric. I have always considered myself eccentric, too eccentric to judge anyone else. Later his eccentricity took over.

"We were terribly self-centered people. I believed two people so self-centered couldn't possibly get along together. I may have been wrong. Maybe that was the best way. We were so busy pleasing ourselves and going on our own way, we had no time or inclination to find any fault in each other.

"I almost never talked about my brother Tom, certainly never with my parents. Never with my brothers and sisters. Somehow, I felt I could with Howard, especially when we were flying.

"We had a lot of time, and I felt he understood because he'd lost his parents when he was young. He said sixteen was a tough age for a boy. I told him how my parents had said we must never mention Tom.

"He said maybe it was because of the way he died that they didn't want to talk about it. I didn't think that was it. I believed it was because they didn't want us growing up in a household of sadness.

"One subject we never talked about was money. I never found it an interesting subject to talk about, and I don't think he did either, or we would have talked about it. He had plenty of other people he could talk about money with.

"He may have enjoyed talking about money with business people who shared that facet of his interest. Personally, I think he wasn't interested in talking about money, only in making it. I don't think he was even too interested in making it. He just happened to make it because he was genuinely, deeply interested in things that made money.

"I was only interested in acting, and I made money doing that, though money was never a motivating factor in my life. Lucky me.

"I have always had enough, more than I needed to spend, and enough to be independent, which is a luxury. It meant I could say no, which I frequently did, and it may not have been the best thing. Maybe I said no to some of what I should have said yes to. I know I said yes sometimes when I should have said no. Judging a script is not an exact science.

"I've been called 'independent' all my life. I like the word, but I think that not having to worry about money contributed greatly to that. Greatly.

"I don't know about how it affected Howard's feelings toward me, but it may have made him feel easier with me knowing that what I felt for him was for him and not for his money.

"Of course, I'm sure I liked the idea of his success and that helped make him a man to admire. But I personally had no use for all that money. If I'd examined my thinking about it then, which I didn't, I might have thought it was a big responsibility.

"Howard once said to me, 'You're like an upside-down cake.' I gave some thought to that. That meant I have upside-down think-ing. I was unconventional. Maybe it came from standing on my head so much when I was a child, and I continued it. A good exer-cise, good for the blood and circulation.

"Howard admired my ability. He never quite mastered standing on his head. Just as well.

"I did it to impress my father, who loved gymnastics, but then I found I enjoyed it. Perhaps I enjoyed the accomplishment of the trick. We were all taught to enjoy the accomplishment of a trick.

"I wondered if long ago that's what Tom was trying to do—accomplish a trick."

# 5

# "Oh, Spence"

"Our screen characters fell in love," Kate told me. "I don't know which came first, our screen characters falling in love, or *us* falling in love. I think it was *us* first, but our screen characters knew it first."

*Woman of the Year* began filming in late August 1941. Joseph Mankiewicz was again the producer.

"It was Kate who personally offered the script for *Woman of the Year* to Louis B. Mayer for M-G-M," Mankiewicz told me. "She said there was a firm price, no negotiation, of $100,000. One hundred thousand dollars was the same sum Kate was receiving as *her* salary.

"Mayer had the greatest respect for Kate as an actress and as a person. He believed in her judgment about films, especially about a part for herself. He said she always understood what she could do, what she could do best.

"Mayer wanted my opinion on the script. He told me that he was certain, at that price, that the writer was one of experience and renown and that they had some reason for not revealing his name. Kate had been adamant on that. She'd made it a firm condition that the script purchase had to be bought entirely for itself and not because of the well-established name of the writer. Kate was an honorable person.

"She refused to tell who wrote the script. That would have been unacceptable if it had been said by an agent, but this was Katharine Hepburn, after all, and she wanted to do the script. When Mayer gave it to me, I read it immediately. I liked it. Mayer and I agreed that it was very well done, and that the writer must be someone special. That idea was confirmed by the price Kate said would have to be paid for the script."

Kate told me, "I'd learned something from Leland and maybe something of Howard Hughes rubbed off on me, too. It's a sort of philosophy. If you don't think you're worth a lot, why should anyone offer more?"

"We all waited anxiously to learn the identity of the prestigious writer," Mankiewicz told me. "It turned out to be a writing team, Ring Lardner, Jr., and Michael Kanin, Garson's brother."

Years later, Michael Kanin told me he was ecstatic when Kate told him that the script was being purchased. "When I heard the price, I couldn't believe what had happened. Only Kate could have done it. What a boost she gave to my career."

"I had to create the mystery," Kate said, "and set the price high because it was the only way there was a chance the script would be done, and I wanted to do it. I also had in mind the actor I wanted to play opposite me. I knew Spencer Tracy would be perfect."

"It had seemed Tracy was not going to be available," Mankiewicz said. "And then, as so often happens in Hollywood, sometimes producing greater casting than anything you could ever have imagined, he suddenly became free. And so we had a new team like Myrna Loy and William Powell were. I think even greater. Tracy and Hepburn. It was greater because there was not only magic on the screen between them, but it was clear there were genuine sparks as well.

"Cukor, who was Hepburn's favorite director and best friend, was busy directing something with Garbo, I think, so Kate suggested George Stevens, a fine director she'd worked with before. Stevens met with almost everyone's approval.

"Tracy wasn't thrilled. He was the only one who wasn't thrilled about the choice of a director, but he was the most important. When he spoke with me about Stevens, he said, 'Stevens is that woman's friend, and he's going to direct the picture as a woman's picture, giving "that woman" all of the advantages, the best angles, close-ups.' He was talking about Kate, calling her 'that woman.' No respect. Plenty of antipathy. But at some point during the film, I noticed that the ice was melting.

"As the film progressed, and the onscreen relationship between Sam Craig and Tess Harding seemed to be changing, the real-life relationship between Spencer Tracy and Katharine Hepburn seemed to be changing, too.

"I have to admit that when they first met, I was surprised that they didn't hit it off at all. It was icy-cool between them. I wasn't expecting love at first sight, but I wasn't expecting *hate* at first sight, either! They were like cats and dogs guarding their territory.

"Kate was wearing high heels, so she was a little taller than Tracy. She said, 'I fear I may be a little too tall for you, Mr. Tracy.'

"And I said, 'Don't worry, Kate. He'll cut you down to size.'

"I thought it could be a problem. Well, that was all right for the first part of the film, but as it becomes a love story, I wasn't certain that, even though both Hepburn and Tracy were fine actors, they could overcome their lack of rapport, let alone the male-female re-action that was supposed to exude sexual attraction.

"As they got to know each other, there was still an edge to their conversation, but it was a different kind of edge. There was sup-posed to be a strong sexual attraction, a battle of the sexes, in which the sexual attraction played a big role.

"Tracy said to me, 'I think Stevens is favoring me in his setups. Can you talk to him so he does better by Kate.' I noticed he wasn't calling her 'that woman' anymore. He was asking me to speak with Stevens about doing better by Kate!

"Well, just a little later, Kate was there asking if she could have a few minutes of my time, alone. Of course, she could!

"She had come to tell me that she thought George was favoring her because they were friends, and she would prefer it if he would shift his emphasis to show Spence more. Could I do that? I said I would speak with George. And I did.

"I went to George and said, 'You won't believe this but,' and I told him about what Tracy said and then what Kate said. He wasn't at all surprised. He'd already heard from Tracy and from Kate.

"He said, 'This morning Tracy got in very early, and he came up to me and said, "You know I think you're sort of . . ." I thought he was going to say, sort of favoring Kate, and he was going to com-plain. Just the opposite. I'd been trying very hard to play no favor-ites between them and be equally fair to each, not because I wanted to please both or either one of them, but because that was what I wanted to do. I wanted to achieve the balance.

" 'In the afternoon, Kate came to me and said, "George, there's something I have to talk to you about." She said *to* you, not *with* you, so I was already worried. Then, she said, "George, dear," and that *really* worried me. Usually the "dear" was a bad sign and meant that she was going to tell me something about how I should direct the picture, something I wouldn't agree with. This time, she was very nice. She said, "Just one thing. I think you've been favoring me, and I hope you'll do more with Spencer. After all, I think this film, even though it's called *Woman of the Year*, is really more about Sam than Tess, and also, could you photograph for *his* best side?"

" 'Actually, I didn't think either one of them had a best side. They both had *two* best sides.'

"Each was concerned that the other should be given the best possible chance in the film.

"George and I looked at each other, and we both understood. Our stars were living out the script in real life.

"Our stars were falling in love!"

## *Woman of the Year (1942)*

When *New York Sun* columnists Sam Craig (Spencer Tracy) and Tess Harding (Katharine Hepburn) feud in print over the relevancy of sports in a world at war, they are ordered by the newspaper to make peace.

Surprisingly, when they actually meet, they are strongly attracted to each other. Though their romance is full of obstacles and surprises, Sam realizes he loves her, and she accepts his marriage proposal. Their wedding night is interrupted by the unexpected arrival of refugees and revelers, but the unwanted guests are finally enticed away to another party, and the newlyweds have their wedding night alone.

Sam and Tess are so busy with their separate careers, they seldom see each other, and he resents being known as the husband of a famous woman. He wants a conventional marriage, with a family. Tess tries adopting a refugee child, but it doesn't work out.

When Tess is named Woman of the Year, she and Sam argue, and he moves back into his own apartment.

At the marriage of Tess's widowed father (Minor Watson) to her Aunt Ellen (Fay Bainter), Tess realizes she has to be with the man she loves.

Early, while Sam is still asleep, Tess goes to his apartment intending to surprise him with a breakfast she has cooked. The breakfast is a comic disaster, with a raw egg ending up on her open-toed shoe.

They reconcile. Sam doesn't expect her to give up everything for him. He just wants her to be Tess Harding *Craig*.

Kate had wanted Spencer to feel comfortable, and she hoped that he would be more comfortable talking about baseball and sports with George Stevens than with George Cukor. "As it turned out," she told me, "Spencer and George Stevens never talked about baseball, or anyway, I never heard that conversation. It didn't matter anyway, George Stevens did a wonderful job, and what really counts is what the audience sees on the screen.

"*Woman of the Year* was a big hit. Then, we went on with George—George Cukor, that is—as director, and Spencer and he became good friends."

"There'd been sort of a front office discussion of how it looked having Spencer Tracy's name precede Kate Hepburn's in the credits," Mankiewicz told me. "Most of them thought it should be Hepburn-Tracy rather than Tracy-Hepburn. So I tested the subject with the concerned principals.

"I asked Kate how she felt about it. Kate always knew how she felt about everything. She said, 'Spence is the bigger star, so it should be up to him. Tracy-Hepburn sounds better and is easier to remember than Hepburn-Tracy, and besides, I don't give a damn!'

"So I went to Tracy, and I asked him whether he minded. He said, 'I don't think many people will notice, but I sure will. Screen credit is not a matter of chivalry. This is a film and not the last life-boat on the *Titanic*.'

"You know," Kate confessed, "professionally speaking, Spence did much more for my career than I did for his. He was a bigger star. No one ever called him 'box office poison.'"


*Woman of the Year* won an Oscar for the best original screenplay. Kate was nominated for best actress, but lost to Ginger Rogers.

"They talk about actors and actresses who fall in love while they're having a romance onscreen, making a movie together," Kate told me. "Sometimes it leads to an affair, sometimes marriage. Sometimes it's a wrap when the movie wraps. I could not imagine any of these things ever happening to me.

"I wasn't usually attracted to actors because I couldn't tell when they were playing a part. It seemed to me that I already knew the only actor I needed to know. *Me*. When I was working, my concentration was too intense on what I was doing, and there wasn't enough of me to go around to moonlight with romantic wanderings, mental or physical. I needed my sleep. I wanted to get to sleep as early as possible, so I would wake up well rested for my day, raring to go. I frequently was the first one on the set.

"I had passed thirty, a birthday which seemed very big at the time, and I had my head on straight, I thought. And then, there he was, Spence. All my logic, out the window. Which window? *Any* window.

"I never wasted any time thinking about reason. I just fell in love with him. If you *fall* in love, it's already not reasonable.

"Sometimes Spence reminded me a little of my father, but he was so Irish, and Father wasn't Irish. Father was Scottish.

"Spencer wasn't one for exercise for exercise's sake. He liked polo. At least verbally, he was not a believer in acting as a truly important calling. Father thought it rather 'silly' work, not at all to be compared to being a doctor, a surgeon, while Spence thought being an actor didn't compare with the valuable service a plumber could offer.

"Spencer had ambivalent feelings about acting, He wanted very much to be an actor when he was young. He was very dedicated, even desperate. Acting and being good at it was very important to him.

"By the time I knew Spence, he had become successful and lauded. He had begun to doubt the worthwhileness of what he was doing. He'd begun to question if it was just the dream of a 'selfish' person. I think a part of him had become a little ashamed of what he was doing. Maybe because it came so easily, so naturally to him and the rewards were so great. He told me he felt 'over-rewarded.'

"I remember him saying, more than once, 'Being a plumber is a much more essential and honorable job.'

"I said, 'But, Spence, think how unhappy plumbers would be if they didn't have any movies to go to.'"

"I think that Spence and I represented the perfect American couple for the filmgoing public of that time," Kate said. "I don't think there's any doubt that he represented an ideal sort of American male. He was strong-looking, with a big head, a boar neck, and a craggy face. He couldn't be called handsome, but he had sex appeal. He was intelligent, but not intellectual. He loved sports, especially those he could play himself. He was a man's man, but he appealed to women, too. I represent a woman he appealed to.

"He really was like a big bear, a kind of teddy bear. I could needle him, irritate him. I could try in every way to get around him. I think audiences found this sort of male-female relationship rather romantic. Even when I'm skittering around, irritating him, everyone knows he's a big bear who could make me tremble with just one growl. And every once in a while he says some insulting thing to me, and I get furious, but everyone laughs. It's so very male-female.

"I don't like talking much about what Spencer and I had because I don't believe in chewing over stuff till all the magic is gone. Being in love in a private way that is yours alone, shared with only one other person, is not so different from the love affair with an entire audience. Each can give you that wonderful feeling you have of being desired, of seeing that highly favorable reflection of yourself in the eyes of the person you love, or in the audience reaction."

"I have always been proud of the ending of *Woman of the Year*," Mankiewicz told me. "I was largely responsible for it. It's the part of the film that people always remember, but it wasn't in the original script that Lardner and Kanin turned in. We showed the film at some screenings, and it really fell flat the way it was.

"It was my idea to have the strong humorous ending with Kate trying to prove what a good wife she can be while wreaking havoc in the kitchen."

Although Mankiewicz is best known for his sophisticated characters speaking urbane dialogue, he got his Hollywood start as the writer of the slapstick farce *Million Dollar Legs* with W. C. Fields.

"Kate loved doing that scene," Mankiewicz continued. "She said, 'Slapstick. Oh, goody.'

"She was wonderful in it, and it totally humanized this apparent paragon of virtue for all of the women in the audience who were feeling diminished when they compared themselves to Kate's 'woman of the year.' Tess Harding could do anything it seemed, and then they found out she couldn't make a simple breakfast, something they could all do. Kate was humanized, and everyone was happy, I thought, until one night I met Michael Kanin in a restaurant and stood up as he passed by to shake hands. He left me standing there with my hand out in space and walked by as if he'd never met me. Worse. I understood. That's how we writers are."

"Just after *Woman of the Year* opened," Kate said, "I was speaking with a woman who was saying to me how proud my family must be of me for that film. But I didn't think they would see it, because they usually didn't. Nobody ever said anything about it.

"*Woman of the Year* was on the screens in 1942, after the attack on Pearl Harbor, as young soldiers and sailors prepared to ship out. The woman said, 'Do you realize that *Woman of the Year* will be the last film some of these young men will ever see?'"

Kate said those words were something she never forgot, and when, in later years, someone talked about *Woman of the Year*, she remembered all those brave young men who saw it and that some of them didn't come back at all, and some of them came back injured, not at all the same as when they went away.

"War is so horrible. But in World War II, we didn't have any choice."

"I think no matter how much speculation there is, and there is no shortage of that, no one knows what goes on in anyone else's bedroom, even if the people themselves tell you about it," George

Cukor told me. "It's almost too obvious to say that only the two people involved, assuming there are two, can tell the true story, and that only from the point of view of each person, assuming he or she has chosen to tell the truth.

"I was a witness to Kate's half of the love story, not because of what she told me, but because of the way she glowed over Spencer Tracy. She was absolutely girlish when she spoke about him or was with him. They were like a couple of lovebirds together.

"Kate seemed to have absorbed nothing from her mother, a feminist. She was Tracy's willing servant, his slave. She loved to serve him. It was a totally different Kate than the person I'd known or knew with everyone else in the world.

"I mentioned it once to Kate and said what would your mother think about your ditsy, gaga way with Spencer. Not much of a feminist triumph.

" 'My mother is the person who would understand perfectly. It's just the way she was about my father.'

"Kate was talking about Tracy once, and do you know she called him 'my big potato, my big Irish potato.' It was said warmly, as an obvious term of endearment, with that girlish sigh."

"When we were alone together," Kate told me, "and sometimes in front of other people, Spence used to make fun of my Bryn Mawr way of saying his name, 'Spen-sah.' He did a great imitation of me. People were appalled. I thought it was funny."


Spencer Tracy was born in Milwaukee, Wisconsin, on April 5, 1900. His father, John, the son of Irish immigrants, worked as a trucker and was a heavy drinker. Spencer's mother was an Episcopalian, but he was brought up as a Catholic and remained one all his life. He had a brother, Carroll, to whom he was close.

As a boy, Spencer attended Marquette Academy, a Jesuit prep school. A fellow student was Pat O'Brien, the film actor.

When he was very young, Spencer considered becoming a priest.

In 1917, he enlisted in the army, but the war ended before he saw combat.

Tracy attended Ripon College, where he enjoyed performing in the theater. His father had no faith in his son's possibilities as an actor. He had hoped Spencer would follow in his footsteps as a trucker, which would guarantee him a good living, such as the one he had provided for his family, but he paid for his son's drama training.

In 1923, Tracy met a young actress, Louise Treadwell, who told him how much she admired his work. They married, and nine months later, their son, John, was born. He was born deaf.

They had a daughter, Susie, but their lives were totally changed by Tracy's wife's devotion to the care and education of their son, to help John have as normal a life as possible.

Spencer and Louise lived apart, though they never said they were separated. Spencer was a frequent visitor for weekends, and divorce was never considered.


"Gretchen was Loretta Young's real name, going back to the days before she became a film star," Douglas Fairbanks, Jr., told me. "I'd known her then, and I always called her Gretch. We were great chums, and she often exchanged confidences with me.

"Gretch said that she'd had a wonderful affair with Spencer Tracy, and that he was the best lover she'd ever had. To make it perfectly clear, she added, 'We had the best sex, the best sex of my life.' She didn't go into detail, but that made it clear enough.

"I was quite tempted to ask her about Gable. She'd had an affair with Clark Gable, too, but I had a personal reason for my curiosity. When I was married to Joan Crawford, my first wife, it was rumored that as our marriage broke down, and I'd been guilty of my own infidelities, my wife had an affair with Gable. I've never known for sure. I knew Gable, and I liked him, but it was a question I could never ask him.

"I knew that Gretch had had an affair with Gable while they were filming. Finally I asked her, 'Did Gable compare with Tracy as a lover?'

" 'Oh, no,' she answered without hesitation, 'Gable didn't compare at all to Tracy.'

"Gretch seemed to have forgotten our own romantic affair, hers and mine. It had been a long time ago, but I hadn't forgotten a moment of it. Possibly a hurt look on my face revealed my feelings to her, and she said, 'Douglas you were the best dancer I ever danced with.'"

In the late 1930s, RKO bought a story idea from novelist I. A. R. Wylie. A Citizen Kane-type figure is murdered. After his death, his widow risks being accused of his murder in order to conceal the truth about his pro-fascist tendencies.

RKO sold the idea to M-G-M, who assigned Donald Ogden Stewart to convert the story into a screenplay. *Keeper of the Flame* was the result. Tracy and Hepburn liked the script and especially the idea behind the script at that moment in history. The war in Europe had been raging for a year, and soon the Japanese would bomb Pearl Harbor, bringing the United States into the conflict.

## *Keeper of the Flame (1942)*

Robert V. Forrest, a millionaire with political ambitions, is murdered. The motive is unclear. He may have been killed for his political views, which have a certain popularity. Calling himself an American patriot, he took an extreme isolationist stand at the beginning of the war in Europe.

Investigative reporter Steven O'Malley (Spencer Tracy), back from a European assignment, is assigned to the Forrest story. In his interviews with the victim's family members and staff, he becomes convinced that something is being hidden about the murder. Forrest's widow, Christine (Katharine Hepburn), appears a suspicious figure, as does Forrest's uncooperative secretary, Clive Kerndom (Richard Whorf).

As O'Malley delves deeper into his investigation of the circumstances of the crime, he finds himself falling in love with Christine, and she is falling in love with him. When all of the evidence indicates her own involvement in the murder, he is forced to make a decision. Should he be true to his integrity as a newspaperman, or should he protect the woman whom he has come to love?

Evidence that would have implicated her is destroyed in a fire, from which O'Malley rescues Christine. Afterward, she tells O'Malley the truth. She did not kill her husband, but she tried to conceal the truth about him and the reason he was killed.

Forrest was a Nazi sympathizer posing as a patriotic American. His real goal was to establish a totalitarian fascist government in the United States. Christine learned this and was trying to protect her dead husband's memory. Forrest was killed by others because of his hidden fascist agenda and his growing influence.

"George [Cukor] never really directed Spencer," Kate told me. "He didn't have to, because he just liked what Spencer did.

"George wasn't at all that way with me. He saw quite a bit to fix. Then, he saw more in the rushes. And he told me all about it.

Plenty of hints. But I didn't mind. I was happy. George was a great director and a great person. I knew he could help me, and that was just what I wanted. I had perfect confidence in him, and I trusted him. But there was one great quality George had. He always made you feel good.

"It's really important that the director doesn't destroy the confidence of the actress or the actor. I don't think there's that much difference between actresses and actors. They have to have egos, and their egos are generally more fragile than anyone would guess. Sometimes the people who cover their insecurity most may seem arrogant, and it's just a cover for this terrible insecurity.

"I must say I was pretty confident, overconfident, considering the odds against me. Fortunately, I didn't know about those, how great the odds against me were. I hadn't really given failure a thought. Early on, it would have been almost impossible to shake my confidence. Then, very quickly, I knew success could happen, and even if I couldn't do it every time, I knew I could do it again.

"I'd experienced how success felt. It felt nice."

In 1942, Kate returned to a Philip Barry play, *Without Love*, which played briefly on Broadway, then toured for four months. She also made a cameo appearance in Frank Borzage's *Stage Door Canteen*.

## Stage Door Canteen (1943)

Eileen (Cheryl Walker), an aspiring actress, serves as a junior hostess at the wartime New York Stage Door Canteen. One of the servicemen who come there, Private Ed Smith (William Terry), nicknamed "Dakota," falls instantly in love with her, but she is not in love with him. He comes back the following night, and she is abrupt with him, for which she is later sorry. When he comes back another night, she finds she has fallen in love with "Dakota." She breaks a Canteen rule and has a date with him. They agree to get married before he is shipped out. They will meet at the Canteen and marry on the day before his embarkation.

Eileen appears at the Canteen on time, but can't enter because her date with a serviceman she met there has been discovered. She turns to the officer of the day, Katharine Hepburn, for help. Miss Hepburn arranges for Eileen to enter without a pass so she can meet "Dakota" and get married before he leaves.

Eileen finds out that "Dakota" won't be there. His outfit shipped out that morning. Miss Hepburn consoles her, as Eileen vows to wait for his return.

This film was essentially a revue of sixty-five stars and well-known show business personalities performing in the wartime setting of the Stage Door Canteen.

*Dragon Seed* was based on Pearl S. Buck's novel about the reaction of rural peasants to the Japanese invasion of China in 1937. As was the usual practice in Hollywood, Asian actors were used only in bit parts or as extras. Having the German-born Marlene Dietrich and Luise Rainer or the Swedish Ingrid Bergman play Asian characters was an acceptable convention. Rainer told me, "I felt foolish the first time I was made up as O-Lan. Then, on the set, I saw that my fellow Chinese were Paul Muni, Walter Connolly, Charley Grapewin, and Tilly Losch. The only one who looked out of place was Keye Luke, who really *was* Chinese." Rainer won an Oscar for her part in *The Good Earth*, another film adaptation of a Pearl Buck novel set in China.

# Dragon Seed (1944)

In 1937, as the Japanese army nears his farm, elderly Ling Tan (Walter Huston) does not see any reason for alarm, but his son, Lao Er (Turhan Bey) thinks otherwise. He plans to leave with his young wife, Jade (Katharine Hepburn), for the interior, where he hopes to join other peasants in setting up a munitions factory.

Jade puzzles Lao Er. Her sense of tradition and acceptance of change seems odd to him. She believes in the new China that is emerging, yet clings to much of the old China. She believes that the two are compatible, a view not shared by her husband or father-in-law.

On a visit to Wu Lien (Akim Tamiroff), a wealthy relative, she is disgusted to find that he is actively collaborating with the Japanese. While his servants are preparing a banquet for the Japanese, she flirts with the kitchen guard (J. Carrol Naish), diverting his attention long enough to poison some of the food. When several Japanese officers die after the banquet, Wu Lien is held accountable and is executed.

Returning to her village, she finds Ling Tan finally accepting the reality that the Japanese are coming and times will be different. He has sold his farm and is joining Lao Er and Jade in their exodus to the interior.

Turhan Bey had been borrowed from Universal by M-G-M for this film. He had a Turkish father and a Czech mother. Although he was only twenty-one, he was smitten with Kate. He sent her love letters and flowers.

"I was about fifteen years older than he was," Kate remembered, "but he didn't seem to have noticed. They were beautiful letters, and I saved them all. They were beautiful flowers, but, of course, I couldn't save them, though I pressed a few. I was very touched by the feelings of this handsome young man. I did, however, speak to him, alone, as tenderly as I could. I suggested that we were in an insecure profession and that he should be saving that money he was spending on the flowers. I didn't tell him he had to stop writing the letters."

This film reunited Kate with Pandro S. Berman, who had produced films of hers for RKO during the 1930s. Their last film together had been *Stage Door* in 1937. In Hollywood, the producer was usually the controlling force on a film because he had the last word in practically everything, including the selection of stars, the director, and all production matters, including the final editing of the film.

During World War II, Washington, D.C., virtually doubled in population. Wartime labor and material shortages prevented new building, and overcrowding was the result. Perfect strangers were sharing everything from taxis to beds. Hollywood made a number of comedies about this problem. *The More the Merrier* was a big hit using overcrowded wartime Washington as a setting. Another Washington film was the next Tracy-Hepburn film, *Without Love*.

## *Without Love* (1945)

In wartime Washington, the housing shortage has forced some "odd couple" living arrangements. One of them is the "platonic" marriage of Pat Jamieson (Spencer Tracy) and Jamie Rowan (Katharine Hepburn). Pat is an aeronautical engineer who has come to Washington to develop a helmet for high-altitude flying that he has invented, but he has no place to live. Jamie is a young widow with a large Georgetown house. Having met Pat and liked him, she suggests a novel solution to his housing problem. Marry her. Of course, it will be a marriage in name only. They marry, and Pat moves in.

Pat is so absorbed in his work that he often brings it home with him. Far from being annoyed by the clutter his tools and scientific instruments cause in her tidy home, Jamie is fascinated by his important wartime work and offers to help. As they work together, their marriage without love develops into one with love.

In the film's cast was Lucille Ball in a supporting role. *Time* magazine noticed her. "Lucille Ball handles her lowly wisecracks so well as to set up a new career for herself."

"What a redhead Katharine Hepburn is!" Lucille Ball told me. "She has all the true redhead characteristics, an indomitable dynamo. She's my favorite actress, and I'd like to have known her well as a person because I think the person must be even more interesting than the actress. She was always very kind to everyone and remembered their names, even the names of their children. She paid attention to everyone working on the film, the cast, the crew. No one was humble in her eyes. I tried to remember that when I had power."

*Undercurrent* was Kate's twenty-second film. This film and *Keeper of the Flame* were her only ventures in the direction of the popular *film noir* genre of the time. The versatile Vincente Minnelli was director.

# *Undercurrent (1946)*

During a swift courtship, Ann Hamilton (Katharine Hepburn), a college professor's daughter verging on spinsterhood, is swept off her high heels by Alan Garroway (Robert Taylor), a wealthy industrialist and inventor of a device that turned his family's company into an industrial giant.

Their marriage is happy until she asks about a brother she has never met. Any mention of his brother, Michael, angers Alan. Michael, he says, disappeared after stealing money from the company.

Still curious, Ann starts making inquiries. One of Alan's old girlfriends, Sylvia (Jayne Meadows), believes Michael is dead and Alan could be involved.

Ann visits a ranch house once owned by Michael. It reflects a personality much like her own. A caretaker confirms Ann's impression.

Alan, aware of his wife's inquiries, angrily accuses her of being obsessed with Michael. Then he apologizes, explaining that they need time away together.

At the family country home, Alan is confronted by the mysterious ranch caretaker, who is Michael (Robert Mitchum). He acuses Alan of murdering the real inventor of the device so that he could claim it. Alan admits the crime and promises to tell Ann the truth if Michael will remain silent.

The unbalanced Alan tries to kill Ann in a riding accident. Instead, he is killed.

Meeting Michael, Ann says she wants to recompense the family of the murdered engineer. She and Michael will be making a life together.

*The Sea of Grass* was shot in 1945, but its release was held back until 1947. M-G-M was disappointed by the picture director Elia Kazan had made for them, and so was he. They had in mind a grand-scale Tracy-Hepburn western, and Kazan wanted something more like a Pare Lorentz Dust Bowl documentary. "I wanted unknown actors who looked like real cattlemen and their leather-skinned women, and I got the full M-G-M glamour treatment," Kazan said. "Mr. Mayer let me know soon that he thought I might be in the wrong business."

## The Sea of Grass (1947)

Cattle baron Colonel Jim Brewton (Spencer Tracy) loses a bitterly fought court battle that opens up his St. Augustine Plains in New Mexico to homesteaders. He is so obsessed with his beloved "sea of grass," that his wife, Lutie (Katharine Hepburn), is no longer able to bear his neglect, and she temporarily separates from him, leaving their young daughter in his care.

Lutie goes to Denver where she becomes involved with her husband's arch enemy, Brice Chamberlain (Melvyn Douglas), the lawyer who championed the cause of the homesteaders and won their case in court for them.

She returns to the ranch pregnant, and Jim believes he is the father. During a difficult childbirth, however, a raving Lutie cries out that the baby boy isn't his. In spite of this, Jim wants the baby, and he accepts him as his own. He says, "A man wants a son."

He and Lutie quarrel, and he forces her to leave, this time permanently. He will not allow her to take their little girl, but she can take her son. She realizes that if she does, however, the boy will not have Jim's protection, money or a future inheritance. Lutie leaves her baby son with Jim, and the boy, Brock, becomes the person Jim most cares about, even more than the daughter who is his and Lutie's child.

Brock (Robert Walker) grows up an insufferable braggart and bully who looks for trouble and finds it. He is shot in a gunfight and dies in his father's arms.

The grown daughter, Sara Beth (Phyllis Thaxter), urges her mother to go back to Jim, because he needs her. After the death of Brock, Jim emotionally welcomes her back.

At the Players Club in New York City, Kazan told me that he was particularly irked by Kate's habit of going into the washroom so that she came out always looking clean and fresh, no matter how dirty the scene was they were shooting. "I tried to tell her, but she didn't pay attention, so then I didn't say anything," Kazan said, "because by that time I didn't care if she came out naked. Neither she nor Tracy seemed to have any respect for my directing. They had decided they were going to do it their way, and they did."

For *Song of Love*, Kate studied piano fingering with Laura Dubman, a pupil of Artur Rubinstein's, so that she could be photographed with her hands on the keyboard. The pianist on the soundtrack was Rubinstein himself.

## Song of Love (1947)

Young Robert Schumann (Paul Henreid) teaches piano to support himself while he composes. One of his pupils, twelve-year-old Clara Wieck (Katharine Hepburn), shows special promise. They fall in love, and she asks him to wait until she is old enough for them to marry.

By the time she is eighteen, Robert has achieved some

success as a composer, but he does not earn enough to support a wife and family. Over the objections of Clara's father (Leo G. Carroll), and with the help of Franz Liszt (Henry Daniell), the couple marry. Schumann is twenty-seven.

Robert's ambition to become a concert pianist was dashed when he injured his hands practicing, so he transfers his dream to Clara, who is truly a virtuoso pianist. Her career, however, is interrupted by seven children and her husband's growing success.

Young Johannes Brahms (Robert Walker), one of Schumann's pupils, is fascinated by Clara. They have much in common, including a dislike of Liszt's flamboyance, even if he is a leading champion of Schumann's music. Brahms falls in love with Clara, and while she has great affection for him, she still loves her husband, who is showing early signs of insanity.

While conducting a performance of his cantata, *Scenes from Goethe's Faust*, Schumann collapses and is hospitalized. Several years later, he dies in an asylum at the age of forty-six.

Brahms proposes marriage to his widow, but she declines, choosing instead to remain lifelong friends. Clara returns to the concert stage and becomes one of the most revered piano virtuosi of the nineteenth century.

*Song of Love* takes fewer liberties with historical fact than was the Hollywood custom of the time. Hepburn is well cast as Clara Schumann, who was famously outspoken at a time when that was truly shocking behavior for a woman.

Besides being a great pianist, she was also a great teacher of piano and the first woman ever to be allowed to teach in a conservatory.

When Clara was engaged as a professor at the Frankfurt Conservatory, the head of the institution, Joachim Raff, was asked by the board why he had violated its policy of not employing women.

"I haven't," Raff answered. "I engage only men. And Madame Schumann, I count as a man."

This story was reported in a letter from Clara to Brahms.

In 1948, the promotional slogan "Movies are better than ever" began to appear in newspaper ads, theater lobbies, and even on the screens. With people still waiting in long lines for the latest Hollywood product, the studios felt the need to remind people that their films were "better than ever." There were two reasons.

First, the Justice Department had just ordered that the studios divest themselves of their theater chains because they constituted a restraint of trade. Warner Brothers, M-G-M, Paramount, and to a lesser extent RKO could no longer count on sure outlets for their continuous flow of films.

The second setback for Hollywood was television. In 1948, movie theaters began experiencing a noticeable drop in attendance on nights they were in competition with popular programs on the new medium.

Since the major Hollywood studios refused to release their old films to television, Tracy and Hepburn would not be seen on TV for more than a decade. In spite of these ominous signs, the studios continued production as if it were 1939.

Frank Capra produced and directed, *State of the Union*, the Pulitzer Prize–winning Broadway play by Howard Lindsay and Russel Crouse.

Kate's name is spelled "Katherine" in the opening credits.

## *State of the Union (1948)*

Republican liberal Grant Matthews (Spencer Tracy), a wealthy aviation manufacturer, is being urged to try for the Republican presidential nomination. Those most influential in his decision to run are Kay Thorndyke (Angela Lansbury) and Jim Conover (Adolphe Menjou). She is a scheming young newspaper heiress, and he is a clever behind-the-scenes politician.

Grant is advised by Kay to reunite with his wife, Mary (Katharine Hepburn), from whom he is unofficially separated. Appearing happily married is important for his candidacy. Mary, still in love with Grant, agrees, although she believes her husband has been having an affair with Kay.

At a televised political event, Kate finds out that there really was an affair and gets drunk, saying all of the things a Republican presidential candidate's wife should not say. Grant, not wanting to lose his wife and not able to reconcile his principles with those of Kay and Conover, withdraws from the race, on camera, characterizing himself as "unworthy," but ready to go on working behind the scenes for ethics in politics.

Angela Lansbury plays a worldly and sophisticated woman, whose clothes emphasize her wealth and power. She was barely twenty at the time.

Van Johnson, who plays one of Kay's reporters, told me that he considered Spencer Tracy the best actor he had ever worked with, and "the best friend to my career and to me I ever had. His belief in me gave me the confidence every actor has to have." While making *A Guy Named Joe* with Tracy in 1944, Johnson was badly injured in a car accident. Thanks to Tracy's insistence that he not be replaced,

Johnson was able to recover and return to the production, a milestone in his career.

The picture coincided with the presidential campaign of 1948. There was a third party on the ticket, the Progressive Party. Its candidate was former Democratic Vice President Henry Wallace, whose platform included a conciliatory approach to the Soviet Union and other ideas that many considered leftist. When Kate appeared to speak on his behalf, she wore a red dress. She said she hadn't given any thought to the color of her dress, except in terms of how it looked on her. She had been deciding between the red dress and a favorite pink dress that she almost chose. Later, she regretted her choice of red, but she said maybe the pink would have been worse. The appearance and the dress led to questioning of her politics, and she said she regretted the speech, which she had given because she thought it was what her mother would have done. "But Mother wouldn't have regretted it."

When Spencer Tracy accepted the role of Grant Matthews, it was assumed that Kate would be playing his estranged wife. Then it was announced that Claudette Colbert would play the part. Colbert withdrew, and Kate was signed. Capra maintained that he and Tracy had wanted Kate to play the part from the beginning,

Director George Cukor felt the ideal place to shoot most of *Adam's Rib* was in New York City. He knew that Kate would be pleased because she could stay at her own Turtle Bay townhouse. Tracy could stay at the Waldorf Towers, which he liked, and which was only a few blocks from Kate's home.

A neighbor of Kate's said that sometimes he would have insomnia or wake up at about five in the morning. He would see the door open at Hepburn's house and Spencer Tracy would step out. She would appear in the doorway, and they would embrace and kiss for a long time. Then Tracy would rush into a waiting black limousine and leave, presumably returning to the nearby Waldorf.

## Adam's Rib (1949)

Doris Attinger (Judy Holliday) shoots her husband, Warren (Tom Ewell), in the apartment of his mistress, Beryl (Jean Hagen). Doris is indicted for attempted murder.

Happily married Amanda (Katharine Hepburn) and Adam Bonner (Spencer Tracy), both lawyers, discuss the case over breakfast. She asserts that gender discrimination should be a mitigating factor, while he argues that the law must be upheld.

As assistant district attorney, Adam is assigned to prosecute the case. Feeling very strongly about women's rights, Amanda volunteers to defend Doris.

At the trial, the issue of feminine inequality is stressed by Amanda, and Adam and Amanda get more tabloid front page space than the trial.

Amanda wins a not guilty verdict for her client, humiliating Adam. He becomes morose, angry, and leaves her.

Amanda waits in their apartment in hopes that Adam will call, while Kip (David Wayne), a predatory neighbor, tries to seduce her. Finding them there together, Adam pulls out a revolver and aims it at them. She says he can't do that. It's against the law, exactly the point he was making in court. Then, he puts the barrel into his mouth and bites off a piece—of licorice. It's a candy gun.

As they review their property and possessions at an accountant's office, all the dreams and happy memories cause tears to roll down Adam's cheeks. Amanda realizes he still loves her. Later, he shows her how he can cry whenever he chooses, on a moment's notice.

Back together, she maintains that there is no difference between men and women, except for one little difference. He says, "You know what the French say: '*Vive la différence!* Hooray for that little difference."

*Adam's Rib* was based on an original story by Garson Kanin and Ruth Gordon, who also did the screenplay. The film was hugely successful.

A young actress named Judy Holliday enjoyed a brilliant success as the lead in Garson Kanin's *Born Yesterday* on Broadway. She was hopeful that she would be offered the opportunity to play her part in the Hollywood film that was being planned, but disappointed to learn that the producers wanted a famous film actress. Kanin, Cukor, Tracy, and Hepburn all liked her and wanted to help. They offered her a perfect part in *Adam's Rib*.

Holliday, however, declined the offer. She told Kanin that it seemed too small a role, a step backward rather than a step forward.

Kanin and Kate flew to New York to persuade her. Kate offered to coach her and to tell her everything she knew about making films, and in their scenes together, Kate said she would arrange for Holliday to be photographed in the best possible way. Kanin offered to build up her part. Holliday agreed, and Kate and Kanin were right. It was the beginning of a very successful career. She would get the starring role in *Born Yesterday*, opposite William Holden and Broderick Crawford, for which she won the Oscar for Best Actress. Her appearance in *Adam's Rib* was more effective than any screen test could have been.

Two puppets, one of Kate and the other of Tracy were suspended over a little stage with a proscenium arch that had been built for the *Adam's Rib* credits. George Cukor had them in his home. "These puppets were originally supposed to appear in the film, but," Cukor said, "their moment never came, and they ended up on the cutting room floor." Only the empty stage appears in the credits. As we walked by them once, Cukor said to me, "Talent and opportunity do not always go hand-in-hand."

Just before she left to make *The African Queen*, Kate went home to spend a few days in Hartford with her parents. She rode to Fenwick with her father, and they returned to Hartford in time to be at tea, the five o'clock ritual with her mother.

Since she would be away on location for some time, Kate was especially anxious to have that tea with her mother. It was during tea that Kate thought her mother was at her most gracious and beautiful, and Kate often pictured her mother that way when she thought of her, in one of the richly decorated kimonos her mother liked to wear when all of the children joined her for tea.

Arriving back in Hartford, Kate and Dr. Hepburn found the tea table perfectly set, as always, and everything ready. But there was no sign of Kit Hepburn. The house was very quiet.

Kate and her father went upstairs and found Kit lying on the bed. She was dead.

Later, it was determined that she had died of a cerebral hemorrhage.

" 'What if we'd been here?' I asked my father. 'Couldn't we have done something?'

"He didn't reprimand me for my what-if.

"He simply said, 'No. Even if I had been standing at her side, there was nothing that could have been done. It was very fast.'"

As her mother's ashes were placed near Tom's, Kate thought about all the things that she wished she had asked her mother. The idea that her beloved mother would never be there for her again made Kate feel "like a little girl."

"I thought that I would be able to think about any problem I had in the future and imagine what my mother would have said, that I would hear her voice in my head. But it wasn't that way. She was gone.

"I was worried that my father could not survive the death of Mother, that their bond was so strong that he would not survive her loss. He would never, I knew, no matter how terrible it was for him, commit suicide, which he believed was an act of intolerable weakness. But I thought his heart might break or stop. He was a man of such strong will power, I thought he might will himself into a heart attack.

"But he did survive the death of my mother. And a few months afterward, he remarried. He married his nurse, Madeleine, who had been working with him.

"None of us children said anything to each other about Father's marriage. We were only concerned that Father survive with whatever comfort he could find in life. What my siblings thought, I don't know. I only know what was in my own head.

"My first reaction, shock. It was so unexpected. I couldn't believe it. I had a very conventional thought. Why hadn't he waited longer? I surprised myself by how conventional I was. Then, I tried to understand, so I could explain it to myself. I had no one else to explain it to. But I wanted to understand it for myself.

"What I figured out at the time was that it actually was because of the greatness of my parents' marriage. That was why he wanted to be married again, and quickly. It wouldn't be like what he had with my mother, with everything they shared, their youth and all of us, their family, but the woman he married was a very nice lady, and a part of his profession, working with him. He wouldn't be alone.

"I was happy for him, I think, and I understood. Well, sort of . . ."

\*　　　\*　　　\*

"When my mother died, and my father destroyed all of her letters, her suffragette material, pamphlets, and diary notes, he was very definite about what he was doing. I didn't ask why at the time. I assumed he thought it for the best, that he was watching over her privacy and her memory."

By the time she thought about it, the bonfire had already consumed her mother's professional and personal memories. It was so final, but Kate was not accustomed to questioning her father's judgment.

Dr. Hepburn had said that his children all should feel free to speak their minds. They had all listened, but they hadn't really felt free to speak if they were going to disagree with Father.

"As a child, I had a dream for my own romantic future. For most girls, their ideas were vague. They just knew they wanted to find someone wonderful. My dream was quite definite. I had my role models I'd been observing all my life, unconsciously at first and then consciously, the perfect marriage. My own parents. I dreamed of having that kind of relationship between two equals who were totally together, as independent persons.

"It's what I thought was the perfect marriage. I was in my forties before I really gave up and began to face that it was never going to happen for me like that. Of course, I'd decided marriage wasn't for me, so if I didn't have a perfect marriage, it wasn't anybody's fault but my own.

"Later, I reappraised it a bit. My parents were dedicated to setting that example for us. We assumed there was never dissension and that my mother always genuinely agreed with Father. My mother loved every one of us, and since she was a pioneer in family planning and my father was a brilliant doctor, we knew there were no accidents among us siblings. We assumed we were all planned and desired.

"It was, however, quite a responsibility especially for my mother. We were actually three families, each of two children. First, Tom and I. Then, Bob and Dick. After that my two younger sisters, Marion and Peg. My mother was pretty tied up for twenty years.

"We children never saw it that way. We knew our mother was also pursuing her interest in women's rights, and sometimes her work took her out of our house and away for several days. This was possible because we had a staff of five in help.

"We assumed my father supported everything she believed in. Now, I don't know about that.

"I don't think he discouraged her, but looking back, I can't say he encouraged her, either. If he had told her to cease and desist, I think she would have done what he asked. But it would have broken her heart.

"The fact that we were so materially comfortable and so economically secure made it possible. My mother did not do windows. There was always help for the house and with the children. She only had the responsibility of overseeing the life of home and family, which she did beautifully, always with perfect grace.

"Was my father proud of her and her aspirations and accomplishments? We children simply assumed that he was, because it was obvious how wonderful she was and we totally respected her, not just as our mother, but as a person, a personage.

"When I look back, I don't remember Father ever saying anything specific to indicate how proud he was of Mother's outside-the-home activities. But he never said anything against them, and if he had objected, Father was never shy about making vociferous objections, so the assumption was he stood behind her, if not right at her side.

"But what I never really understood was why, after her sudden death, far, far too early, he destroyed all of her papers?"

The *African Queen* adventure began while Kate was touring in *As You Like It*. Producer Sam Spiegel called and asked her if she had read

C. S. Forester's 1935 novel, *The African Queen*. Forester was best known for his popular Captain Horatio Hornblower novels. When she said she hadn't, Spiegel asked if he could send her a copy. He wanted to make a film of it.

"At the moment," Kate said, "I didn't have another film, so an actress who doesn't have her next project is always glad to hear the phone ring."

Spiegel had just bought the film rights and wanted her to play the part of Rose Sayer, a British spinster who is a missionary in Africa. She loved the book.

Director John Huston had at first thought an English actor should play the part of cockney Charlie Allnut, but he changed his mind the moment Humphrey Bogart's name was suggested. The character had to be a British subject, even if he sounded like an American, but the problem was easily resolved by changing the character's nationality to Canadian.

"Bogey was perfection for his part," Kate said. "There was nobody else in the world who could have been Charlie. Nobody. I was very good, but he made me look better and *be* better, because he was so great. He made me feel I was Rosie. He *was* Charlie. That's the ultimate.

"What was especially smashing about Bogey as an actor was that in real life, Bogey wasn't any of those characters he played so fabulously. He wasn't a tough guy. He wasn't a private eye. He was a patrician, a bit snobbish, from a very nice New York background."

In the Hollywood of 1950, when *The African Queen* was made, any suggestion that a film be shot on an actual jungle location was met with the stock phrase, "Shoot it in Griffith Park." Producers felt that audiences couldn't tell the difference between Africa and a park in Los Angeles, at a fraction of the cost. Katharine Hepburn believed differently, and she made that clear from the beginning when she spoke with Spiegel.

"I was responsible for what we all went through in Africa. I told him that we simply *had* to go to Africa. *The African Queen* couldn't just be a studio picture.

"When I met our director, John Huston, I said the same thing. John said, 'What do you think of our going on location to some place that looks like Africa, but is a little closer and more comfortable?'

" 'Oh, no,' I foolishly said. 'If we pretend, the audience will know. They'll know. And *we'll* know. If we have to pretend about that, it will distract us from getting totally into our characters.'

"Well, I lived to eat my words. And I wish I'd *only* eaten my words, and so did my stomach, which paid the price during filming and long after. I'd always believed I had a cast iron stomach. Well, I didn't, or maybe even cast iron wasn't invulnerable to corrosion.

"I remember I thought when we left Africa for London [to finish filming], my stomach would regain its composure and revert to its old good habits. Wrong again. I don't mean to be indelicate.

"But I can't say I'm sorry. The experience was memorable, so special that I can't say I would like to have given it up.

"I think I made some enemies, Betty Bacall for instance, at least in the beginning. I hope not. I liked her, and we've been friends ever since. She accompanied Bogey on the trip. The experience was pretty hard on all of us, Bogey, too. You probably think that being Bogey, he had to be stoic and never complain because it would be bad for his macho image. But he had quite a bit to say, quite a bit not exactly suitable for saying in a lady's presence."

At first, Kate had some misgivings about producer Sam Spiegel's choice of a director. Huston and screenwriter Peter Viertel were taking a long time to finish their adaptation of the Forester novel.

She became even more apprehensive when Huston and Viertel left for Africa without giving her a final script.

"It made me feel insecure," she said, "to be going there to darkest Africa with bugs I couldn't have imagined in my worst dream, to arrive and not have seen a script. It gave me the heebie-jeebies, whatever they are.

"I said to myself, 'Kath, do you want to go to Africa?'

"Kath said, 'Very much.'

"So I didn't have anything to lose.

"Bogey told me how upset Ingrid Bergman had been when they were making *Casablanca*, and she thought they were deliberately keeping the ending of the film from her, 'So,' Bogey said, 'she didn't know if at the end she was going to get Henreid or me. She found out later they were keeping it from themselves, too. They hadn't figured out how to end it themselves. Well, they finally decided to try it both ways, and then they knew. They got it right. So don't worry, Kate. I know John, and he'll get it right.'

"I've worked with some fine directors," Kate continued. "George Stevens, David Lean, Joseph Mankiewicz, but my favorite is George Cukor. He was glorious beyond words, as a director and as a friend. But no director ever gave me a shorter, simpler bit of advice that answered my need than John Huston when we were there in Africa.

"I told him that I didn't quite know how to play my character, Rosie. I was stuck in the African mud. I hadn't grasped her character. I didn't really understand what made Rosie tick. 'Can you explain Rosie to me?'

"John looked at me for a moment, and then he said, 'Eleanor Roosevelt.'

"That did it. I understood exactly what to do. I'd found my character, or anyway, John had.

"Sometimes he spoke so slowly my mind wandered. By the time he got from A to Z and made his point, or some point, if he ever did, I'd forgotten what it was the point of. I hoped the slow way he spoke was not an accurate indication of the speed with which his mind worked, or it would be a lot longer shoot than I'd planned for.

"I tend to speak fast, and mostly not in simple sentences. Simple-minded, maybe. At my worst, the language I speak would be called Blurt.

"At first, I thought maybe John was making fun of my style, of *me*. I discarded that thought and decided he was gathering his wits, and I assumed he had some. I considered that avoidance of putting a period to the end of his sentence might be cover, so I wouldn't have a chance to speak, unless I interrupted, which I wasn't above doing, and said that dirty word—script.

"It was my preoccupation, and he probably considered it my obsession. Where was the script? I'd read the novel, but that would not suffice. Forester was still alive, but he wasn't involved.

"When I finally said the word, he didn't seem at all taken aback. I assumed it was expected, and he said, 'Don't worry, honey.'

"When he called me 'honey,' he hardly knew me. I considered saying I'm not your honey, but I bit my tongue, because I didn't think that would be good for the director-actress relationship I was hoping we were going to have. The term of endearment, I suppose, was meant to be ingratiating. I wondered how many honeys he had. What I knew was, I wasn't one of them."

Kate noticed right away the rapport Bogart and Huston had with each other. Even in the depths of the jungle, they liked to get together and discuss totally irrelevant matters with fervor.

"I was chatting with John and Bogey," Kate remembered, "about some subject, like the difference between men and women, and one of them said something about how hard it is to understand a woman, and how women don't understand a man. I said something clever like, 'If you want to know about men, you have to ask a plain woman, not a beautiful one.'

"Then I departed quickly so I wouldn't be called upon to explain what I meant. It sounded good, so I thought I'd stop while I was ahead.

"I wasn't yet out of earshot, I've always had very good hearing, when I overheard some words not intended for my ears. At least I don't *think* they were.

"Bogey was laughing. He said, 'Kate said we have to ask a plain woman. Well, we've got one handy.'"

## The African Queen (1951)

The Reverend Samuel Sayer (Robert Morley) and his sister, Rose (Katharine Hepburn) are operating a missionary outpost in German East Africa when war breaks out in 1914. Their only contact with civilization is a monthly visit by the *African Queen*, a small river boat, piloted by Charlie Allnut (Humphrey Bogart), an alcoholic Canadian drifter.

After German soldiers burn the village, Sayer's health deteriorates. Dying, in his delirium, he says he took Rose with him because she was "not comely among maidens." When Allnut returns, she leaves with him.

Allnut suggests they hide in the jungle, but Rose wants to take the *African Queen* down the river to Lake Victoria and sink the German gunboat, the *Louisa*, which is preventing the British advance into eastern Africa. Although Allnut reluctantly agrees, he doubts she is tough enough to endure the ordeal.

Rose surprises Allnut with her courage and enthusiasm, and she admires his skill.

After nearly being killed by German troops and surviving the rapids, they fall in love. All seems over when they get stuck in leech-infested mud, but a rainstorm floats them out onto Lake Victoria.

Armed with makeshift torpedoes, they wait for the *Louisa*, but a rainstorm capsizes them.

Charlie is captured and sentenced to hang as a spy. When Rosie is brought aboard, they proudly tell the disbelieving German captain (Peter Bull) how they came down the river to sink his ship.

Before the execution, the captain grants Charlie's last request, marrying the doomed couple, There is an explosion, and the *Louisa* sinks. The *African Queen* with its torpedoes has collided with her.

Removing their nooses and diving overboard, Charlie and Rosie sing, as they merrily swim away to happiness together.

For the 1951 Academy Awards, Kate was nominated for Best Actress and John Huston for Best Direction. Bogart won the Best Actor Oscar for *The African Queen*.

When I asked cinematographer Jack Cardiff what it was like working with Katharine Hepburn, he said, "She certainly had a lot of freckles. She tried to cover them as best she could with makeup, but by the time of *The African Queen*, Kate had accepted them, as well as other imperfections."

Guy Hamilton, who later became a successful director himself, was John Huston's assistant director. He had retired to Spain when he talked with me about the difficulties the crew faced shooting in the Congo.

"I went out every morning very early with Huston to look for the location we were meaning to shoot, in what was Kenya at that time.

But John was more interested in shooting elephants. Really. So he popped off to the Belgian Congo, which was then next door. There, you could shoot anything, including the natives, and John thought this is where we should shoot film.

"It was in the middle of absolutely nothing. We were absolutely miles from anywhere, surrounded by lepers. Sam Spiegel, our producer, kept well away after learning that. We had to go up and down the river, and the only thing we had was the *African Queen*, which was a small boat, and what it towed. We had to build rafts to put bits and pieces of the *African Queen* on. And then, another raft that would have makeup, hairdressing, props, etc., and then the lights and electricians. The generator made too much noise, so the sound cable ran on little canoes at the back.

"The point of this story was that Katie Hepburn had it in her contract that she had to have a private loo, and that responsibility was handed over to me. Now, I've got enough problems with the *African Queen*, towing every morning this terrible convoy, and at the back, another four canoes, with a couple of planks across, and a little raft and hut, and inside was an electric fan. And there was Katie Hepburn's loo. Why she couldn't go into the bushes, as everybody else did, I do not know. But every morning, as we went up the river or down the river, as we went around bends, we were forever hooking something on to the banks or the trees or something. And, of course, inevitably, it was always Katie's el-fan loo, private lavatory, etc. etc. I wasn't going to stop the convoy, 'cause we'd just got underway, and I gave orders 'Cut it, forget it.' And regular as clockwork, Miss Hepburn used to say at ten o'clock, 'Where is my loo?'

"I said, 'Katie, I'm terribly sorry but we had to abandon it on the way.' My relationship with Miss Hepburn, gone wrong, took many, many weeks to recover.

"I was there with the art director long before the unit arrived, because they were building a hut, a bungalow for Katie, a bungalow for Bogie, a bungalow for John, and then for the crew. We were paying the local ladies to carry water, at a penny a load, which they carried on their heads. They poured it into a big tank, and that was the chore when we finished the day, getting all that organized. I suppose I was there about a month before the crew came down, and then I was with the crew for about four or five weeks, and then I went down with the dreaded thing that got me evacuated back to London. I got the job of preparing the arrival at Isleworth Studios for when the crew returned. By that time, I was reasonably fit. Reasonably. The studio period was about another six weeks.

"Africa was really hard work, because we were working with Technicolor cameras, which in those days was a great monster. It was three-strip. When you reloaded it, you didn't just reload one reel of film. You had to put three reels of film in, and then the blimp, because of the dialogue in close-ups. The blimp silenced the sound of the camera's motor. So, that was very, very heavy, and very hard work.

"As we went up and down the river, occasionally we used to get very bored, because we would say, 'John, we could take you outside Shepperton Studios, up the Thames, and show you scenery which is *exactly* the same as we've got now. And John would say, 'African it up.'

"From the beginning John had wanted Africa. White hunter, black heart, you know, is pretty much the correct story. We used to go with bits of Kleenex and rush into the bushes and make little bits of Kleenex look like white lilies. When you looked through the camera, at least it looked African. We were in the Belgian Congo, and it didn't look African enough.

"It was a great experience for us all. I remember, I think it was Lake Albert. We all piled onto a motorboat, and we were going up

Lake Albert. There were hippos banging into the boat, as you went along the river bank, and there were alligators. Everybody was sort of pulling back. But then, you're making movies, and in no time at all, the clapper boy was leaning out and a hippo would pop up, and we would say, 'Sit down!' It was exciting."

"Before I left London," Kate said, "I filled a suitcase with tins of British cookies, the ones they call biscuits. I've always loved those cookies, and I stock up whenever I'm in London or any British place. My favorites are from Fortnum & Mason. They're great for breakfast, and for a bedtime snack, too. I've always thought they would make a wonderful meal, but I never really expected to be eating them as a meal, especially for more than one meal.

"Those attractive tins not only keep the biscuits nice and fresh, but the tins themselves are usually so attractive, they stimulate your appetite. Eye appeal is so important. And they're nice for keeping things in afterward.

"And chocolate bars. Heaven! There's nothing more soothing than a nice dark chocolate bar. Umm. You don't ever need to be hungry.

"Then, there's ice cream. Lovely. I could never get enough. But ice cream is more fragile. You need certain facilities to make it and keep it.

"In Africa, we couldn't have ice cream. The closest you could come was to dream about ice cream. My first choice dream would have been to eat ice cream all night. Pleasurable, but not fattening. I thought as hard as I could, just before I fell asleep, about ice cream, but it didn't work.

"I filled my suitcases with British tea biscuits and chocolate bars, not because I saw myself needing them, but because I knew I'd be wanting my favorites. I didn't know I'd be *needing* them!

"I took so many that I knew I'd be horribly embarrassed if anyone looked into my luggage and found the number of cookie tins I'd brought. I should at the very least have turned red with embarrassment.

"As it happened, I hadn't brought enough. I ran out of cookies before the end of the filming in East Africa. I'd seen the cookies as treats, not as my main source of sustenance. When my supply was gone, I became dependent on local food to which I was not accustomed, and my stomach even less.

"One of my most memorable images of our time in Africa had nothing to do with the film," Kate recalled. "Well, it might have, if I'd made a wrong noise. They would have had to finish the film without me, so it would have been a very different film. They would have had to rewrite the script, with an early death for Rosie.

"We were walking through the jungle, avoiding some elephants, as I remember. That was when I saw a boar. That's B-O-A-R. I'd seen plenty of bores, B-O-R-E-S.

"This boar was crossing the road in front of our little group. He was very big. Then I saw that he had a young family traipsing along behind him, or rather behind her. Obviously, she was a mother. I thought, 'What a lovely photograph!' I reached into my bag and took out my camera. I moved a little closer. She turned and looked at me with the most tender eyes. I wanted to get closer, so my picture would show her eyes.

"She moved. I heard John's voice calling me, softly.

" 'Back up, Kate, slowly,' he said softly. 'Very slowly.'

"Well, John Huston was my director, so I followed his directions.

"The boar, followed by her babies, moved on. And John had saved his film and his star. Me.

"He explained that, in this case, the female of the species can be more dangerous than the male when she is protecting her babies. Later, he got me a gift, a little statue of a boar.

"I love rain. I love all of the different sounds it makes. Rain is different in California from the way it is in Connecticut, but the torrential rain in Africa, hitting palm leaves—now *that* is *real* drama!

"Sometimes we take on our parts, and sometimes our parts take on us. I did my best to take on the part of Rosie, but I think Rosie took over me."

"Filming *The African Queen*," Jack Cardiff, the legendary cinematographer, told me, "there were so many ways to get sick or die, one had no wish to contemplate them all. There were more than enough to go around among all of us, and there were a lot of us. I had a vision of my name, rather faded, on a wooden cross there in the Congo mud.

"Many of the local people worked for us. They were very anxious to be employed because they had few opportunities to supplement their meager style of life. We were offering them a chance for some small luxuries, while we were living there on a standard which we who knew only luxury, our life in London and other good places, could barely endure.

"Many of them suffered from strange diseases which made it hard to look at them. It doesn't sound right, but some of them were really deformed by the disease. It was not something with which I was familiar, nor did I wish to become familiar with it. I was a little embarrassed about prying into these people's private lives, but what the disease had done to them was too obvious to pretend I didn't notice. We didn't like to give the disease its proper name. Leprosy makes one feel ill just saying the word. It's a shivery disease.

"We heard eerie sounds which I could not recognize, sounds like nothing I'd ever heard before. I inquired about it and I was told,

'It's only the gorillas.' I accepted the answer at face value and didn't go looking for face-to-face encounters."


"When *African Queen* finished its location filming in Africa, and we all left, despite the hardships it had presented, I felt a sadness about leaving. I said to myself, 'Kath, I know I'll be coming back,' and then I said to myself, 'No, you won't. You won't have any reason to come back.' That voice in my head said, 'Africa is so far away.' That increased my longing, even before I left.

"I took with me a lot of souvenirs. I bought masks I didn't have wall space for because I wanted to take the place away with me.

"I also had my stomach blight as a souvenir. I hoped it wouldn't last as long as the masks.

"Our plane stopped in Cairo, but we weren't allowed to leave the airport. Terrible. An opportunity missed. John [Huston] told me not to worry. He'd pull some strings. I guess he didn't have hold of the right strings. We had to stay in the airport. I didn't think we looked like terrorists who had come to blow up the Pyramids. Not even Bogey.

"It was explained to us that it wasn't to protect the Pyramids from us. It was to protect *us*. They didn't want to lose any celebrities in Cairo, and they didn't want the responsibility of protecting us.

"We went on to London to complete the film."


"Once your digestive tract forgets how it's supposed to work, and it goes into eccentric behavior, one doesn't wish to discuss this behavior with anyone, not even one's doctor. Of course, one didn't have a doctor at hand in Africa.

"Then your digestive tract remembers bad habits it got into, and you have to retrain it.

"It's all terribly inconvenient and boring, but necessary. Life is much happier without this kind of complication. I was very grateful to this marvelous British doctor in London who restored me to what I had previously taken for granted. He wasn't squeamish at all, as you can imagine, and we even became friends, after the memory of how we met faded a little for me."

When Angela Allen arrived to do the continuity for *The African Queen*, she and director John Huston met for the first time. Obviously, he approved of her work, because he would work with her for thirteen more films. I spoke with her in London just before Christmas of 2008.

"It was my job to make sure all the scenes matched," she told me. "I arrived on the plane ride to Africa with some members of the cast and crew. Katharine Hepburn was onboard. I had all the passports, and I saw that hers showed her birthday was just about to happen. But before I could say more than a few words, she said, 'Shut up. I don't want anyone to know it's my birthday. I hate a fuss.'

"I didn't say anything, but I think the real reason she didn't want me to mention her passport and her birthday was because she didn't want anyone to know her age. I was surprised when I'd seen it, because I'd thought she was younger. I think she was forty-six at that time. She was very intimidating.

"I was very young, I was twenty-one, when I was selected by Sam Spiegel in London to go out to Africa and do the continuity for *The African Queen*. The director hadn't met me before I arrived in Africa, so I hoped he'd like me because he'd be rather stuck with me. John [Huston] had already gone out to Africa by that time.

"I was the youngest in the business, and it was certainly my first time in Africa. I didn't go to university. Couldn't have afforded it back in those days. I started working when I was eighteen, and

I'd been on the second unit of *The Third Man* with Carol Reed. And then I'd done another film, with [producer] John Woolf, called *Pandora and the Flying Dutchman*. It was the same company that was doing *The African Queen*, and that was the reason they took me up for it.

"And so to Africa. I've still got photos of us in our tweed suits when we all left London to go to this incredibly hot country. Katharine Hepburn joined us on the plane, and we went through Khartoum and then Léopoldville.

"So, we all flew in this plane together to Léopoldville, and we stayed there. I think we were there two or three nights. To get to our destination, we had to travel in a train that could catch fire, because it was kind of a wooden train. It was full of every creepy and crawly that bites. Then we had to drive to the camp. The camp was in the middle of the Congo. It had been hacked out of elephant grass, and that's where we lived. They had, shall we say, huts. Sort of individual ones, you know. Katie had hers, and Bogey with his wife, Betty Bacall, John his, and then there was kind of a dormitory. The next morning, I saw I was bitten from the top of my legs to my ankles.

"I'll tell you, it was very primitive. We used to wash with sort of red water. That seemed to be the natural color of the water. The shower was a bucket. You know, you'd be in the shower and the locals would come and drop buckets of water over you. Sanitation wasn't fancy. Nothing glamorous.

"You've probably heard the famous story about when the boat sank. It did actually sink. When we got to base, the next morning, there it was lying on its side, actually, drawing water. The entire male unit had to bring it upright and pull it.

"Where Katie was concerned, she was very bossy. I mean, she would say to me, 'Go tell him to learn the next scene.' So, I'd say, 'Bogey, she wants you to learn the next one.'

"He said, 'Christ, if I learn that one, I'll have forgotten the first one.'

"She wanted him to know the three scenes right off. She really *was* bossy. She used to tell everyone, or try to, not that we listened, what to do and how everything should be. When we went up the river, she lived with us 'cause there was nowhere else for anybody to live. Of course, she had her private hut. She was a very strong-minded woman, and she'd sort of give the orders sometimes. The most frightening for me was when John wanted to do a retake, and I said, 'You have to change to the other outfit . . .'

"She said, 'No, I don't!'

"I said, 'Well, yes, you do. It doesn't match what you were wearing before.'

" 'No, I don't. I was wearing so-and-so.'

"And I thought, here am I, twenty-one, with this big star, and she's quite intimidating, and I'm having to say, 'You're wrong, I'm right.' I have to say it, because that's what my job is.

"In those days, you know, there was no video, no Polaroid. It was only what I'd written down. It would have taken a phone call to London, where there was a mammoth operation, so I couldn't call the editor and say, 'Am I right?' I just had to hope that I *was* right. I thought I was, but she was so intimidating. When I think about it, I probably should have been quiet, but I was a mad girl who stuck to her guns, because otherwise, it makes them all doubt. From then on, she never argued with me over things like that.

"Fortunately, Mr. Huston believed me, and I *was* right.

"Kate got on with John and Bogey, and Betty. She was a bit angry the first morning, because John didn't appear. He'd gone off looking for elephants. I don't know why. There weren't any around there. Anyway, he came back and said, 'I knew we couldn't shoot today, because the weather wasn't good enough.' Katie was a bit put out about it.

"Then, we had another scene where John had a habit of listening but not always watching. He said, 'Fine, fine. Print it.'

" 'You weren't watching, John,' Katie said.

" 'Yeah, but I was listening,' he said.

" 'But you weren't watching,' she said.

"So, she insisted on having another take. The first one seemed good to all of us. And as we turned the boat around, we took the top off of something on the boat. It took about five hours to mend, and we had to sail all the way up the river again. You know, the first take had been fine, but she was insistent. She was very domineering.

"But she got on fine with Bogey and Betty, and with everybody, really. Nobody fell out at all. We couldn't afford to because we had to all be there together and make it work. Katie realized that this was a totally different experience, I think, from anything she'd ever had before. You know, what was the point? You really had to get on with it. And she did. She was a woman who always learned her lines. She was very disciplined in that sense of the word. In the evening, she'd eat with John, Bogey, and Betty. Then she'd probably go to bed earlier. The boys would play cards and drink, and she'd go to her cabin.

"We all knew she was with Spencer Tracy, but it wasn't something you ever mentioned. I mean, there were pictures of him in her cabin, but you never spoke about him.

"I did double for her, because we didn't have anybody else. I was the only woman there, so I did get to double for her. I took the boat down the river where the real crocodiles were. I got the real crocodiles. There wasn't anyone else to do it. I was directing the second unit at that point, so I did my job, and I jumped in to double.

"Funnily enough, much later, years later, many people said to me, 'Oh, do you know you look like Katharine Hepburn?' And when Katie got to know this, she said, 'Oh, poor Angie.'

"I was shooting a film with John Frankenheimer in London and someone was going home who knew Katie very well. He said, 'Oh, I'm going to tell her I've just seen you on the bridge.'

"And Katie said to him, 'Is she still being told she looks like me?'

"I also worked with Duke Wayne. When he met her in London, I was working on the film at the time, and he came back and said, 'Oh, you look like Kate Hepburn!'

"And I said, 'Oh, not another one.'

"I can't see it. Other people can.

"I didn't have contact with her after *The African Queen*. Then, I didn't work with her again. One wasn't a personal friend, or anything, which one might be with others.

"She was very polite and everything else. Oh, yes, she told me not to get married. Definitely not. Then she said you should be married once—briefly. It wasn't because I took her advice, but I didn't marry. Not because of her."

When I asked her if Jack Cardiff had any problems photographing Kate, she said, "Oh, no, no. She never interfered with Jack Cardiff. She had so much respect for him. We didn't have rushes out there, so there was no way you could check to see if there was anything wrong. As far as I know, she never complained about that part of it at all in all the time we were there, and I think we were there almost three months altogether. I think it was eight or nine weeks in Africa. I honestly can't remember exactly. The various places in the Congo, Uganda, and up the Murchison Falls. Then, we came back to London and we worked in the studios here.

"I don't know if I was glad to get back to London or not. For me, it was my first time in Africa, I was young. It was an experience. You know, I got on very well. They used to tease me like mad. I got on with John. Obviously I did, 'cause I did fourteen films with him. He was loyal to me and I was loyal to him. We got on because I knew his style of shooting. The production controllers would ask him, 'What are you going to do today?' and he'd say, 'I'm not going to discuss it. You go and ask her. She knows exactly what I'm going to do, and I'm not going through it all again with you.' He and I had a good working relationship.

"And I thought Humphrey Bogart was lovely. I mean, he was very professional. He was always on time. He did whatever John wanted. He was not an ad-lib type of actor, 'cause I worked with him on that, and we did *Beat the Devil*, which was ad-lib. The others used to love to write their own lines and leap around. But he'd say, 'No. Where do you want me to be?' With Katie, they'd never worked together before, but the friendship started then and has endured. After he died, she was still friendly with Betty.

"I never called her Miss Hepburn. I called her Katie. I don't recall ever calling her Miss Hepburn, though I may have the first couple of times. Can you imagine all of the boys having to call her Miss Hepburn? Maybe some of them did, but she couldn't be quite that grand. I don't think John would have stood for it.

"Betty was there as a wife. Everybody called her Betty. Oh, she's a grande dame. She can be very princess-like when she wants to be. I've seen her since. I've met her on many occasions. She would always say, 'Oh, do you remember *The African Queen*?'

"I remember when Katie got sick, like everybody else. I didn't, but she did, like a lot of them did, half the crew. We had to close down for three days. Bogey, he wasn't sick. Well, then, Bogey and John used to say they weren't sick because they didn't drink water. They drank whiskey. Well, they were quite right, 'cause the water was bad."

"I didn't know why I wasn't sick. I kept going with the few that were standing when all the rest of them were down with something.

You just put up with it. Then, you were young and enthusiastic, and everything was an experience. You had to be careful of everything, like the snakes. We had crocodiles around there. Wild elephants would come. You'd see the baboons in the trees. It was their territory. They'd come and watch us shooting. They used to call out and make sounds, their remarks. Baboons, evidently, remember people, I'm told. We didn't have any incidents, but the prop man had some words with one, and the baboon got his revenge on the poor man the next day. He picked him out of everybody. It wasn't like he didn't know who it was. The baboon saw him and was screaming and jumping around.

"We used to go out with the hippos in the water there and they'd rise up, and they'd rock the boat. Then they'd watch us from the riverbank."

"I remember once," Guy Hamilton told me, "around Murchison Falls, going away over the lunch break where we had sandwiches or whatever it was, and I went around the corner. Murchison Falls is very beautiful and it's right on the equator, and I thought, 'Here am I, on the equator, in the middle of Africa. Probably no white man has ever been where I am. And then I tripped over a tin. It was a movie tin, a bit rusty, and it was from M-G-M's *Trader Horn*. Metro had been there before me.

"Katie was so professional and a very special lady. We all absolutely adored her. There's one story I can tell you that says it all. I mean, we were miles and miles away from telephones or anything like that. Later, we moved on and we stopped at some hotel where there was a telephone. The telephone rang and they said it was for Miss Hepburn. I happened to be nearby. She shot past me and grabbed the phone. And she said:

" 'Oh, Spence.'

"I mean, there was so much emotion in her voice. She obviously hadn't heard from him or spoken to him for some time. It moved me, because you knew that this was someone who she deeply, deeply cared about, the gentleman on the other end. She was deliriously happy. It was all there in the way she said those two words: 'Oh, Spence.'"

## 6

# He Never Said, "I Love You"

In 1950, Kate was Rosalind in *As You Like It*, a Theatre Guild production that played in New York and on tour. Michael Benthall, who would later direct her in *Coco*, directed. Joseph Mankiewicz was there at Kate's personal request.

"I'll tell you a little tale which will give you a unique insight into Miss Hepburn," Mankiewicz told me, "although her reaction was not uncommon among actresses, or actors, either, for that matter.

"I've had the experience a few times of being asked by an actress to give her my 'honest' appraisal of what I thought of what she had done. Once, I answered Luise Rainer's question fairly. I thought she had done well, or well enough. I said something complimenting her on what a fine job she had done in her screen test, but I think I didn't speak with enough authority, or enough enthusiasm. Or perhaps I spoke with too much brevity. Miss Rainer, with those wonderful eyes and her delightful accent, and her cajoling way, attempted to persuade me to answer her question *truthfully*, 'absolutely truthfully.'

"Truth. That's a word that can really get you into trouble. She said, 'Call me Luise.' I did. 'Luise,' I said, and I proceeded to give her a few tips. The sweet look remained on her face, but her eyes blazed. I don't think she ever forgave me, and I don't think she needed any tips. She won Oscars as Best Actress, two years in a row.

"When I talked it over with Moss Hart, he gave me some advice. If the actress is in rehearsals or previews, you can dare, but once she is performing, just rave. And then rave some more. I agreed. But I forgot too easily.

"Kate Hepburn was going to be performing in *As You Like It* in Los Angeles at the Biltmore Theatre. I was very happy when she sent me tickets. She sent me a pair of tickets, not just for one performance, but for several evenings, with a note explaining.

" 'You probably think I've sent you all of these tickets to give you the choice when you want to come to the play. Well, that's a part of it, but the real reason I didn't just ask you when you wanted to come is I don't want to know which night you're there. Just give the other tickets away. And the night you come, be sure to come backstage to see me. That's very important to me.'

"I did exactly as she said. I went backstage alone. Quite a few people were waiting there to see Kate. She didn't emerge for quite a while. When she did, she nodded to me, acknowledging my existence. She went back into her dressing room to see the remaining people she hadn't yet seen. When she finished seeing everyone, she came out and beckoned me in.

" 'I wanted to be alone with you, Joe, so that you can feel free to tell me the total truth.' There it was, that terrible tricky word. I proceeded to fall into the trap.

"I began by telling her the truth. She was wonderful, I told her. She preened. 'Oh, do you really think so?'

" 'I do,' I reaffirmed my positive appraisal, adding, 'And the audience thought so, too.'

" 'I felt that,' she said, 'but being in the audience you could feel their response.'

" 'I'm not exaggerating,' I said, 'when I say they loved you.' Then I stuck both feet into my mouth, and if I'd had three feet, the third would have been there, too. I have been praised for many worthy attributes in my life, but I don't remember anyone ever saying I was a wonderful diplomat. People said I was a straight shooter, but I didn't want to shoot anyone, and sometimes the person I ended up shooting was myself.

"I said, 'They would have loved you whatever you did because they've all seen your films, and they're happy to see you in person.'

" 'Is there anything specific you noticed that might help my performance?'

"I sensed a palpable chill.

" 'No, nothing,' I said. 'You were perfect in every respect, except . . .'

"I stopped. I have always been guilty of talking too much, but knowing that has never helped me to stop doing it, to stop while I was still ahead.

"She pursued it. "'Except?'

" 'Well, there were a few times when I thought you swallowed a few words or used gestures that could have been bigger, because acting in films is so different from being on the stage . . .'

"I don't think she ever forgave me. She certainly never sent me any more theater tickets again."


*Pat and Mike* was one of Katharine Hepburn's favorite films. She said it was because she had always been proud of her athletic ability, and this film gave her the chance to show off. "Father told me I wanted to be an actress because I am a show-off by nature. He was right. I knew I was a wonderful natural athlete, and I'd been practicing all my life, or at least since I was three."

George Cukor told me that Kate came to him and asked if he wanted to have a professional athlete do some of the golf and tennis scenes for her. "It seemed a foolish question," Cukor said. "We would have had to do everything in long shot, and there was no need. We had our pro in Kate. I told her what a foolish idea it was.

"She was quite pleased by my reaction. Her athletic prowess had inspired the script, which was tailored to her very special abilities. I think all that she wanted was a bit of reassurance."

## Pat and Mike (1952)

College physical education teacher Pat Pemberton (Katharine Hepburn) is called upon by her fiancé, Collier Weld (William Ching), to help fill out a foursome in an important game of golf. As a member of the school board, Weld is wooing a wealthy couple, the Bemingers (Loring Smith and Phyllis Povah), for a sizable endowment. Pat is a superb athlete in all sports, but she can't play at all when she knows her fiancé is watching. Pat embarrasses him twice. First, she plays badly, second she talks back to Mrs. Beminger and then shows how well she *can* drive a golf ball.

When Weld is not watching her, Pat plays like a professional—something that small-time promoter Mike Conovan (Spencer Tracy) notices. He signs her up and then starts to train her. She quickly rises as a professional tennis player and golfer, but Mike has to be careful her fiancé isn't in the audience. If he is, her tennis racket gets very small and the net very high.

When she qualifies for a championship golf tournament, two unwelcome "partners" appear, Spec Cauley (George Mathews) and Hank Tasling (Charles Bronson). They have "invested" in Pat and now they expect to cash in. They want her to throw the tournament so they can bet against her.

Pat, of course, refuses to play along, even though it's a chance for her and Mike to win big, too. When Mike delivers her ultimatum to the two thugs, they start to beat him up. They are stopped, however, by Pat, who beats *them* up instead. Everyone lands in the local jail.

Not able to get Pat to cooperate, the two crooks try to use the unsuspecting Weld to distract her, but it fails, and Pat and Mike become a permanent couple.

In *Pat and Mike*, Tracy speaks his famous line "She ain't got much meat on her, but what she's got is cherce." This line was written by Ruth Gordon and Garson Kanin.

Tracy would refer to Kate as his "bag of bones," even "my old bag of bones." Kate said, "There were people who thought that was terrible of him, an example of male chauvinism, and they were appalled, and expected me to resent it."

"Far from it. I loved it. The key word was when Spence said, 'my' bag of bones. I was happy. I was *his* bag of bones. It was a term of endearment coming from him. It was said during the days of our courtship. When he said it in our last years together, after he was very ill, and when I was more than twenty years older, it meant even more to me. It meant that, for him, I hadn't changed."

After *Pat and Mike*, Kate flew to London to make plans for another classic revival directed by her friend Michael Benthall. He had become head of the Old Vic in that time since they had done *As You Like It* together. Although *The Millionairess* was virtually unknown, it *was* by George Bernard Shaw, for whose work Kate had acquired a passion from her parents. Shaw was their favorite playwright, and they would read aloud together, at night in their home, from his plays.

*The Millionairess* had a curious background. Although written in 1935, the play had never received a major production in London or New York. Shaw had written it especially for Edith Evans, but she never performed it, nor had any other prominent actress when Kate expressed interest two years after the playwright's death. Shaw himself had stated that he considered Katharine Hepburn to be the ideal actress to play the lead. That meant a great deal to Kate and certainly influenced her. She believed that it also would make an excellent film vehicle for her, and she had talked with writer-director Preston Sturges, who shared her enthusiasm for the project. She had the greatest respect for Sturges's work.

She opened with costars Robert Helpmann and Cyril Ritchard in June 1953 at London's New Theatre to respectful, but not rave, reviews, for the first major production Shaw's play had ever received. Kate was surprised, disappointed, but not deterred from going to Broadway with the play.

During the subsequent Broadway run, Kate worked with Sturges on what she considered a "brilliant" screenplay adaptation. This was several years after Sturges's meteoric rise and fall in Hollywood.

"That was the greatest disappointment of my career," Kate told me. "We'd done the funniest script I've ever read, but Hollywood wouldn't trust an over-the-hill director even with a queen-of-the-hill actress. The New York reviews of the play were unfavorable, and no one wanted to finance *The Millionairess*, even with George Bernard Shaw's name on it. Even with *my* name on it. I really believe the failure of our project killed Sturges. The poor man literally died of neglect. He wanted so much to work."

In the meantime, director David Lean was considering a film project based on a play by Arthur Laurents called *The Time of the Cuckoo*. It was about a middle-aged unmarried secretary who finds *her* brief encounter in Venice with a married Italian. The film was titled *Summer Madness* in England and *Summertime* in the U.S.

Kate remembered her reaction to a phone call telling her that David Lean had agreed to direct the film, and that he wanted her to be in it. "I would be the star. The film as he was planning it would be all about *my* character. I couldn't contain my excitement. I didn't even ask what I'd be paid. I just said I wanted to do it.

"Fortunately I didn't go as far as to say, 'I would work for free to work with David Lean.' Worse yet, I could've said, 'I'd pay to work with David Lean.' I only thought those thoughts.

"But I was told I'd said *more* than enough. Too much. I'd spoiled the negotiation. I didn't care. I was glad. They might have negotiated me out of the part. That happens sometimes, and an actor never knows what wonderful opportunity was lost.

"They added that the film was going to be made in Venice. Well, well. No hardship that. And to put the cherry on the sundae, and fresh whipped cream, too, I had some time on my hands because Spence had agreed to do a film which was going to keep him busy.

"I negotiated to get expenses paid for Constance Collier and her personal companion, Phyllis [Wilbourn]. I said that Miss Collier was essential to my professional well-being, as my drama coach. Well, that was stretching it a little. Phyllis was essential to both our personal well-beings. 'Without Phyllis,' I said, 'who would carry my baggage?' I don't think Phyllis ever carried anything for me except my purse, my umbrella, or our lunch. I was much stronger than she. There was no objection to what I wanted.

When Constance Collier died in 1955, Wilbourn considered an offer from Greta Garbo before going to work for Kate. She stayed with Kate for the rest of her life.

Kate said, "Constance called Phyllis her 'be-with,' a British phrase I'd never heard before, that said it all. It said it all for me, too."

"We started our *Summertime* life in Venice in the Grand Hotel.

"I found a house close to the studio on the island of Murano. You know, where they make the glass. I bought a lot of that glass for everyone I knew, including myself. Too far from town. Then, I found a great apartment on the Grand Canal, by the Gritti Palace, which came well furnished with a cook, butler, maid, and, can you imagine this, our own gondola with our own gondolier. That was equivalent to having a car and chauffeur.

"David was living in the Gritti. He loved that. Room service. I was to be a secretary or a teacher taking a holiday in Venice. There were two love affairs; one was mine with Rossano Brazzi in the story, and the other, David's with Venice.

"David was such a perfectionist, and he was always right, which was handy because that allowed him to be a perfectionist. I remember he wanted red goblets for a scene and couldn't find them. His simple answer—he had them hand-blown. They were wonderful. I was hoping to get them when the film ended, but they sort of disappeared. I hope David got them. If I'd had them, I would have offered to give them to him.

"David was one of my favorite directors and one of my favorite people. Sometimes when you get to know a person whose work you have admired, you are disappointed in the person and it can be so deeply that it influences not only your future appreciation of the person's work, but even your memory of your past enjoyment of the person's work.

"With David it was the exact opposite. I couldn't respect and enjoy his work more because I already did, the maximum. As for the person, with David the person and his work were one."

# Summertime (1955)

Jane Hudson (Katharine Hepburn), a middle-aged, unmarried secretary of refined sensibilities, romantic yearnings, and limited opportunities, looks forward to her lifelong dream, a summer vacation in Venice. The Italian city has always embodied for her the essence of romance, which is conspicuously absent in her prosaic life. Her dreams of romance and passion have faded all too quickly with her disappearing youth. She hopes in Venice to recapture those dreams. Where she comes from, she is a spinster.

Jane is noticed in Venice. First, by a child of the street, Mauro (Gaetano Autiero), who becomes her protector and guide, and then by the handsome proprietor of an antique shop, Renato de Rossi (Rossano Brazzi), with whom she falls in love, and he with her. Miraculously, she has found her romantic ideal exactly where she expected to find him.

Her dreams are shattered, however, when she learns from Renato's son Vito (Jeremy Spenser) that his father is married. Still, she cannot stop loving Renato, and they continue seeing each other. Finally, she agrees to join him for a holiday on the island of Burano. There, even romantic passion cannot make her totally forget the hopelessness of their relationship.

She leaves Venice, however, fulfilled, with fond memories. She has experienced her romantic dream. It will always remain that, a romantic dream.

Kate was nominated for an Oscar. She lost to Anna Magnani in *The Rose Tattoo*.

In 1990, David Lean was awarded the American Film Institute Life Achievement Award in the ballroom of the Beverly Hills Hilton Hotel. At a small dinner afterward, I was talking with director Billy Wilder when Lean motioned to Wilder and me to join him at the table where he was seated in a wheelchair. There were two empty seats beside him.

Lean's first words to Wilder were, "I've got work!"

"Do you need an assistant, David?" Wilder playfully replied.

Wilder and Lean had a wonderful rapport. Lean's health was poor, and while the tribute had made him happy and proud, it was also an ordeal. He had been worried about the long walk into the ballroom with every eye on him. He had been ill and hadn't been walking, so he was nervous about both speaking and walking. He did both, however, successfully.

"What did you like best about the evening?" Lean asked Wilder.

"Personally I'm always too nervous to enjoy being honored, but tonight is fine because it's *you* on the hot seat, not me," Wilder answered.

"I can tell you, Billy, exactly what I liked best about all of this," Lean said. "It makes me bankable."

"Of all the great films you've made," Wilder continued, "my personal favorite is *Brief Encounter*. I would like to have made that film. But then, I would like to have made *any* of your films. So, do you have a favorite?"

"I can choose one without any hesitation," Lean said. "*Summer Madness*, or as you call it here in America, *Summertime*.

"It starred my favorite actress, Katharine Hepburn, and it was set and filmed in my favorite place, Venice. And the subject is the most basic and pervasive one of all: not love, but loneliness. The idea of treating loneliness appealed to me."

I had heard Lean say the same thing the year before, when I talked with him in London.

"Loneliness," he told me, "is in all of us, and it's a more common emotion than love, but we speak less about it. We're ashamed to admit we ever feel it, especially us men. Men feel it just as much as women. Loneliness is not considered manly, but loneliness affects both men and women. There is a tendency in all of us to feel ashamed if we are lonely, that it is our fault for not being more beautiful or more successful or whatever. We hope for a not-too-brief encounter.

"*Summertime* is about a lonely woman who falls in love. You know, I put more of myself into that film than any other. That is the way I feel. Having Kate Hepburn meant so much to me. *Summer Madness* started with my falling in love with Venice. I felt like I discovered Venice. It seemed to me that no one had ever seen Venice the way I saw it, and I wanted to share what I saw with others. Things aren't good if you only see them yourself. It's the sharing that makes it complete. The director's dream is to share his vision with his audiences, with the world.

"I feel there is nothing more basic in the human personality than loneliness, something that certainly has always haunted me, personally. Kate Hepburn is a great natural and spontaneous actress. She would never admit to being a lonely person, but professionally no one can convey it better.

"I was shooting a scene with Kate, and she tripped. I thought it was an accident, so I got ready to reshoot the scene. And then she tripped again. Then, I understood. She had tripped in character, and it was good. It showed her character as clumsy and nervous. I don't know if she planned it, or it just happened to her. We never discussed it because if she didn't bring it up, I didn't want to stop her spontaneity, and I didn't want to encourage her to do too much of that kind of thing, visual ad-libbing. I think if she had preplanned her tripping in the scene, she would have told me. Maybe the first time, she really tripped, and then she decided to do it again because her tripping had been in character, and it felt right.

"Jane Hudson is a lonely woman who finds in love the remedy for the malady she didn't fully realize she was suffering from—an empty life. She wanted to find love, but if you are not open to it, I don't think you can find it. She had given up, or she thought she had given up. Apparently, there was still a spark of hope. Love and romance find her. Katharine Hepburn was capable of playing a woman who was smart and independent and had scared off men all her life. She felt she knew what she wanted."

The final screenplay writer, H. E. Bates, wanted the character of Renato de Rossi to be a gigolo, but Lean rejected this concept. "For Jane to be deceived by a gigolo wouldn't have suited the image that Katharine Hepburn brought with her. The man has to be worthy, not only of Jane Hudson, but of Katharine Hepburn, as well.

"Kate was a very rich woman with at least two houses in America and servants, but she wasn't at all pretentious or demanding, there in her old clothes. She was no diva. Not a fashion plate. She was an original.

"She knew it all, about filmmaking, lighting, and that kind of thing. She always hit her marks. Amazing. Unbelievable the way she could hit them so exactly.

"She could hit her marks like no one else, but she could be scary. Not with me. Never with me. A lot of people were scared of her. She rather enjoyed that. It tickled her.

"She was so full of energy, especially in the morning. You had to watch out with her in the morning. Her brain was racing, and her tongue was going even faster.

"We became fast friends. I liked Katharine Hepburn very much before we made the film, but she became my favorite actress as we made it. I was grateful to have her there, not only for her impeccable performance and professional support, but because she was fun to be with, with her constant stream of running chatter. Not everyone was fond of her running talk, but I was fascinated. I wish we could have worked together again.

"I thought Kate and I had a friendship that would go on and on," Lean said, "but you know how it is with careers that take you in different directions."

Kate told me, "You won't believe this, but there were a lot of local merchants, some of the shopkeepers, who got ideas for a financial opportunity when they saw our camera setting up. They told us that we were costing them money by keeping people away from their shops, ruining business, even if it was late at night, when their shops would have been closed. When we tried to film, they made a terrible racket. Hammering, clattering, shouting, and playing music very loudly.

"We tried diplomacy and reason, which didn't get us very far. Then, one of our more clever people got the brilliant idea of trying money.

"That did it. We were able to go on. Can you believe that?"

I said yes, I could. I told her that I had been on the set at Cinecittà in Rome when Federico Fellini was directing *And the Ship Sails On*. He was directing many extras, who played the parts of the people in steerage class, and they were being paid by the hour. If the scene went only a few minutes into the next hour, the extras would be paid for the full second hour.

The group would do everything perfectly, and then, just before the scene finished, someone would do something disruptive so that the scene was spoiled.

Fellini was enormously frustrated, but he explained to me that there was nothing he could do about it. He would speak cajolingly to them, he would admonish, but no matter how many times he tried, it would be to no avail. They would look blankly at him or smile sheepish smiles, but only when they had gone a few minutes into the next hour would they finish the scene perfectly.

The most discussed scene in *Summertime* is the one in which Katharine Hepburn's character is so intent on taking a photo that, as she steps back to get a better shot, she backs into the canal.

"I did crazy things," Kate told me, "adolescent foolishness, when I was at Bryn Mawr, at a time when I should have attained a certain maturity. Perhaps I never did attain maturity, only old age.

"It particularly stands out in my mind, the day I went swimming in the Bryn Mawr fountain, nude. I took off all my clothes and got into the fountain. I could have been thrown out of school, disgracing my parents and myself.

"The person I am now can't really explain the person I was all those years ago. I suppose I wanted to show I was free, not totally free, because no one can be totally free of the world we live in, but there are bonds we like and those we don't. I defied convention. I've always been an impulsive person, especially physically. A weak brain. I didn't use my brain until after I left school, and even then, not sufficiently.

"Filming in Venice, I did my own stunt, falling into the canal. I remember Rossano Brazzi telling me, 'Don't do it. It's dangerous.' But he didn't say what the danger was. Like people who warn you with a 'Watch out!' and they don't say what you should watch out for, so you freeze in your tracks and get hit in the head by the falling object which they were warning you about. They should have been more precise. Like, 'Move to the right,' or, 'Move to the left,' or a simple, 'Run for your life!'

"Mr. Brazzi suggested I let the stunt person do the fall. Well, it didn't seem right to me to have someone do a stunt for me, just because it was dangerous. Besides, I was probably a better swimmer than she was, and falling into the canal didn't look dangerous to me. What I didn't know was that the danger wasn't in the swimming. It was lurking in the water in the canal.

Tom and Kathy Hepburn. Her beloved brother's apparent suicide in 1921, just before his sixteenth birthday, changed Kate's life.

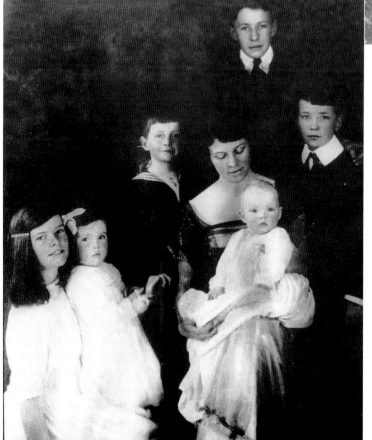

The Hepburn family in 1919. Bottom row, left to right: Katharine, Marion, and baby Peggy. Middle row: Bob, Kit Hepburn, and Dick. Tom is at the top. Dr. Thomas Hepburn was behind the camera.

At Bryn Mawr, Kate became serious about theater, finding what she wanted to do in life. Pandora in the Elizabethan pastoral play *The Woman in the Moon,* was her first major role. She always enjoyed going barefoot.

Kate, who arrived in Hollywood an unknown stage actress, was cast opposite John Barrymore in her first picture, *A Bill of Divorcement* (1932). After the premiere, Barrymore said she stole the picture.

*Christopher Strong* (1933) was the closest Kate came to playing aviatrix Amelia Earhart, whom she greatly admired. At the time, she was involved with aviation enthusiast Leland Hayward. Howard Hughes taught her how to fly during their long affair.

Conditions at the RKO Ranch were primitive and rushed. Kate does her own makeup just before a scene in *Christopher Strong*.

Adolphe Menjou, Douglas Fairbanks, Jr., and Kate in *Morning Glory*. For her performance in this 1933 film, she won a Best Actress Oscar, the first of four, a record.

Director George Cukor confers with his "little women," Kate, Frances Dee, Joan Bennett, and Jean Parker for the 1933 film of the same name. Cukor was already Kate's favorite director and one of her closest friends. Cukor considered Jo the closest to her own personality of any part she ever played.

Though famous for her casual wear, Kate enjoyed dressing fashionably when she chose to do so. This photo was taken near her New York Turtle Bay townhouse in 1933. She knew where she was going.

Fred MacMurray with Kate in *Alice Adams* (1935). Director George Stevens was chosen over William Wyler in a coin toss.

For a while in her childhood, Kate had decided she wanted to be called "Jimmy." In 1935's *Sylvia Scarlett,* she remembered that time, when she played a girl masquerading as a boy.

It was suggested that Kate was having an affair with director John Ford when they made *Mary of Scotland* in 1936. Kate said it was "an affair of the mind."

In *A Woman Rebels* (1936), Kate wears feminine costumes while vociferously proclaiming herself a liberated Victorian woman.

Kate was a great natural athlete, but she rarely had the opportunity to display her abilities in films. In *Bringing Up Baby* (1938), she and Cary Grant "meet-cute" over a disputed golf ball and continue a series of misadventures leading to romance.

*Bringing Up Baby*, one of the legendary screwball comedies, was a flop when it was released, even with Kate and Cary Grant. RKO attributed it to her being considered "box office poison," never imagining how popular the film would be with future audiences.

Director Howard Hawks chats with Grant and Kate on the *Bringing Up Baby* set.

In *The Philadelphia Story* (1940), Ruth Hussey loves James Stewart, who thinks he loves Kate, who thinks she hates Cary Grant, and to prove it, she is about to marry someone she doesn't love.

In *Dragon Seed* (1944), Kate plays Jade, a young Chinese wife who confronts outdated tradition and the Japanese invasion with the same defiant spirit. It was based on a best-selling Pearl S. Buck novel.

George Stevens (center) was not considered a comedy director, but Kate thought him one of the best. *Woman of the Year* was his third Hepburn film.

*Woman of the Year* (1942) was the first Spencer Tracy-Katharine Hepburn film. Tracy made the decision that it should be billed as Tracy-Hepburn, not Hepburn-Tracy. Kate agreed. The magic between them onscreen was matched off-screen.

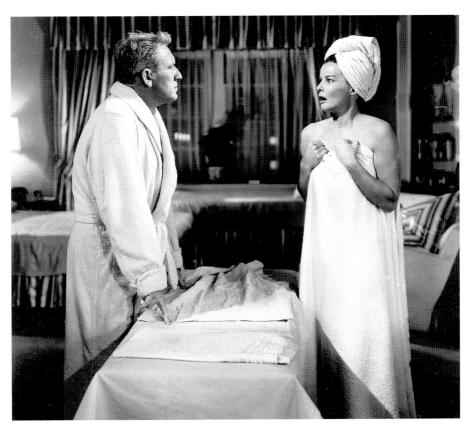

In *Adam's Rib* (1949), Tracy and Hepburn argue as they never argued in real life. Kate preferred not to argue and was the submissive person in their relationship. She said she believed she loved "Spence" more than he loved her, and that was fine with her.

"She ain't got much meat on her, but what she's got is cherce," was a line people remembered from 1952's *Pat and Mike*. In real life, Tracy occasionally referred to Kate as "my old bag of bones." She didn't mind as long as he said, "my."

While shooting *The African Queen* on location in Africa in 1951, everyone except Humphrey Bogart and director John Huston got sick. "It was because they never drank the water," Kate explained, "only alcohol."

During the 1950s, Kate graduated to spinster parts. In *Summertime* (1955), she plays a disappointed spinster who finds romance, at least temporarily, with Rossano Brazzi.

Kate refused a double for this famous scene of her falling into a polluted Venice canal in *Summertime*. An eye infection that she developed afterward lasted for years, and she blamed the dirty water.

Both Kate and Elizabeth Taylor were nominated for Best Actress Oscars in *Suddenly, Last Summer* (1959), but Simone Signoret won for *Room at the Top*.

Spencer Tracy had only a short time to live while he and Kate were making *Guess Who's Coming to Dinner* in 1967. Many didn't believe he would be able to complete the film, but he was determined. He died only a few weeks after his last scene.

It was Kate's idea to cast her niece, Katharine Houghton, as her daughter in *Guess Who's Coming to Dinner.*

Peter O'Toole flew from London to Los Angeles, a plane trip he hated, to persuade Kate to appear with him in 1968's *The Lion in Winter*.

When making *Rooster Cogburn* (1975), Kate liked to lean close against John Wayne. She admitted it gave her a thrill.

Jane Fonda, Henry Fonda, and Kate on location for 1981's *On Golden Pond*. Jane Fonda produced the film partly to give herself the chance to share a closer relationship with her father. Kate was happy to be included in this family reunion, for which she won her fourth Best Actress Oscar.

Kate made an extremely rare appearance to honor her friend George Cukor at the Film Society of Lincoln Center Gala Tribute to him in 1978. She wore sandals with her toes showing. [*Photo by Charles William Bush, collection of Charlotte Chandler*]

"I didn't understand that. I don't think any one of us did fully, even Rossano Brazzi.

"I had no fear, but if I had known just how toxic the garbage in the canal was, or what kind of problems it would produce for me for the rest of my life, I would have been afraid. I still wouldn't have let someone else do it for me, although it might not have been as hard on someone tougher-skinned than me. My skin has always been sensitive.

"I certainly would have put up a bigger squawk about it and suggested they use a dummy. As it was, they did use a dummy, and the dummy was me."

"Kate would not accept a double," Lean told me. "All sorts of precautions were taken to protect the star. Mats were spread on the water so that as little of the polluted water would touch her as possible. The fall was planned near a stairway so that Kate was able to scamper out. There were two cameras shooting it, so that the scene would not have to be reshot. Both cameras got it. It was perfect."

Afterward, there was speculation that the skin problems Katharine Hepburn had were attributable directly to her *Summertime* adventure—or *misadventure*.

Kate said she did not know what to believe herself. "I never had very good skin," she told me, "and I loved to be outside in the sun. No one to blame but myself.

"Have you ever had a pedicure?" she suddenly asked me.

I said I had.

"Aren't they divine?

"After that experience, I had one as soon as I could," Kate said. "It was very enjoyable, that pedicure. "But whatever the problems, whatever the price, I wouldn't have missed *Summertime* and David Lean."

*     *     *

"Quite a while after *Summertime*," David Lean told me, "I was in Los Angeles for the Oscars, and Kate invited me to a restaurant to have dinner with her and Spencer. They seemed to get along wonderfully together, great rapport, so comfortable with each other. I was envying them their happiness and wondered what their secret was. I've certainly found my marriages and relationships all very complicated.

"Toward the end of dinner, Kate said to me, 'What are you thinking, David? Are you noticing how happy Spence and I are together?' she asked, reading my mind."

At that, Lean said he noticed Spencer Tracy looking less happy as he studied his empty plate. Lean said, " 'Yes, your relationship *is* impressive.'

"Kate said, 'It is. But I sometimes think what would it have been like if we'd been able to marry when we first met.' She laughed. 'I think we would've been divorced by now.'"


"I've never been a jealous person," Kate told me. "I never wanted to be anyone but me. When people talked about envying someone or resenting someone who was favored by someone they favored, they were showing jealousy. I only understood it intellectually, but when I was away for a while, I heard from some people who acted like they were my friends, but weren't, that Spence had been seen having dinner with Grace Kelly.

"Neither one of us ever imposed any restrictions on the other, but one evening when I got back, I couldn't resist saying in what I hoped was my most casual throwaway tone, 'Do you like Miss Kelly?'

"He didn't hesitate. 'She's a beautiful young girl. Very young. Very beautiful, and very talented.'

"Why did he have to say *very young?*

"It was clear he was impressed by her. I was sorry I'd asked."

"I started out my career just hoping I'd get work," Kate said. "When I had success, I knew I wanted not to be typecast, and when I had some choice in parts, I set about trying to get variety, to test myself.

"I was very fortunate that as I became a lady of a certain age, an actress of a certain age, I had grown into a spinster, and there seemed to be many parts for spinsters, for which I was grateful. Better to be typecast than cast aside.

"And then, I noticed there are spinsters, and there are *spinsters*, and that indeed there are many varieties of women who are lumped together as spinsters. I was, at that point however, grateful for my professional spinsterhood. In *The Rainmaker*, the character I played was pretty close to me."

Kate said she particularly enjoyed her comedy scene in which she parodies the kind of girl she isn't, one who pretends in order to get a man.

"I never believed in pretending in order to get a man, because I think it gets you what you don't want. If a girl can pretend well enough, she gets a man who wants the girl she pretended to be."

## The Rainmaker (1956)

Bill Starbuck (Burt Lancaster) roams the the 1930s Midwest as a peddler of whatever people think they need. His next town, Three Points, Iowa, needs rain. A drought is killing their cattle.

The Curry family, local cattlemen, is more concerned about still unmarried Lizzie (Katharine Hepburn). Her father, widower H. C. Curry (Cameron Prud'homme) and two brothers, Noah (Lloyd Bridges) and Jimmy (Earl Holliman), pin their last hopes for Lizzie on deputy sheriff File (Wendell Corey), the town's only eligible bachelor.

Starbuck arrives at the Curry ranch offering to bring rain for one hundred dollars. Ignoring Lizzie's and Noah's misgivings, H. C. accepts the proposition.

There is an argument about Lizzie's inability to get a man. She is told by H. C. to use her "feminine wiles."

During a visit, File admits to Lizzie that he is not a widower. His wife left him. Even his dog left him. Lizzie tries out her feminine wiles, but he likes her better the way she really is.

After File leaves, Noah tells Lizzie to face being an old maid. She rushes outside, ending up in the tack room with Starbuck, who tells her a woman *is* beautiful if she *believes* she is. Starbuck confesses he is a fake, but his dream is to be a *real* rainmaker.

He kisses Lizzie. For the first time, she believes she is beautiful. They make love.

File comes to arrest Starbuck. The Currys deny having seen him, but Starbuck gives himself up. They convince File that Starbuck should be allowed to leave.

As he is departing, he invites Lizzie to come with him. At the same time, File asks her to stay, and while she is tempted, she chooses reliable File. Starbuck returns the hundred dollars and leaves.

Lightning and thunder announce an impending rainstorm.

Burt Lancaster had heard rumors that Kate could be difficult, bossy, demanding, and so on, but his agent, Ben Benjamin, remembered how much Burt liked working with her, "a real professional," Burt said.

*The Rainmaker* was based on N. Richard Nash's successful 1954 Broadway play. Joseph Anthony, who directed the play on Broadway, was brought out to Hollywood by producer Hal Wallis to direct the film. Cameron Prud'homme repeated the role of H. C. Curry that he had created on Broadway. *The Rainmaker* was later made into a musical called *110 in the Shade*.

Again, Kate was nominated by the Motion Picture Academy for the Best Actress Oscar. This time she lost to Ingrid Bergman, in *Anastasia*.

"I thought *The Iron Petticoat* would be my *Ninotchka*," Kate told me. "Sort of.

"Well, it wasn't *Ninotchka* and I wasn't Greta Garbo. Wasn't Garbo fantastic? I love that picture.

"There were hints that the actor they had in mind to play opposite me was Cary Grant. I'm sure they had him in mind, but he didn't have *them* in mind. I doubt he was ever approached about the film, and if they did, it was no temptation for Cary. He didn't have the drive to go on working like I did.

"In the film, I was supposed to soften and become romantic and become a real woman, transformed by my love for the handsome, exciting, romantic hero I have fallen in love with, who has fallen in love with me.

"Garbo had Melvyn Douglas, a good actor, but he really didn't have the looks for the part. I thought it wouldn't be so difficult to find someone who filled the bill if they didn't get Cary, who was perfect. Perfect.

"I loved the part, and I had faith in my ability to do the Russian-type accent. I just hoped no one would compare my physical appearance to Garbo. At my youthful best, I was never beautiful like Garbo. To tell the truth, I was never beautiful, period, and at the point I was doing *Iron Petticoat*, I wasn't even beautiful like Katharine Hepburn. Youth had gone.

"No one did make the comparison. It would have been too silly.

"I signed the contract without knowing who would be my leading man, and though I don't know it for a fact, I rather suspect my leading man didn't know *I* had been signed until it was too late for him. They signed, can you imagine, Bob Hope.

"No one could deny he was a talent in what he did. Not I certainly, though personally, in truth, I wasn't a big fan of his humor. I respected his entertaining for the armed forces during World War II. I was so sad for our poor young boys who were lost or hurt. So young.

"He was not *my* idea of a heartthrob. I'm sure I wasn't *his*, either.

"Among things he wasn't satisfied with were his part and his lines. He really wanted to play Bob Hope, and he did. I think it was the only part he *could* play. Well, it was what audiences expected and wanted, wasn't it?

"For this film, however, it wasn't what audiences wanted. They didn't want it and the critics didn't like it. Largely, the critics ignored it. What could anyone say?

"Mr. Hope came with an entourage, his gag writers, to punch up his lines. His jokes overwhelmed my character. I didn't care. I wished he would overwhelm me right out of the film. We didn't have good rapport in our parts or in real life. I did my best. Maybe what he did was his best. We went through the motions.

"I thought the result was like our being in two separate films."

# The Iron Petticoat (1956)

Soviet Air Force Captain Vinka Kovelenko (Katharine Hepburn) has nothing against the communist system, but is angered and humiliated at being ignored for promotion and military honors by her comrade commanders. Finally, she can take it no longer, and she flies a MiG to West Germany, where she lands at an American military base. There, she is treated as a defector and put under the command of Captain Chuck Lockwood (Bob Hope). Besides extracting as much military information from her as he can, he tries to indoctrinate her into the benefits of capitalism. Since she is not really a defector, but a woman angry at her Soviet superiors, she counters his arguments with those of her own, which extol the benefits of communism.

He has greater success when they go to London. There, she indulges herself in all of the forbidden pleasures of the West while falling in love with Lockwood. Lasting happiness is postponed, however, until they thwart a plan by the Russian embassy in London to abduct her and take her back to Russia.

"Mr. Hope thought I had no sense of humor, and as far as he was concerned, I suppose I didn't. He would tell me jokes on the set, and I knew what his jokes meant to him, so I smiled and laughed a bit. To him, they *were* him. So, I did my best to tolerate them.

"I don't want to sound frivolous or petty, but I'm afraid I was influenced by the chance to be in London. I love to travel, especially all expenses paid, and there was no place I liked being more than England.

"I liked England. Bob Hope loved England. He'd been born there.

"I believe, I *hope*, audiences have forgotten I ever made that film. I try not to say bad things about pictures I chose to make and took the money for making them, but this one doesn't count.

"I met Mr. Hope sometime after we worked together. He was very cordial. I was, too. He seemed to be a very nice man. I think he was when we didn't have to be a romantic team bringing life to a dead project. Maybe he'd even been told to pep it up a little.

"My character was supposed to change because of love, my falling in love with Bob Hope. I wasn't that good an actress, and he was supposed to be a man women fell in love with, and of all these women, he chooses *me*. Oh, come on now. No one could have been *that* good an actor."

I remember Bob Hope talking with Groucho Marx about Katharine Hepburn in Groucho's home. I didn't hear the beginning of the conversation, but I heard clearly Hope's comment that "Katharine Hepburn's got zilch sense of humor." He didn't call her Kate.

*Desk Set* was an expanded version of William Marchant's play *The Desk Set*, in which Shirley Booth starred on Broadway. It was the seventh of the eight Tracy-Hepburn pictures and the first they appeared in together in color and widescreen.

## Desk Set (1957)

Bunny Watson (Katharine Hepburn) is a memory expert, a genius at what she does. She works for a large broadcasting network and can answer any question asked her or channel it to one of her expert staff.

Then an engineer, Richard Sumner (Spencer Tracy), invents a computer that, in theory at least, will make

Bunny's job and those of her staff obsolete. Bunny, not so sure of Sumner's claims, challenges him on everything, often proving him wrong. He seems to enjoy it, and so does she.

One of Bunny's old boyfriends (Gig Young) notices this, and becomes interested in her again. She only laughs at his proposal. Her eyes are on Sumner, and his on her.

All of the problems are solved when Sumner tells the company that his computer won't operate efficiently without Bunny and her staff. Everyone will keep their jobs, efficiency will be increased, and Bunny will have more time to spend with Sumner.

"I always say I don't like the movies made from my plays," Tennessee Williams told me at his home in Key West. "Do you know why I say that?"

"Could it be because it's true?" I offered.

"My reason," he said, "has always been because I wanted to attack those films before the others, the critics especially, attacked them."

In 1959, Kate went to London to play Mrs. Venable in the film version of Tennessee Williams's *Suddenly, Last Summer*. Sam Spiegel produced, and Joseph Mankiewicz directed. Williams, himself an experienced screenplay writer, had written the film adaptation with Gore Vidal.

Kate loved London, but hated being separated from Spencer. She had been involved with Shakespeare and hadn't been on the screen for almost two years. From 1959 until 1960, she had been doing *The Merchant of Venice*, *Much Ado About Nothing*, *Twelfth Night*, and *Antony and Cleopatra*.

She prepared by reading all of Tennessee Williams's plays, prose, and poetry. She had been impressed by Williams before that, but reading his body of work led her "to be more impressed than I could ever have dreamed."

Williams said that Katharine Hepburn was a playwright's dream. "I love her diction. She made my lines sound better than I thought they would." Two years later, he wanted her to play the part of Hannah Jelkes in *The Night of the Iguana*. There was a great deal of negotiation, but Kate said she only wanted to agree to six months. Bette Davis agreed to play the other leading part, Maxine Faulk, but both she and Kate were overlooked for the John Huston film version, in which the Maxine Faulk character was played by Ava Gardner.

Williams had based *Suddenly, Last Summer* to some extent on his own family. His mother, Edwina, subjected his sister Rose to a lobotomy, which left her with the mind of a child for the rest of her life. "But I think Miss Rose has been happy," he said hopefully, though with some doubt in his voice. He told me that Mrs. Venable had characteristics of his own mother, who saw things only from her own point of view. "But maybe that's all any of us can do.

"It was my characters who really wrote the plays. The trouble was some of them weren't very talented. They *wanted* to do it, but some of them didn't know *how* to write a play. What could I do? I didn't want to hurt their feelings."

Kate had first agreed to play Mrs. Venable as she had been created by Tennessee Williams, but after giving it some thought, she decided that the part was not right for her as written, and she wished to make changes. Mankiewicz strongly disagreed.

"Kate wanted to appear insane at the beginning and be mad all the way through, which would not have worked for the film, not to have allowed development of her character.

"It was a terrible idea, even for Hepburn, because if she began by revealing the entire truth about her character, she would have nowhere to go with her performance. It was important that Mrs. Venable not seem crazy at the beginning. That was to be revealed at the end. But Kate was worried that an unsympathetic role might make some members of the audience feel that she had actually *become* that person.

"The play existed as a Tennessee Williams creation, and there were many who would have considered changing it a sacrilege. The studio would never have agreed."

## *Suddenly, Last Summer (1959)*

Young Sebastian Venable, a well-known American poet, dies in Spanish North Africa under mysterious circumstances. His death is recorded officially as cardiac arrest, but he had no history of heart illness, and his body was badly mutilated, what the Spanish police described as "somewhat damaged." With him at the time of his death was his beautiful cousin, Catherine Holly (Elizabeth Taylor).

Sebastian's death has been such a traumatic experience for her that her speech is often rambling and incoherent. From what she says in lucid moments, one gathers that Sebastian was involved in some way with the gangs of boys who inhabit the beach and exist by exploiting the tourists in whatever ways they can.

Strongly dedicated to protecting Sebastian's memory and reputation is his wealthy mother (Katharine Hepburn). Mrs. Venable will go to any lengths on behalf of her son, even possibly subjecting Catherine to a lobotomy. This procedure, it is predicted, will calm her shattered nerves. It will also leave her with the mind of a small child.

Called in for consultation is Dr. Cukrowicz (Montgomery Clift). He is skeptical of Catherine's need for such an extreme operation. Before he will consent to it, he insists on giving her a truth serum that may explain this neurotic state.

Under the influence of the drug, Catherine recounts Sebastian's involvement as a pedophile with the boy gangs. He contacted them first through his mother, who made the arrangements, and then through Catherine, whom he charmed into finding boys for him when Mrs. Venable began to have misgivings. His sadomasochistic tendencies did not endear him to the boys, and suddenly, last summer, they took their revenge.

Mankiewicz was concerned that Miss Hepburn, in her mid-fifties, would feel uncomfortable playing next to the young and beautiful Miss Taylor. It might be disappointing to her as a star and especially as a woman.

Kate believed that Mankiewicz had chosen to photograph her in the harshest way possible. She felt that this was totally unnecessary and merely "to cover his lack of talent" by emphasizing the unflattering comparison between her and Taylor. She especially hated the lighting. "It made my freckles look like age spots on my hands."

She also thought that Mankiewicz was too hard on Montgomery Clift, who had recently had a terrible automobile accident. The accident had nearly cost Clift his life, and it had certainly cost him some of his good looks, which plastic surgery hadn't been able to restore. Kate, like Taylor, felt that Clift needed "gentle" direction.

Mankiewicz, speaking with me about Kate's performance in *Suddenly, Last Summer*, said, "She was damned brilliant.

"She and I were friends from *Philadelphia Story* days," he said, "but she was cooler toward me after *Suddenly*. A domineering way she had that seemed rather cute and funny when she was younger had been so catered to that, by the time she did *Suddenly*, she'd become as mannered a person as she was as an actress.

"She had so many ideas from her long experience as an actress that she really wanted to direct herself without taking on the responsibilities of the director. We had a battle of wills. Once it degenerates into that, the director can't afford to let the actress win or he's not the director anymore. Not only does she know that, but everyone in the cast and crew quickly knows that you aren't.

"Some of the ideas she had were good and some weren't. Fortunately, she took a stand on some that were really wrong, so I was able to say no. It was important that I could say no to her, or she would have taken over."

Mankiewicz agreed to shoot the scene of Mrs. Venable descending in the elevator both ways, his way and Kate's way. He told me he never planned to use her way, and it was only a ruse to pacify her.

Kate told me she realized much later that "it was only a trick Joe played on me. I was very gullible, and I put my heart into that scene, thinking that he could be persuaded by seeing how well *my* way worked. I didn't understand that I didn't have a chance. He was bullheaded. A completely closed mind. If he had told me he was going to do it *his* way, I'm sure I wouldn't have liked it. Well, I *didn't* like it. But when it came to me that he was only willing to waste a little film on me to shut me up, well, I couldn't forgive that, could I?"

"Kate was miffed," Mankiewicz conceded. "She felt I favored Elizabeth Taylor because Liz was so beautiful, and so young. Well, perhaps as a man it was true that I preferred to look at Miss Taylor, but as a director that would not influence me. Kate made certain that I preferred to *listen* to Liz, who wanted my directions and didn't talk much. Kate also thought I might favor Clift. That was farthest from my mind, except for hoping he would hold together for the length of the production. I depended on Liz to keep Monty on track. They were such great friends.

"The thing Kate never forgave me for was some close-ups of her hands, which made her seem older by contrast to Elizabeth Taylor."

For their roles in *Suddenly, Last Summer*, both Katharine Hepburn and Elizabeth Taylor were nominated for Oscars as Best Actress. Mankiewicz told me he couldn't understand why *he* was overlooked. "I was, after all, the director who steered those performances." The film did well financially and Mankiewicz was more sought after, so he wasn't totally overlooked.

It was generally believed that neither Taylor nor Hepburn won the Oscar because they split the votes, allowing Simone Signoret to win for *Room at the Top*.

During the time she was filming *Long Day's Journey into Night* in New York, Kate spent weekends with her dying father and Spencer, who were on opposite coasts.

"I would leave Friday after we finished filming in New York to drive to my father in Connecticut. At the same time, Spencer wasn't well at all. I was told his health was deteriorating rapidly. So, Saturday after I had been with my father, I frequently flew to spend some time with Spence, and I left Sunday to be back on the set." Arriving in time for her call on Monday morning, she would film all day.

"*Long Day's Journey into Night*," Kate told me, "was the mirror image of my own agony during that time. I am not an Actors Studio kind of actress who drew on happenings in my own life to come up with the feelings needed for my character. It's not usually happiness that actors have trouble with, but it's playing sad, having your heart break in a giant screen close-up. I've never had that problem because I could cry on a dime. I needed hardly any time at all to burst into tears, two-eyed, any flow desired, and my only problem was sometimes I cried so profusely that after the director said cut, I needed a few minutes to stop crying. My red eyes would be genuine, no makeup needed. What surprised even me was I could do it even at my happiest moments. Around the set, people asked me how I did it. Young, even not so young, actors wanted to know my trick, so that they could do it. I had to say I didn't know how I did it. I don't think they believed me.

"My performance of suffering was much appreciated, and some of those who had said I was more of a personality than a real actress suddenly acclaimed that performance, saying I was 'a real actress.' My agony had won them over, and they said I could appear haggard, too, if I wanted. Well, I was genuinely in agony and more than a little haggard. The two men in my life I loved were dying.

"My father was dying a prolonged and horrible death over many months, almost a year, and there was no hope of his getting better, only the knowledge that he would be worse.

"He said to me, 'I'm glad that I'm the one who has to suffer like this, rather than your mother.'

"I found myself praying for Father's death. For myself, I wanted him to be in the world, but for him, I wanted the pain to end. I shouldn't use the word 'praying,' because Father wouldn't have approved. He didn't believe praying served a constructive purpose. He came from a family that had ministers in it, but he said that the pain and suffering he had seen as a doctor endured by people who didn't deserve it had caused him to disbelieve in a kind and merciful God, and he refused to believe in any other.

"I couldn't let everyone down for Long Day's Journey. Not only did I have the pivotal part, but I knew what financial backing there was had been raised on my name. We had all taken almost nothing in order to be able to make the film. I believed in it, but I didn't believe there would ever be any big profit sharing. There would be no gravy train.

"I remember how Spence had laughed and sneered at my pitiful $25,000. I'd wanted him to play opposite me, but he said he had bills to pay and if he worked, he had to earn real money. Maybe he said that because he knew he wasn't well enough to do the part. I believe he was more comfortable in California. He hated flying from the West Coast to the East Coast and back. But he didn't like to say that because he wouldn't have wanted me to think he had any fear of flying.

"I never minded flying. I could always sleep or read a script. Spence had terrible insomnia and he couldn't sleep through a night on the world's most comfortable mattress.

"When I traveled during those weekends to Connecticut and California after a week of shooting, I could sleep standing up, as they say.

"Spence felt guilty about my having taken time away from my career to be with him. I think he overestimated the status of my career at the moment. I don't think I would have been buried under a landslide of fabulous parts. Our mailman wasn't bent under the weight of great scripts arriving for me. I didn't care. I was where I wanted to be, doing what I wanted to do, being what Father said I was, 'a natural caregiver.'"

## Long Day's Journey into Night (1962)

The Tyrone family is spending the summer of 1912 in a Connecticut seaside cottage. The youngest son, Edmund (Dean Stockwell), who has literary aspirations, may be tubercular.

The father, James Tyrone, Sr. (Ralph Richardson), lives in a world of memories. The mother, Mary (Katharine Hepburn), developed a drug addiction after Edmund's difficult birth. She feels responsible for Edmund's condition. Her father died of tuberculosis, and she fears the disease has been passed on to her son.

James Tyrone, Jr. (Jason Robards, Jr.), is an alcoholic. One of his few pastimes in life besides drinking is looking after his younger brother and encouraging him in his ambition to be a writer.

While Tyrone Sr. rants on about his long-past triumphs on the stage, Edmund tries to comfort his mother, and Tyrone Jr. drinks.

Soon, he gets so drunk, he reveals his real feelings toward Edmund. He hates him and wants him to fail.

As day turns into night, the Tyrone family returns to normalcy and prepares for tomorrow's long day's journey into night.

Robards reprised his role from the 1956 Broadway premiere of the Eugene O'Neill play. The playwright had stipulated in his will that the 1940 play was not to be performed until twenty-six years after his death, presumably because of its autobiographical implications. He died in 1951, and his widow was able to change this provision. The enormously successful Broadway production was directed by José Quintero.

The film, directed by Sidney Lumet, was shot in Manhattan and the Bronx in thirty-seven days for $435,000. Kate was nominated again for an Oscar but lost to Anne Bancroft, in *The Miracle Worker*.

On November 20, 1962, Dr. Thomas Norval Hepburn died.

Looking back on her life, Kate reflected on the importance of her father in her early life. "He was, after all, the first man in my life and the patriarch of our family.

"I took his discouragement of my career as an actress in a very positive way. It meant that he had some hope for me, after all, that I *could* do and be something better.

"I like to think I would have tried acting once I knew it was what I wanted to do, no matter what. If Father had said, 'Go ahead, dear, with my blessing,' maybe that could have stopped me, being the kind of defiant, contrary-natured girl I am. Words like those might have sent me into a panic. Well, no need to worry. It was the opposite of what he thought and of what he said, and he made himself very clear at every opportunity, all his life.

"I revered him, so I set out to show him he was wrong and to win his praise, or at least his approval in recognition for my talent. I don't think my father ever admitted to being wrong about anything because I think he never believed he was.

"By never giving me any approbation, by withholding his approval, he gave me something to always strive for. Wasn't I lucky!

"My father told me when I was about to choose a career that I should choose one that would last a lifetime.

"I've had a big career, not just long, but big. Longer than I could ever have imagined. Bigger than even a very optimistic young girl could ever have dreamed of, even when I *was* a very optimistic young girl."

"When he died, I was terribly sad, heartbroken, but along with the terrible loss I felt at his passing, I also felt the loss of the pressure to prove to him that I was a great actress. Showing him became an unattainable goal.

"After the funeral, I thought, 'It can never be.'

"Father never came to California to see me in my movie star milieu. One could say he always meant to make the trip but just put it off and never got around to it. He was a very serious doctor, and he never wanted to leave all the patients who depended on him. And they did depend on him.

"He really had no interest in California because I think he believed he had the best of the whole world right where he was, traveling between Hartford and Fenwick. He really had no need to come and see me because I made the trip there so often.

"The real reason, I think, was he didn't want to encourage me to go on living in California. He was waiting for me to give up my so-called career in California. I know he considered my acting rather a waste of my time, though he never suggested, after a certain point, when he had really given up on me, what else I might do with my life that was *less* of a waste of time.

"Father may not have been proud of me, because of the career I had chosen, but I believe he was proud of my success, though he never mentioned it. Everyone in the neighborhood knew about his daughter. Everyone at the hospital and all of his patients knew about his eldest daughter.

"My father liked success, and when they admired me, he was getting secondhand admiration.

"When he died, I felt terrible. There I was, an orphan. I was sad, but maybe not as sad as I thought I'd be. It may be because it was so long since I'd been in constant contact with my father. I have a sneaking feeling it was because he married so quickly, only months after my mother's death. I had some trouble adjusting to that. I didn't dislike my father's wife, but I thought my parents had the most perfect marriage. You know, when two became one.

"Madeleine was a nice lady. It was only after she and my father were married that I looked at her. I'd never really noticed her until Father said he was going to marry again, and it was Madeleine, just after Mother died. I saw that look of love and worship on her face whenever she looked at my father. I'm sure my father was well aware of it, and though he almost never showed any emotion, even at my mother's funeral, because it was against his personality and philosophy of stoicism, I think he relished her obvious hero worship.

"My mother had always placed her own feelings and thoughts second to those of my father. She had made it seem that they were totally unified and agreed on everything. I don't think that was exactly so.

"Despite her lofty education and high intelligence, Mother lived in a man's world, accepting her place as a woman. We children knew our parents had a love-marriage. Their noisy lovemaking at night was well understood by all of us from a very early age. Father particularly made no attempt to restrain his obvious gusto. Mother was more decorous, but there were squeals and sighs aplenty. All of us knew very early how we happened to come into the world. Born of love. Goody!

"But I never saw Mother look at Father with worship. If she ever did, it was only in private, when they were alone. I don't think it was really in her character, and I don't believe it was what my father would have liked. Maybe it *was* what he really liked. Who knows?

"Perhaps he was getting old. He looked wonderful, but you never know everything about anyone, even your own parents, maybe *especially* your own parents. As the years ahead of you seem fewer, we all feel different inside, no matter how well you carry it off on the outside.

"I had my own theory. I felt the reason my father didn't want to wait longer was because he missed my mother so much and was so lonely. Madeleine was his nurse, so she shared his work, which he loved so much. He may also have thought about the future and that he might need someone who was a good nurse to take care of him, and he didn't want to be a burden on any of us.

"I know my father's dream was that I follow in his footsteps. I admired him and what he did, but I knew what I wanted.

"My mother didn't say anything. She would never have supported me against what my father wanted, but she didn't add her voice to discouraging me either.

"It was the first time I deliberately went against his wishes. I never wanted to disappoint him. I was disappointing and displeasing him, but I couldn't help it. I had to try for what I knew I wanted."


"William Rose, who wrote *The Ladykillers*, wrote the script for *Guess Who's Coming to Dinner*," Kate said. "Stanley Kramer would be directing, and I liked the idea.

"There was a lovely part for Kathy [Houghton], my niece, Marion's daughter. She would play Spencer's and my daughter. I loved that. She's beautiful and she definitely had a family resemblance. It was my idea.

"But I didn't really like the name of our daughter in the script, so I said to Stanley, 'Could you ask the writer if he'd mind changing the name?' Stanley asked me if I had a reason why I didn't want to use the name that had been chosen. I said yes, of course.

"I had a good reason. Spencer and I would never have chosen that name, Joey, for our daughter if we had had one, and our characters certainly wouldn't have chosen that name. Spencer and I felt that our films were our children. I thought this film would be our last child, a late-life child.

"Willie Rose later said to me, 'These films are like *my* children. That's why I can't just accept other names, no matter how much I might like or respect those who suggest them. It would be like giving me advice on how to bring up my children. I don't really want to hear it. I feel I know what's best for my own child, and I always harbor some small secret resentment against those who want to make a change, even one so apparently slight as changing the name of a character. The characters' names are the way I have come to know them, and I become attached to them, so how could I change the name, especially of a major character? The character would become a stranger to me.'

"I knew well at whom this small diatribe was aimed. I had my answer. The name didn't get changed, but Willie and I became good friends anyway."

## Guess Who's Coming to Dinner (1967)

Arriving in San Francisco after a short Hawaiian vacation, twenty-one-year-old Joey Drayton (Katharine Houghton) and Dr. John Prentice (Sidney Poitier), who is in his middle 30s, prepare themselves to meet her parents. They have just become engaged, and Joey wants the blessing of her parents, if she can get it. She is traveling with Prentice to Geneva, where he is about to assume an important post in the World Health Organization.

Her parents are Matt and Christina Drayton (Spencer Tracy and Katharine Hepburn). He is the publisher of a liberal, crusading San Francisco newspaper and she owns an art gallery specializing in the avant-garde.

When they meet their daughter's intended husband, his age is of no consequence. It is his race that tests their liberal sensibilities. He is African-American.

Once they have come to terms with this, they discover that only half of the problem has been solved. Prentice's parents (Roy E. Glenn and Beah Richards) arrive from Los Angeles with his father strongly objecting to the marriage, feeling that his son is throwing away his career. Unexpected discrimination forces Matt and Christina to lobby in favor of what they aren't at all sure of themselves. Matt's clinching argument to the two gathered families is that the couple love each other, and it's their business what they do with their lives.

"The part of my daughter," Kate said, "was a difficult one. A young unknown actress needs more opportunity to win the sympathy of the audience. Otherwise, too much has to depend on her youth, innocence, and beauty. She had one good speech to win the audience, but it was cut. Instead she only talks with her father about the differences between the principles he taught her and the way he's behaving.

"Without Stanley Kramer, the film couldn't have happened. It was his idea in the first place, and he carried it through against obstacles you cannot even imagine."

Karen Sharpe Kramer, the director's widow, told me "Stanley always appreciated Kate's importance. He couldn't have obtained the backing without her. Even so, Stanley, Kate, and Spencer had to delay collecting their salaries until Spencer had completed his last scene. We all knew he was dying. I think he did the film for Kate, because he couldn't leave her anything in his will."

Kate was godmother to Stanley and Karen's baby. The baby was a girl, and a box arrived at the Kramer home, a gift from godmother Kate. It contained Kate's own christening dress.


"I was struck by the fantastic energy Kate had," Sidney Poitier told me. "She never ran down.

"I'd hoped to get to know her better than I did because I'd admired her as an actress, and then, I was very struck by her personally, but her time was pretty taken.

"The illness of Spencer dominated everything. I knew his health was very poor and many of the people who knew what the situation was didn't believe we'd finish the film, that is, that Tracy would be able to finish the film. Those of us who were close knew it was worse than they thought. Kate brought him to and from the set. She worked with him on his lines. She made sure with Stanley [Kramer] that his hours were right for what he could do, and what he couldn't do was different each day. There were days when he couldn't do anything. There were days when he was great, and I got the chance to know what it was like working with Tracy.

"Kate was also trying to help her niece, who was a nice, beautiful girl without much experience or confidence, but I thought she had talent, and I tried to help her.

"The film was a real strain because you couldn't help but suffer for Spencer, and then you couldn't help but suffer for Kate, who was suffering for both of them. But I was always glad I did it."


"It came clear to me," Kate said, "that no matter how much I wanted to put aside the truth of how ill Spence was, neither one of us could ignore it. I couldn't ignore it and I couldn't face it.

"I thought about when Spencer was gone, how I would feel, what I would be willing to give for one more day. One more hour. I didn't want to have regrets, to think about the time I might have with him instead of one more film or one more play.

"It wasn't a sacrifice I made for Spence. It was the only thing I could do for myself. It was selfish. I wanted to be with him.

"I don't think I consciously formulated the thought that as long as Spencer would be working, he had a purpose to go on, that his future would be more certain. I believed that Spence wouldn't let me down. He had a strong will, and couldn't die because he wanted me to get paid. And he didn't want to let the others down, either."

George Cukor told me, "Tracy could be very social with his old friends, but he didn't enjoy big parties with strangers. As his health deteriorated, he didn't want to see people very much, or really, I think, he didn't want people to see *him*. His whole image was one of vigor and stamina, not exactly of physical beauty, but masculinity and strength. A part of his image was that he had no vanity, vanity being considered a feminine trait. But I think he was vain enough. It's just that he was only vain about what he *had* to be vain about.

"During the day Tracy had the television on a lot. I don't think it was so much because he enjoyed the programs as much as because he didn't want to be alone with his own thoughts."


"I thought about why Spence let me persuade him to do *Guess Who's Coming to Dinner*," Kate said. "He liked the idea of the film. He was great friends with Stanley Kramer and thought he was a wonderful director. When we met Sidney Poitier, Spence liked him.

"Those were all reasons to do the film, but they weren't enough to convince Spence, not at that point. What stopped him was clear. He didn't feel well enough to think he could do it, and moreover, he wasn't certain he'd even live through it. He didn't want to die before it was finished and let everyone down.

"Why did he agree to do it when I asked him to, in spite of how sick he was feeling, and he didn't have the energy, and he didn't want to embarrass himself even in the days before he was in such fragile health? There was only one reason I can imagine.

"Me. He did it for me.

"When Spencer had finished his part in the film, he seemed very happy about it. Well, maybe 'happy' isn't the right way to express it. Spence had never been a bouncy, gushy personality, but he was very warm, and he transmitted a feeling of joy to me in our early days. 'A person doesn't have to say everything,' he said to me. I think he said that because I was 'going on,' as he called it.

"I can always see in my mind Spencer on the day he finished his last shot of the film as we walked off to the car, so I could drive him home. He turned and looked back at everyone all gathered there watching us leave, and he smiled and waved goodbye."

"In our private life, Spencer didn't talk a lot, but what he said counted. It suited me because I always preferred a man who didn't talk too much, for two reasons. One, it doesn't seem manly to me for a man to babble, and second, if he talked a lot, we would be talking at the same time. You know, the way birds do.

"I think I don't talk as much now as I once did. I don't think I have the same drive to communicate because so many of the people I wanted to communicate with are gone to where no one can communicate with them."

Kevin Thomas, longtime critic and writer for the *Los Angeles Times*, remembered a moment that characterized Katharine Hepburn.

"I was invited to a cast and crew party for the completion of *Guess Who's Coming to Dinner* at the old Columbia lot. Everyone who had been involved in the production was there, except Spencer Tracy.

"There was a small platform, a kind of makeshift stage. The director of the film, Stanley Kramer, came out to speak. He was very emotional. He started to cry. He began to speak about what a privilege it had been to work with Katharine Hepburn and with Spencer Tracy, and he added, very emotionally, something to the effect of what it had meant to direct Spencer Tracy in his last film.

"There was a kind of hush, and then, sort of a commotion. From the audience, leaping like a gazelle, Katharine Hepburn landed gracefully on the stage. She laughed her wonderful laugh and grabbed the microphone and put her arm around Kramer.

"Smiling, she said, 'We all know how Spencer is. For years, every time he makes a film, he announces that he is retiring and that this is going to be his very last film. Then, he comes back for just one more.' She treated it all lightheartedly, like a great joke.

"She never gave a performance more worthy of an Oscar. Everyone knew that Spencer Tracy wasn't well, but only a few people in the inner circle knew that he was at home dying.

"It was an unforgettable, brilliant moment. She turned it around and saved the day from being a premature funeral.

"A few weeks later, Spencer Tracy died."

In the middle of the night of June 10, 1967, Kate was in bed in the small bedroom at the back of the Cukor cottage when she heard a cup fall in the kitchen and then the terrifying sound of Spencer falling.

She rushed into the kitchen, but before she could reach him, it was all over. He had died of a heart attack.

There were some who said it was a shame that she hadn't had a chance to say goodbye to him. But that was all she had been doing for the past few years, saying goodbye to Spence in *her* way, in *his* way—in *their* way—which was never to say goodbye. Kate was only grateful for the way it happened. Spence could scarcely have known what happened. He had not suffered.

Kate called George Cukor in the main house and Albert and Margaret, the devoted couple who worked for him and lived on the grounds. She called her personal assistant Phyllis, who was staying at Kate's house, which she rented in order to give herself a public address of her own, and a place where Phyllis could stay. She also called Howard Strickling, the head of M-G-M's publicity department, who had been dedicated to keeping the Tracy-Hepburn relationship out of the press.

Kate had planned to leave with her few personal possessions and go to her house just blocks away. But she thought about how she had spent so much of her life with this man, almost thirty years, and she decided not to run away.

She called Carroll Tracy, Spencer's brother, a difficult call. She knew how much Carroll loved his brother.

Then she called Louise Tracy, Spencer's wife, and gave her the address where to come.

The press was told that Kate and Mr. Cukor had arrived at eleven A.M. after the body was gone, and had left before the press arrived.

Unlike the way her parents would have felt, Kate wanted to be at the mortuary where Spencer's body was. She went in after it had closed, when everyone who had come to pay their respects had gone.

She placed a small picture she had painted in the casket with him. The next night, the casket was sealed by order of the family. Kate wondered if her painting was there to accompany Spence, or if it had been found and taken away.

On the day of the funeral, Kate and Phyllis followed the cars to the Immaculate Heart of Mary Church in Hollywood. As the church was in sight, Kate turned around, and she and Phyllis went back to the cottage. Kate knew she could not be at the funeral, but she wanted to be as close as she could be.

After the service, some of Kate's and Spencer's closest friends who knew about their relationship came by the cottage to see her, among them Garson Kanin, Ruth Gordon, and director Jean Negulesco and his wife.

A few weeks after the funeral, Kate called Louise Tracy. She asked if there was anything she could do, and suggested that they might be friends.

Kate was surprised by Louise's response. After a momentary pause, Spencer's widow said, "I thought you were only a rumor."

After Tracy's death, *Guess Who's Coming to Dinner* opened, and the film was the most successful Tracy and Hepburn had ever made, together or apart. It was nominated for ten Oscars, among them Best Picture, Best Director, Best Actor, Best Actress, and Best Screenplay.

William Rose won for his screenplay and Kate won for Best Actress. It was her tenth nomination, and it had been thirty-four years since Kate had won her first Oscar as Best Actress in *Morning Glory*.

Kate was not happy because Spencer had been nominated for Best Actor, but had not won.

One time when I was in New York having tea with Kate, she showed me a large cup that had been broken in several places and glued back together. It was missing a piece.

"This one isn't for you to drink from," she said. "I just wanted to show it to you. Spencer was holding it the night he died. I heard it fall and break, and he fell. I rushed from my room, but it was too late. I'd lost Spencer. I had my memories and the cup. I thought I picked up all the pieces, but apparently I missed one.

"Do you know . . . Well, no, of course, you wouldn't know, but Spence never said to me, 'I love you.' I'm quite sure he never said it, not once, because I'm sure I would have remembered it and re-played the moment over and over in my head.

"Now, Spence never went in for a lot of mushy stuff, and I wasn't a gusher myself, but I did say to him on numerous appropriate and spontaneous occasions when I was carried away, 'I love you.' With-out being conscious of it, I was probably angling for some sort of like response from him. It didn't work.

"I'd always said I didn't care about men saying words to me like 'I love you' because words like that came most easily to men I didn't usually care for. Anyway, I always believed I considered all of the romantic nonsense words silly. Until Spence . . . Then it was all different.

"I would have done anything for Spence. Why? It was a mystery to me."

# 7

# The Madwoman of Fenwick

"I'll tell you about Peter O'Toole, who was in *Lion in Winter* with me," Kate said. "He can be summed up in one quick little story I'd like to tell you, and then you'll know him.

"I was waiting for my makeup, and I was in the next scene. I was getting nervous, so I went to see why the makeup man was so late coming to me.

"I found out rather quickly where he had been detained. He was applying makeup for Peter O'Toole, who didn't have a scene until later.

"I was pretty put out, and I didn't make a secret of it. I grabbed hold of that makeup man, who obviously was much chummier with my costar than with me. I told him in words he couldn't misunderstand that I was *not* pleased. Then, Peter O'Toole laughed, not *with* me, but *at* me, so as I departed with the makeup man in tow, I gave Mr. O'Toole a little slap on the side of his head. Well, maybe it wasn't little, but it wasn't much either.

"The makeup man was hustling to get me ready when Mr. O'Toole came limping along. He was using a crutch, and limping badly, and his head was bandaged as though he was suffering from a terrible wound.

"*That* is Peter O'Toole.

"Peter had Irish charm, *too* much charm, and I'd guess too much Irish—whiskey. He was just what I needed to put life into the old gal."

Jane Merrow, who played Princess Alais in the film, talked with me about working with Kate.

"I was very nervous about her to start with, as we all were, because of who she was. Peter O'Toole told us we were like children in a family. But, as it turned out, she was just as nervous as we were.

"He knew. He was a very sympathetic type of man. He would tune into people very well. He'd know what was going on with them, and he adored Kate. So, once we all warmed up to each other, and we were relaxed, we all got on extremely well. We really did get along rather like a family, which was amazing, because often when people work together like that, the film doesn't turn out very well. We all have too much of a good time.

"I wish, in a funny sort of way, that I'd known her later. I think I was too young to gain enough from her experience. Well, I wasn't *that* young, but I was too immature though I did learn an awful lot from her.

"The biggest thing I learned was about being a professional actor. I was a stage actress, which I think is important. I went to the Royal

Academy of Dramatic Art and did all the technical things. I thought I was pretty good. I don't mean in terms of my acting ability, but in terms of my approach.

"But I found my approach was rather lacking compared to hers. When we first got together to rehearse, Kate knew not only her own lines, but she knew all of ours. And none of us knew our own lines at that point. This was just rehearsal. We hadn't started shooting. So that was a bit of a shock. Then, we were rushing home that night making sure we knew our own lines.

"Her research, her approach to her work, and her focus and everything was so extraordinary. I think I've developed a lot more of that myself now. But when you're young, you're kind of callow.

"We all met, first of all, in a wonderful London restaurant called the White Tower, in a private room. There was Kate at the table, and the rest of us came in and met her. You suddenly see one of these great icons in your life and there's this extraordinary feeling.

"Peter had flown out to Los Angeles to ask her to do this film. This was just after Spencer Tracy had died. It was a fragile point in her life. Peter *hated* flying, but he did the trip from London to L.A. to give her the script personally. She said she would do it, but only if he would supervise the casting of all the other important characters. She trusted his judgment. So, he personally tested every single actor for those roles. It was an amazing feat.

"In my first test, I had hair blowing all over my face because it was a very windy day. We were doing some lines from a play that I was doing at the time, and in the middle of the testing, Peter said, 'I don't believe you.' I was just sort of rattling off what I was doing at night, and that was what I meant about callow youth, overconfident about what you're doing, and you don't think about it. That was the first big lesson. From then on, my lessons went very well, and I learned about acting from those two, Kate and Peter, more than I have ever learned from anyone.

"What I learned from Peter is that if you're lying or you're wing-ing, the camera will pick it up. From Kate, I learned about prepara-tion and about working as a team, which was amazing. We had one scene together, just she and I. It was a very intimate scene between Eleanor of Aquitaine and Alais. She said to me, 'You lean forward on my lines, and I'll lean forward on your lines. So we'll go into camera at the same time.' We worked as a team, and that's what I loved about her. She would work with you to the nth degree to do it right.

"Kate liked to wear pants and be comfortable. 'I don't have to worry about looking glamorous anymore,' she said. 'I want to be comfortable.' But she really was an *extremely* feminine woman, and she did flirt with men. I watched her. Oh, she loved men. And good for her!

"She was never rude to people. She wasn't rude because she was a very kind woman. I think sometimes people took her sharpness in the wrong way, which was their problem, not hers.

"She had a great sense of humor and fun. When we first arrived in France, we went for a ride in our chartered airplane, which she called the 'Death Ship.' She said, 'I've had my life and everything else and I'm ready to go, so we're all going on the Death Ship!'

"While we were in France, she said, 'Do you want to go and have a drive, and look around?' because she had a car and chauffeur with her. I said, 'Yes, I'd love to.' We went and drove around, and we got out and looked at everything. In the end, we went to one more place, and she said, 'Aren't you going to get out of the car?' I was exhausted, and she was still raring to go.

*The Lion in Winter*, based on a 1966 play by James Goldman, is drawn from events that took place in 1183, during the reign of Henry II of England. The title refers to Henry's approaching old age.

# The Lion in Winter (1968)

In 1183, King Henry II (Peter O'Toole) wants to decide the succession to his Norman empire—England, Ireland, Wales, Scotland, and part of France.

To attend, his queen, Eleanor of Aquitaine (Katharine Hepburn), must be temporarily released from the castle in which she has been confined for the last ten years for her complicity in a revolt against his rule. Also there are their three sons, Prince Richard the Lion-Hearted (Anthony Hopkins), Prince Geoffrey (John Castle), and Prince John (Nigel Terry), King Henry's mistress Princess Alais (Jane Merrow), and her brother Philip, king of France (Timothy Dalton).

His family is cunning, politically ambitious, and untrustworthy, though they all respect Henry as husband, father, and a great king. The king, however, is exceedingly disappointed in his offspring.

Eleanor claims still to love him, but her only importance to him now is that, as ruler of Aquitaine, her signature is needed to make his control permanent.

Alais also claims to love him, but behind her naïve charm, is a ruthless, power-hungry vixen. She is pregnant with, she hopes, the next male heir to the throne, and she wants King Henry to divorce Eleanor.

Richard is the heir apparent, but Henry favors John. He wants to marry off Alais to John to solidify his relations with France and still have his mistress. Geoffrey favors John, whom he believes he will be able to manipulate.

When Henry discovers that his sons are all conspiring with the weak young French king, he has them imprisoned together in a castle dungeon. Alais demands that he kill them. He agrees, but can't go through with it, and he frees them.

At the boat that will convey Eleanor back to her prison, she extracts the promise from Henry that she will be released for Easter.


Kate said to me, "They know they can't live forever, but they are struggling over their immortality. Their sons represent their future, even though they don't particularly recognize themselves in their sons. It's a common occurrence.

"My own family was exactly the opposite. We all came from the same tree, and we all recognized each other as the children of our parents.

"When Henry asks Eleanor what she wants, she says she wants the Aquitaine. It's clear, though, she really wants back everything she gave away in her dowry, because the marriage hasn't brought her what she thought it would. But what she wants back most, although she never says it, is her youth, filled with promise. She wants the good days back because she knows they existed, even though she can't quite remember them, and he can't either.

"Henry doesn't understand this. He simply says, 'You've got your enigmatic face on,' and her children say, 'What shall we do with Mother?' and they are serious. Sometimes, it's what's *not* said between people that is important.

"The fate of the British and French empires, and perhaps the whole world, is being guided by a small squabbling family. Meanwhile, the common people are just going about their business, trying to eke out the best lives they can, hoping they don't have to go to any bloody battles, wars, or crusades. That's how it is. It's not easy to have a voice, even if you know what's going on, and it's not easy to know what's really going on. Most people don't want to know.

"When I learned I was going to be Eleanor of Aquitaine, I read everything about her and the history of her time that I could find.

"Eleanor was an acting performance for me, a character quite different from my own self. She was angry, but not as angry as I would have been if I'd been married to a king who kept me locked away in a castle cell for ten years. Abominable."

For the first time in Oscar history, there was a tie for Best Actress, Barbra Streisand winning for *Funny Girl* and Katharine Hepburn for *The Lion in Winter*. Each actress received 1,515 votes.

Kate was not at the ceremony to receive her third Oscar because, it was announced, she was working on *The Madwoman of Chaillot* in France. Director Anthony Harvey accepted for her. No matter what, she would not have attended. She had not gone to receive her first two. "Of course, I never knew in advance I was going to win, only that I was nominated. Well, a nomination was enough to get me to run for cover. If I'd known I was going to win, I would have run faster and, until recently, I could still run pretty fast.

"I never cared a lot about winning honors for myself. I enjoyed it a little, I guess, especially in the early days, if it made it easier to get work. They say winning is more fun than losing, and it's one of the few things that the ubiquitous 'they,' whoever *they* are, is right about. Personally, though, I felt a strong sense of competition in athletics, but I never felt it in trophy winning for acting. I don't believe you can readily say that one actor was so much better than the other nominees, and especially you can't say the person was better than all of the people who never got nominated at all, some of whom made films very few people ever saw. People can only vote for what they've seen and what they should have seen.

"What I mind is when someone I know, a friend, or someone who was great in a part and who wanted the award badly, loses it. It's sort of sad, even if the person didn't exactly deserve the award.

"My regular reaction to going to awards shows was *not* going and saying to myself, and to anyone who cared to listen, 'Thank God I don't have to go.'

"It wasn't the only reason I didn't like getting awards. I felt that it opened the door to more focus on my private life. During the years with Spencer, I particularly didn't want that."


"I looked forward to meeting our star, Katharine Hepburn," Anthony Hopkins told me. "I wondered what she would be like, whether she would be like her screen persona or something different. I did not expect her to be modest, retiring, demure. And she wasn't.

"She was a very take-charge lady. She gave her best, and she expected everyone else to do that. No excuses. She knew how to do your job. If you ever didn't get it right, she wasn't shy about letting you know, but in a constructive way. She'd never say, 'That won't do.' She'd give you a clue as to how you could do better, but she would always be a trifle obscure, so you'd have to figure something out for yourself. She believed unless you figured it out for yourself, based on her clue, you weren't really getting it.

"The first time she heard my part—which, I must say, was not the best part I ever hoped to have, though I was impressed by the idea of the film, I really put my heart into what I was doing. I think I got a little too much into it. Anyway, too much of something. Miss Hepburn looked at me in the stern way I remembered some of my schoolteachers who were not entirely pleased with me looked at me.

"'Don't act,' she told me. 'Just speak the lines.'

"I received the message. After that, I must have done much better, because she became friendly. She had a wonderful sense of humor, but I couldn't always tell when she was joking. That was a challenging aspect of her humor. You wouldn't want to make a mistake.

"At first, I was rather quiet with her and mostly listened. That seemed to satisfy her quite well at first. Then, I noticed she seemed to be getting a little bored. So I was bolder and more responsive. Then, I found her very friendly. She spoke a great deal about Spencer Tracy, who had just died. She liked talking about him, and it was clear he was very much on her mind. But it didn't interfere with her work. I think she was glad to be working. It probably kept her mind off just thinking about him and his death.

"I hoped I would work with her again. I didn't but I was glad to have that opportunity, and to work with Peter O'Toole, too, who is truly one of our best actors.

"A number of times I've been asked about working with Kate, and I've been asked to say what it was that gave her such star quality. She certainly had that. I'd say she was electric."

About *The Madwoman of Chaillot,* Kate said, "I have to admit that sometimes an appealing foreign locale for a shoot could be persuasive with me, something of an inducement. Another wonderful chance to see the world, all expenses paid. *Madwoman* offered that.

"I could've paid my own way, and Phyllis's, too, but 'all expenses paid' is more enjoyable. Phyllis was always ready to throw some things into a bag and take off with me. That made it so much nicer, to have a companion at the ready. I wonder why John Huston thought immediately of me for the part of the madwoman?"

In the mid-1980s, Giulietta Masina, on her way back to Rome after an appearance at the San Francisco Film Festival, stopped in New York City. Her husband, Federico Fellini, about whom I had been writing, called me from Rome and asked if I could invite her to lunch, adding that she didn't know people in New York City.

While she and I were having lunch, she asked me if I knew that Katharine Hepburn lived in New York. She said she had been in *The Madwoman of Chaillot* with her and that la Signora Hepburn had invited her to come to her house for tea if she ever came to New York. She added that she didn't know if she really meant it or whether it was one of those things people just say.

I told her I was certain that Katharine Hepburn meant it. She would never have invited her if she hadn't meant it. I told her that I could call.

"Oh, no! I could *never* do *that!*" Masina said. "I didn't really know her well. She is such a great star, and I am well known only in Italy." I told her she had many dedicated fans in the United States who loved her unforgettable performances in *La Strada, Nights of Cabiria,* and *Juliet of the Spirits.*

"I don't speak English, only a little," she said, "and I understood it less well." Giulietta did speak English, but she had no confidence in her ability.

She asked me if we could pass by the house in a taxi after lunch. I told her that we could walk. She said, "No, no. La Signora Hepburn might look out the window and recognize me. She might feel forced to invite me in. I would be so embarrassed.

"La Signora Hepburn was very interested in my husband, Federico. She told me she liked his early work, but she felt he'd gone downhill. I couldn't believe she would say something like that to me, even if she thought it. She was very . . . I don't know the word in English."

I suggested the words "frank" and "blunt," and explained, and she nodded. She said that la Signora Hepburn had asked her if she thought her "genius husband" would be visiting her during the filming, because they were not so far from Rome. Giulietta explained that for Federico, if he couldn't walk to it from their apartment, it was far, so she wasn't expecting him.

As it turned out, Fellini did surprise his wife and arrived in time to have lunch with Katharine Hepburn. The very reserved Masina took a seat at another table in order to give Kate and Fellini a chance "to make the connection."

Back in Rome, Masina told me, "I asked Federico what he thought about la Signora Hepburn. He said she had 'a haunted look in her eyes, like she didn't get enough sleep and had bad dreams.'

## The Madwoman of Chaillot (1969)

Countess Aurelia (Katharine Hepburn) is known as "The Madwoman of Chaillot" because of her eccentric behavior in behalf of just causes. She is appalled to learn that the city of Paris may soon be turned into a gigantic oilfield. She must do something about this, so she enlists the aid of her three best friends, Josephine (Edith Evans), Constance (Margaret Leighton), and Gabrielle (Giulietta Masina). Together they will thwart the evil forces dedicated to destroying a world of beauty.

With the help of other concerned friends, they lure the potential despoilers of their beloved Paris into the basement cellar of her large house, promising to show them evidence of oil there. In a mock trial, the accused are convicted for their evil intentions and then led down even deeper into the dark catacombs below where they believe there is oil. She leaves them sealed in to perish, feeling she has made a step toward saving Paris.

Kate said, "The ending of *Madwoman* was acceptable for the French, who saw the play existentially and metaphorically. American audiences were more literal. They saw my character as a murderess, and her behavior not endearing, not acceptable.

"People ask me why I accepted such a part. Well, why not? I'm already the Madwoman of Fenwick."

John Huston signed Kate to do the Jean Giraudoux play on the condition that shooting would not start until she finished *The Lion in Winter*. While Huston waited, he became increasingly dissatisfied with the screenplay as it was developing and found an excuse to drop out of the project. Kate stayed and reported on time at the Nice studios. The new director was Bryan Forbes.

In 1969, Kate returned to the stage after a nine-year absence. Her last appearance in the theater had been in 1960 at the Stratford, Connecticut, Shakespearean Festival, in *Antony and Cleopatra* and *Twelfth Night*. This time, it would be in a Broadway musical, her first.

Producer Frederick Brisson had originally intended *Coco*, a stage musical based on the life of Gabrielle "Coco" Chanel, for his wife, Rosalind Russell. Lyricist Alan Jay Lerner favored Katharine Hepburn. Neither actress resembled Coco, who in her eighties expressed a preference for "Hepburn," believing it was Audrey Hepburn.

Lerner sent Kate a script, and she liked it. She wanted her old friend Michael Benthall as director. They hadn't worked together since *The Millionnairess* in 1953. She agreed to do *Coco* if she could sing the part satisfactorily, both to their standards and to hers. She had never sung professionally on the stage.

Garson Kanin knew Kate during the months she struggled with the decision whether or not to do *Coco*. As the time drew near for her to decide, Kanin said, "I asked her if it was the singing that was causing her concern." Kate told him that the real problem was something else. "What Kate was so unsure about was wearing high heels! She said, 'I never like doing what I'm not good at, and I'm not good at wearing high heels onstage. I think you have to wear them all the time to be comfortable in them. It's been years since I've worn them, and they're really hard to walk in. I could end up falling on my face, or on something else, onstage.

" 'I'd have to get the shoes a size larger, so I'm not in pain, because that shows for the audience. I'd have to learn again how to walk in them. I'd have to start practicing now.' She did. I think the decision was made talking it out with me. George [Cukor] already had been all for it, and he had the most influence with her."

It was arranged for Kate to audition for Lerner and Brisson in Irene Selznick's apartment on Fifth Avenue in New York. They assumed she would wear Chanel. She wore pants and a sweater.

Her singing was better than expected and it sounded like Katharine Hepburn, which was what was important. She agreed to a six-month contract.

"I was always a good cover-upper," Kate said. "I just made up that word. I had terrible stage fright, but no one guessed.

"My image, I've been told, was that of someone who was fearless, who had total confidence. Well, that shows what a really good actress I was. I've always been afraid when I performed on the stage, and I've had my qualms on the movie set, too.

"The worst terror I've ever felt was before *Coco* on Broadway. I'd never even worn Chanel clothes until I did the play. Very nice clothes, indeed. My friend Laura Harding loved Chanel, and I was very familiar with the Chanel style. The clothes were wonderfully well made. Some people thought I wore pants because I was hiding terrible legs. Well, actually, I'd always had exceptionally good legs and wasn't afraid to show them in swimsuits and tennis skirts. It was just I found pants more comfortable. When

I wore Chanel suits in the play, everyone had a chance to see my very good legs. Showing my legs was about the only thing I wasn't worried about.

"I wanted Douglas [Fairbanks, Jr.] for the part of Louis Greff," Kate told me. Greff, a lawyer, was Coco's old friend and business partner. "I did my best for him, and for me, because he was perfect for the part, and I loved him as a dear friend. He was always fun, and we had wonderful rapport. I was shocked when he wasn't chosen.

"They chose George Rose. It was a completely different interpretation of the part. It couldn't possibly have been more different, but it was very, very good."

Fairbanks told me he'd had high hopes for the part and was very disappointed. He loved the stage as much as Kate did.

George Rose, the British stage and screen actor, explained to me his unusual curtain call at the end of each performance.

"It was determined that I should enter just before Miss Hepburn in the curtain calls, which were to be on the play's most elaborate set, which was full of mirrors, platforms, and steps. Then, I would signal her entrance, and she would stroll in slowly and gracefully to tumultuous applause.

"I decided to enter at a trot, running in as fast as I could from upstage right to the apron, where I would signal her entrance. When I first tried it in rehearsals, the director, Michael Benthall, said, 'You can't do it that way, George. It doesn't fit. You'll be out of step with everyone else.' Straightaway, I knew what he meant, all those models trying to rush in on high heels with tight skirts. But before I could do it again at a more normal gait, Kate spoke up.

" 'Let him gallop in, Mike. I love it. It's so different from Greff, the audience will love it, too.' Then, she turned to me and said, 'But, George—please don't stumble. This damned skirt is so tight, I won't be able to bend over to pick you up.'"

Rose's exuberant curtain call entrance, his short legs spinning, as he raced onstage, and then his elaborate gesture toward Kate as she entered, was unforgettable.

Also memorable were her asides to the audience, explaining details they might not understand. "They ate this up," she said.

"Throughout my life in the theater, I've known people who loved to stay up all night," Kate told me, "and sleep away the entire next morning and maybe part of the afternoon, too. I found that some of my colleagues, who needed little sleep, could stay up to all hours and most of these people experienced a great rush of adrenaline which continued after they left the stage, whether their performance and the play was well or poorly received. They couldn't turn off after a performance. They wanted to go out together and talk until the rush of adrenaline ran down. After a performance, I was quite ready to go home and go to sleep.

"My favorite performances were matinees, if you must know. I was most wide awake and most full of energy. I loved the theater, so I learned to be able to do it, every night, long past what would have been my ideal bedtime.

"I never totally adjusted. No matter how late the performance, I can go to sleep as soon as I get to my bed. I wake up just as early as if I'd gone to bed early and had the right amount of sleep. I have my built-in alarm clock. I believe it's because I never wanted to miss anything. That's the way it was, whatever the reason."

After her last performance in *Coco,* she told the audience:

"I started rehearsal, and I was very, very frightened, and all these people whom you see in back of me *really* gave me the faith to go on. Then, there was the terror of the opening night, and for some wonderful reason, for me, you people gave me a feeling that you believed I could do it. I've lived a very, very fortunate life, because

I had a father and mother who believed in me. I had brothers and sisters who believed in me, and a few friends who have believed in me, and I cannot begin to thank you enough and I hope that you learn the lesson I have learned. And that is, I love you and you love me, and bless you!"

Fear was a bond she and Spencer Tracy shared. "We were both terrified people. I was terrified only about performing and he wasn't, but he worried a lot personally. Spencer was terribly afraid of flying, and he was afraid of falling asleep at night and having nightmares, and afraid of not being able to fall asleep at all.

"I've had bad dreams myself all my life. It might be one reason I'm always so glad to get up early. It's my way out of a dream I'm happy to leave. When I asked doctors about why I had them and what could I do about them, they told me my mind was too active. Well, that didn't sound so bad. I wondered how you slow your mind down. And do you want to? Then, I thought a little more about it, and I wondered how does that explain why the dreams were bad ones? They weren't nightmares, but I didn't enjoy them. Why didn't my too-active mind produce good dreams, especially since I have a happy, lucky life which I enjoy? I didn't remember the dreams when I awakened."

Apart from Katharine Hepburn, *Coco* was distinguished for its costumes and sets by Cecil Beaton, and choreography by Michael Bennett. Lerner was no longer working with Frederick Loewe; his musical collaborator was André Previn.

The most spectacular staging effects in *Coco* were provided by tall mirrors that lined a sweeping upstage staircase. The technical miracle was that while the mirrors reflected the descending models in multiple images, they never glared into the audience.

The noted British critic Sheridan Morley characterized Kate in *Coco* for me as "a diamond in a rhinestone setting."

*Coco* opened on December 18, 1969, and ran to packed houses for six months, 329 performances, until the expiration date of the contract to which Kate had agreed. Then the seemingly more appropriate Danielle Darrieux replaced Kate. There were favorable reviews but the show closed within a few months.

Kate was nominated for a Tony but lost to her friend Lauren Bacall, who was appearing in *Applause*, a stage adaptation of Joseph Mankiewicz's film *All About Eve*. After her last performance, Kate gave each member of the cast and crew a small painting done by her. Each painting was different.

In *The Trojan Women* (1971), Kate played Hecuba and Vanessa Redgrave, Andromache, in Edith Hamilton's translation of Euripides.

"It was truly downbeat," Kate said. "The men and boys have already been killed or taken away, and we women are left to our own devices. We try to plot revenge because we know our fate will be dire—slaves or concubines, or death. All bad choices.

"Except for enjoying Vanessa Redgrave's company, and buying some Spanish antiques at bargain prices, now I don't know what I was doing there.

"I was always a sucker for Euripides, and I was pleased to be at work. I was told we'd be working near Madrid. That sounded good. I didn't check it very carefully.

"Three hours from Madrid. Too far, but unbelievable tea and antique shopping. Great candlesticks."

*Rooster Cogburn* was the closest Kate ever came to making a classic western, although *Sea of Grass* and *The Rainmaker* portrayed Western characters in Western locales. The plot borrowed heavily from

*True Grit* and *The African Queen*. "I didn't care, though," Kate said. "After all, how many spinster ladies get to play the romantic lead opposite Bogey or Duke Wayne?

"For me, personally, the most enjoyable part of working on *Rooster Cogburn* was leaning against John Wayne. It was like leaning against a tree trunk, but better. He had such a hard body. Very exciting. I was happy I still felt that way, a sign of life in the old girl.

"I leaned really hard against Duke whenever I could, but I don't think he noticed. I was well past that point where he would have noticed me as a woman, and I doubt I was ever his type.

"Better he was unaware, or I might have been embarrassed. Duke Wayne did evoke some joyful memories for me."

The character of Rooster Cogburn was drawn from the *True Grit* novel by Charles Portis. Kate's character owes a great deal to Rose Sayer in *The African Queen*.

## Rooster Cogburn (1975)

Eula Goodnight (Katharine Hepburn), a spinster, enlists the aid of woman-hating old Reuben J. "Rooster" Cogburn (John Wayne) to track down and bring to justice the gang of outlaws who killed her father. Their search leads them through the wilds of nineteenth-century Oregon, including a perilous ride down river rapids. Overcoming each obstacle, they find unexpected romance.

Not too long before shooting began, Kate had undergone a hip replacement operation. In spite of this, her age, and her aversion to horses, she insisted on doing all of her riding sequences herself. Thus, John Wayne, a skilled rider, had to adjust to her erratic horsemanship, but he was a good sport about it.

\*      \*      \*

When I interviewed Christopher Reeve at his home near Williams-town, Massachusetts, in 1987, he was filled with energy and enthu-siasm, looking forward to the future. Though Reeve was strikingly handsome, more handsome in person than on the screen, when I asked if we could take some photographs of us together, he said, quite seriously, "I'm not very photogenic."

Talking with me about his theatrical appearance with Katharine Hepburn, he said, "I appeared onstage with her in *A Matter of Grav-ity*. I didn't act *with* her. I acted *near* her. It was one of the great experiences of my life, and she was an unforgettable person.

"I'll tell you something funny. A newspaper column implied that we were having an affair. I was twenty-two and she was sixty-seven. It sure wasn't true, but I'm proud that anyone would think that."

Then he told me the story of his audition for the part he played.

"In 1975, when I had the chance to audition for a new play by Enid Bagnold called *A Matter of Gravity*, I was thrilled and nervous. Thrilled because the part I would be auditioning for would be with Katharine Hepburn, nervous for the same reason. I wanted the part in her play, and I knew a great many other actors would want it, too, every actor who could possibly qualify and some who didn't. The competition would be fierce.

"I had the greatest admiration and respect for Miss Hepburn as an actress. Like every other young actor who was in New York, or who could get to New York, I knew the play would be a rare opportu-nity to perform for audiences coming to see Katharine Hepburn. But even more important to me, I felt there would be so much to learn working with a great actress. I was sure there would be a hundred other actors trying out. I was wrong. It was more like two hundred.

"I arrived at the Edison Theatre in New York City to try out for the producer, Robert Whitehead. His casting director was there, and I was told that Miss Hepburn herself was also seated out there in the dark. She was actually listening to every actor. What a fabulous thing to do! It was unbelievable, but of course it made me even more nervous. I tried to think what I could do to get control of myself or I might throw my chance right there.

"I tried a breathing exercise I'd been encouraged to use when I was studying at Juilliard, for moments of tension. It didn't work. I thought of myself flying a plane. That made some people nervous, but I loved to fly, and it always calmed me. It didn't work, either.

"I couldn't fool myself. I knew just where I was, and I understood all too fully what the opportunity meant to me and how long the odds were against me, even if I was my best, the best I'd ever been.

"Even now, looking back, I can't believe what I did. I stepped forward and made what seemed one of the great mistakes of my life. It wasn't like me at all. I said, in a voice that was so steady I wondered whose voice it was:

" 'Miss Hepburn, I have greetings for you from Beatrice Lamb. She's my grandmother, and she was a classmate of yours at Bryn Mawr.'

"After I spoke, I had a sinking feeling. It was like my voice had spoken without me, totally on its own. I heard what it was saying, but I couldn't take back the words I'd spoken so loudly and clearly.

"Then my sinking feeling got worse. It was a long time ago. Probably Miss Hepburn wouldn't even remember my grandmother, although my grandmother was a very striking woman when I knew her. She was just a girl when Miss Hepburn knew her. They were both just girls.

"I'd stretched the truth a little. My grandmother hadn't exactly sent specific greetings that particular day, but she had told me that she had been at Bryn Mawr at the same time as Katharine Hepburn, and that she had known her. My grandmother was always very exacting about the truth, but I felt stretching the truth a little, even in her name, wouldn't matter if it helped.

"It had been quite a spontaneous outpouring on my part, but afterward, I understood it could have sunk my hopes, depending on how Miss Hepburn took it. I'd always had a tendency to speak, maybe blurt is the better word, and think about what I said afterward. I hadn't thought about what I would do if there was no response from the audience.

"Miss Hepburn might punish me for my being so forward and trying to win her with my flaunting of my connections. If nothing happened, I'd have to begin my part without a cue.

"Then, it came, the reassurance, if you could call it that.

"From somewhere in the back of the theater in the darkness, I heard that unmistakable voice. It was the first time Katharine Hepburn ever spoke to me. The voice in the darkness said, 'Oh, Bea—I never could stand her.'

"I don't know what I'd expected, but as I was to learn later, Katharine Hepburn was unpredictable. I gathered my wits, which, at that moment, I didn't feel I had many of, and I went into action.

"I began moving the furniture on the set, so it would accommodate the reading I was going to give. I shouldn't really call it a reading, because I certainly didn't plan to read. I didn't even have the script with me. I didn't have notes. I wasn't an actor who had to write notes on my hand or the cuff of my shirt. Time enough for that in my old age. I was still too far from that not to trust my memory. Not only did I have an exceptionally good memory, but I'd worked really hard on my lines. I always worked hard, but I'd worked even harder than usual, and the tryout wasn't very long.

"Moving the furniture around turned out to be good for me. I'm a physical person, and I always feel good when I'm moving around. It gets the adrenaline flowing.

"Adrenaline took over. I felt in control of the space, which made me feel much better. The more you're in control of your environment and the more familiar you are with your setting, the freer you are to go into your character. Even more important is knowing your lines. Without rewriting them, they have to sound like *your* words, not something just memorized.

"The stage manager was to read with me. I noticed he was just sitting there, reading for the others in a bored way because he wasn't an actor and he'd been reading to cue all the actors who were trying out.

"I'd always liked to spend some time on a set before I had to perform there, but this situation didn't offer that opportunity. I felt I couldn't keep people waiting any longer, and I couldn't stall any longer.

"The stage manager was yawning. I knew I had to keep my concentration, so I quietly asked him for his help. That seemed to wake him up. I didn't freeze, and I know I was about as good as I was capable of being under those circumstances.

"I finished the reading and started to walk off the stage. I was stopped in my tracks by that great voice of Katharine Hepburn, saying, 'Rehearsals begin on September seventeenth. Be on time.'

"Those were some of the most wonderful words I've ever heard.

"I don't remember if I said anything, like 'thank you.' That wouldn't have been anywhere near how I felt, but it would've at least been polite, and I wouldn't have made my grandmother ashamed of my manners.

"There was one small problem. I'd also won a part in a television soap opera, *Love of Life*, which I'd been doing for a while. Maybe 'won' isn't the right word. I liked being a working actor and could certainly use the money, which was unbelievable, although I wasn't enchanted by my part or the soap opera. I saw it as a stepping-stone as long as I didn't slip on the soap. And the extra money and time gave me the chance to get my pilot's license.

"That reminds me of something that happened a few years later. I went to John Houseman, who'd worked with Orson Welles both onstage and in films, and had become the head of Juilliard. I asked him if I should accept the Superman role. He said in his droll manner, 'Well, you can have a nice career as a serious actor. Or you can have a piss-pot full of gold.'

"I probably disappointed him, there in my Superman outfit. Maybe I disappointed a lot of people in my life. I never wanted to.

"Well, anyway, my role in the soap opera, a character named Ben, was getting popular, and I had more scenes, so I had to drop out of Juilliard [where Reeve was studying acting]. I was sorry about that, but I tried to turn a disadvantage into an advantage by using my free time in New York City to try out for plays. If I got something, I was certain I could arrange to get written out of the script to make my dream as a 'serious' actor a reality. I'd enjoyed being on the show, but I always knew that at any time my character could be written out, and I wouldn't have the security of being in a soap opera.

"I'd have to give *Love of Life* notice so they could get rid of Ben. Characters were always coming and going, and mine could take a freighter to South America if they wanted to reserve the possibility that he might ever be back. Or they could get rid of him permanently in an accident, or maybe he could be murdered. I didn't mind. He was quite a self-centered fellow, a cad. There were certainly enough characters in Ben's life who might want to get rid of him.

"I went to the powers-that-be, and I explained that I couldn't manage to rehearse for the play and finish my contract, especially since the play wouldn't be trying out in New York City. But, unfortunately for me, we had a hit soap opera, and they believed I was a crucial part of making it a hit. Our ratings had zoomed, and I was getting a ton of fan mail.

"So, when I tried to have myself, my character that is, murdered or mysteriously disappear or be called away to Timbuktu, I was surprised to find I could not get out of the contract to save my life, my dramatic life in the theater. No matter how much I implored, the answer was no. Anyway, to save my opportunity of a lifetime, I turned to Miss Hepburn.

"I called her, and she said, 'Don't you worry. I know exactly how to handle this. I'll call them with my sharp-tongue-lashing approach.' I figured *that* would scare the pants off *me*. I didn't worry, and she did call, but she didn't have any more success than I'd had. I guess their pants didn't get scared off as easily as mine.

"So during 1975 and 1976, I'd get up at five to catch the six o'clock train to New York, do the television soap opera, and then get back on the train for the evening performance in New Haven, or wherever we were. I never got enough sleep, and I never had time for meals.

"For breakfast, I had coffee and candy bars. For lunch, I had the same. More candy bars on the way back to wherever we were performing. I had plenty of energy, and the coffee and candy bars kept me extra-stimulated. I became a candy bar authority. I knew every brand and kind intimately. They kept hunger away.

"Whenever I was hungry, I just ate another candy bar. It was actually a luxury for me to be able to eat all of those chocolate bars without guilt because I wasn't eating anything else. I didn't think I ever could, but after a while, I did get kind of tired of chocolate bars, but there wasn't time for anything else. I was going hard, but at my age—I was only about twenty-two—I loved what I was doing. I knew I could handle it.

"One night in New Haven, I added some extra drama to our show. I'd been up since five and barely made my six o'clock train. I filmed at the studio and got my afternoon train. I was there more than half an hour early, with candy bars and coffee as appetizers, entrées and dessert along the way.

"I got to the theater and was ready for my entrance. My character was a student visiting his grandmother. It was a great entrance. Miss

Hepburn was always such a generous spirit about giving opportunities to other actors.

"I burst through the French doors making my usual exuberant entrance. I ran forward, calling out, 'Grandma,' with warm enthusiasm. That was the last thing I remember.

"The next thing I knew, I was lying on a couch, my legs hanging over the side. An actor's nightmare. I realized I had fainted onstage, falling flat on my face. I was out cold. I'm not sure how long I was out, but it was too long. Besides the mortification of having fainted, until then I'd felt I was invulnerable, almost immortal. I'd lost that, forever.

"When I woke up, I heard a voice which wasn't mine speaking *my* lines. My understudy had gone on for me. And he was making mistakes in the lines but the audience didn't know it, because they didn't know what he was supposed to be saying. Obviously he hadn't expected that I was going to give him that opportunity. Fortunately for me, I could tell he wasn't as good as I was. There was that. But then, of course, he hadn't had the benefit of all of the rehearsals and performances I'd had.

"Do you know what Miss Hepburn had done? She'd said to the audience, 'This boy's a fool who doesn't eat enough red meat.'

"She loved red meat and thought lots of good red meat was the key to energy and well-being. I knew it wasn't a diet of chocolate bars, which I had learned the hard way. I didn't hear all of this because I was out cold, but people reported it to me later. Some of them thought it was funny. I didn't. I was pretty embarrassed. But I guessed it was a lot better that she turned it into something light for the audience, so they weren't *too* concerned about me.

"I was worried that Miss Hepburn would be disappointed in me. Angry. She might even fire me, though I didn't really believe she'd go as far as that. When she came to see me, I was pretty embarrassed. I tried to say how sorry I was, that it would never happen again, but she cut me off.

"She said, 'You're just goddamn lucky you're a little bit better than he is.'

"She never mentioned the incident again. That's how she was. I always felt that she particularly liked me and cared about me. It wasn't anything I could exactly put my finger on. It was a kind of cool warmth. She wasn't ever mushy. Just a feeling I had. It could have been my imagination or maybe wishful thinking.

"She put a lot of time and effort into helping me get my character and express him on stage. She would say to me, 'It isn't what you're feeling that counts. It's what the audience is feeling that counts.' I took it very personally. Sometimes I wondered if it was me or my character she cared for, because I was playing her grandson.

"She really got deep into the play. Sometimes I felt she believed she really *was* my grandmother. I wanted to be just as deep into my part as she was, but I never achieved that. I always knew in my own head who I was, as distinguished from the character I was playing. I told it to Kate. She said she would be embarrassed to tell anyone how much she got into the character, but when she left the theater, she left her character in the dressing room, waiting for the next show. She said she knew people who took their character home and inflicted that character on their family and friends. She said to me, 'You don't ever want to do that, and especially when you're driving.'

"I saw her many times after *A Matter of Gravity*, but not as many as I wish I had. She invited me to have tea with her at her house in New York City. I went a few times, but mostly I put it off because it always seemed I had so much to do. Lost opportunities.

"Sometimes, I'd send her postcards from where I traveled and tell her about my progress. She always answered.

"One day, over homemade ice cream at her house in Turtle Bay, I made sort of a pig of myself, eating so much ice cream. That seemed to please her. 'You have ice cream on your nose, Christopher,' she said, and she reached over to wipe it off.

"The small familiarity gave me the courage to refer to the moment when I auditioned and boldly, much out of character for me, dropped my grandmother's name. After I'd said it, I thought it would cost me the part.

"She said, 'What you showed me was you were already in character for the part of my fool of a grandson. Your audacity was perfect. You sounded right, the right speech for the character of my grandson, and your looks didn't hurt you either. It never hurts to be beautiful.'

"Our relationship was cooler than it might have been, I think, because I didn't go on to California to complete the run of the play. My reason was purely selfish. I wanted to go on to something else. I've gone over it in my mind. I let her down. I owed her more and I should have stayed with the show. It's a regret I'll always have. I didn't have a good perspective. I forgot about what getting that part meant to me when she chose me.

"Years later, I saw Kate in New York at the theater. Whenever we could, we both loved going to the theater. She was seated farther down in front and hadn't seen me. I was happy to see her, but then I felt a little uncomfortable. After *A Matter of Gravity* had closed, I'd sent her flowers for a while, and then I'd sent her pictures of my kids, and kept her apprised, but after a while, I'd sort of stopped doing it. I got busy with things that seemed important, but now I don't remember what they were. I was a little hesitant, but I *had* to say hello. I couldn't be there in the same theater with her and not speak. And what if she'd seen me? Or if someone told her they'd seen me there? It had been a while since I'd seen her.

"So, during an intermission, I went down the aisle and stopped in front of her. Before I could speak, she looked up and said, 'Oh, Christopher, you've gotten fat.'

"That was Kate. And I'm sorry to say that was me. I'd gotten fat, but nobody else would say it to me like that, except my mirror.

"We used to have long heart-to-heart talks about what the theater meant to us, plays we admired, parts we dreamed of playing. What came clear was that we both passionately loved being actors. We didn't care about producing, directing, or writing. We liked the idea of acting in films, but our hearts beat faster for the theater.

"Kate said, 'I'll never retire. I'll be playing in my wheelchair.' I said, 'I feel exactly the same way. If that's the only way, I'll be performing in a wheelchair.'"

During the Los Angeles run of *A Matter of Gravity* at the Ahmanson Theatre, Kate was working at home in the Cukor garden, something she enjoyed, when she fractured her ankle. She went onstage in a wheelchair. The audience *more* than accepted her the-show-must-go-on spirit. "I was applauded," she said, "for my performance, I hope, and for my moxie."

Although largely recovered before the end of the run, she continued to perform from the wheelchair because she still wasn't able to do the entire show standing and moving about, but she was able to spring out of her wheelchair and take her curtain calls standing. "That always brought an ovation from the audience, which was standing, too."

During the last years of his life, Christopher Reeve performed confined to a wheelchair. While riding, he was thrown from his horse and paralyzed from the neck down. He made a valiant effort to continue his career, playing several parts from a special chair, something beyond a wheelchair, more a life support system. He kept an optimistic spirit and the hope a cure would be found, that he would walk again.

It did not happen. He died in 2007.

\*     \*     \*

After the run of *A Matter of Gravity*, Kate had tea with the play's author, Enid Bagnold, in London. "Good strong British tea and lovely little petit fours. I tried not to appear too greedy.

"Miss Bagnold, who was in her eighties, or not far from it, was full of praise for my performance in her play. She said there was a rather personal question she wanted to ask me. I said, 'Shoot!'

" 'May I ask you from where you get your fantastic energy? Do you have a secret tip?'

" 'I do,' I said. 'My secret is a hot butterscotch sundae, cold vanilla ice cream with hot butterscotch over it. I have it for dessert at an early dinner, just enough ahead of the curtain, not too close.'

"Enid Bagnold nodded and said she would be having one herself soon. Then she said she hoped I wouldn't mind a beauty tip.

"I said, 'I'm always ready to be more beautiful. Shoot.' So she shot."

The suggestion was that Kate have a face-lift. Bagnold recommended "a subtle one, sort of modified, but you will prolong your career, and it will make you feel good in your real life. too."

Kate did not get angry. She got a face-lift.

"I went to Scotland, taking faithful Phyllis with me. I felt good with Miss Bagnold's suggestion of a doctor. My father felt it was very important that you got the suggestion of a doctor from someone who had good judgment and some experience.

"I just wanted a little something around the eyes, a touch here, a bit there, a bit of tightened skin.

"Afterward I was terribly worried that I'd be asked, 'Did you have a face-lift?' No one ever asked me. If they had, I would've said, 'I had my spirits lifted.'"

In 1972, Kate turned her attention to television films, the first being Edward Albee's adaptation of his own play, *A Delicate Balance*, directed by Tony Richardson.

"*A Delicate Balance* was a lovely play," Kate said, "very internal, with a lot of close-ups, which meant I had to watch out for my neck or the audiences would be watching it. I'd kept my trim figure, but a neck some had called swanlike in my youth, with age had become scrawny and chicken-like. I was in control of my elegant wardrobe, and I made certain I only wore high necklines and fussy collars that not only covered my neck but distracted from it.

"I was very happy with Paul Scofield, a great actor, as my character's husband, and with being reunited with dear Joseph Cotten, who was my first C. K. Dexter Haven in *The Philadelphia Story* on Broadway, before I made the film. Well, all the cast was wonderful."

Speaking with me, Edward Albee said, "I was pleased to have my play filmed. Having Katharine Hepburn be the matriarch meant not only that a wonderful actress would give life to my character, but that more people would see my play than would ever see it because it had won a Pulitzer Prize."

In 1972, Kate agreed to play Amanda Wingfield in Tennessee Williams's *The Glass Menagerie* for a television film to be shot in England. "It was another chance to be in London, all expenses paid. Goodie!" The part was offered to her by Anthony Harvey, her director from *The Lion in Winter*. "The southern accent presented a problem I knew I could handle."

She loved the play and its author, considering it to be one of his masterpieces, and she had seen Laurette Taylor, the first Amanda Wingfield, onstage. "She was my ideal," she said. "I'm so grateful to have met her."

Kate brought to England an old dress she'd saved after she had worn it in *The Philadelphia Story*. She insisted on wearing that dress. "It gave my character an air of worn-out, threadbare desperation."

Tennessee Williams told me that "Miss Hepburn" brought out

dimensions in the character of Amanda that he had never imagined were there. "Kate Hepburn surprised me with her determination to make the impossible possible. One sensed that her Amanda would not be defeated, even in defeat. She would continue stubbornly fighting her hopeless cause to her last breath."

The film was released for television in 1973.

In 1974, early in his first term as president of the Motion Picture Academy, Walter Mirisch asked Kate if she would present the Irving G. Thalberg Award to Lawrence Weingarten, who had been one of her *Adam's Rib* and *Pat and Mike* producers.

Weingarten was terminally ill. Asked who he would most like to have present the award to him, he said that there was just one person, Katharine Hepburn.

Although there had been innumerable requests for her to be an Oscar-presenter, Kate had never considered doing it. She had won Oscars and been nominated many times herself, but she had never attended the awards ceremonies. It was unpleasant to sit there waiting to see if she won, humiliating if she lost, and agony if she *did* win and had to go up onstage and "play" Katharine Hepburn.

Her immediate response to Mirisch was a well-practiced "I don't do awards shows. And I don't have anything to wear."

Mirisch offered her a dress and a dressmaker, which she didn't accept, but she did agree to present the award. She wore black pants and a jacket.

I was in the audience that evening, and a palpable gasp and ecstatic response when Katharine Hepburn was announced as presenter was unforgettable. The audience rose, applauding respectfully for Weingarten, but carried away by enthusiasm for Katharine Hepburn, who was appearing at the Oscar ceremonies for the first time.

\*        \*        \*

A very young and energetic Dan Woodruff went to work for George Cukor at his Hollywood home in the mid-1970s. Woodruff had been working for the Academy of Motion Picture Arts and Sciences, but found himself in need of another job. Texas-born "Danny," an actor and aspiring director, became a friend to Katharine Hepburn when she was living in the cottage on Cukor's property. "Kate's cottage had a small living room, two bedrooms, a kitchen," Woodruff remembered, "and one or two bathrooms. It had a wood-burning fireplace, and I remember there was a wooden goose hanging in the living room. It was suspended from a cane. Kate really liked that goose. It might have been a swan. She told me that she'd bought it for Spencer. It lived there with Spencer and then with both of them and then just her. Finally, when George sold the cottage, it flew back to New York with her to live there, first in Turtle Bay, and then in Connecticut at Fenwick." In his late teens, Danny was the only one who could keep up physically with Kate, although he admitted that "occasionally she wore me out." He also liked to get up early in the morning as soon as it was light, "but I never got up earlier than Kate."

"Kate collected antique teacups," Woodruff remembered. "They were all or mostly from England. She used them all the time to serve tea. She really liked teatime.

"When she first served me, using one of the beautiful cups, I wanted to say, 'Don't you have something else, a little plainer?' It was a pretty big responsibility. I didn't think I was a careless person. I'd been brought up not to drop the dishes, and then George's house was filled with wonderful things. The dinner dishes and glasses there were great, and I never had an accident.

"Before I could say anything to Kate, I noticed that the saucer didn't match the cup, except that both were antique. Then, as I lifted the cup to drink, I noticed that the handle had been glued on and sort of reconstructed from at least two pieces. Obviously, someone less careful than I was had used the cup before. I held the cup with both hands and avoided the chip on the rim of the cup as I sipped the tea, which was very good. What was really delicious were the home-baked cookies, a specialty of Kate's.

"After tea, she said she would wash the cups herself, declining my help. Usually, people who collect antique cups rarely, if ever, use them, I was thinking. It was as if Kate had read my mind. She said, 'Nice things are meant to be used.'

"Kate didn't like to eat out very much. She'd done it a lot when she was young, but she said she got used to not going out much when she was together with Tracy. She could be very domestic. She liked to cook, and she was good, though she didn't have a big repertory. It was all simple, homey, and I think it tasted better because you could see her cooking it and serving it. She especially liked to make meat loaf. I ate quite a lot of meat loaf.

"What she liked to eat best was simply prepared, best quality meat. She got to know a butcher she liked wherever she lived, and they would become friends. She would go and have long conversations with him about the different cuts of steak. She would *really* cultivate the butcher. She was a fussy shopper.

"She enjoyed big salads, good beef, ice cream, her own brownies, and the cookies she baked. And she loved chocolate. George and Kate both could really go at a box of chocolates.

"We used to go out riding our bicycles together. I remember a few times when she fell off her bicycle. She was never a crybaby. She just picked herself up, and she got right back on. She rode really well.

"The first time it happened, I heard this loud thud behind me. I was concerned, especially when I saw her there on the ground. She looked terrible, but she fell well. Not gracefully, but she didn't hurt herself.

"She said, 'I've always been a good faller. I never cared how un-attractive I looked when I fell. I was concerned with not breaking anything. That's what counted. And I was always wearing pants, so I could protect my bones instead of my modesty.'

"Kate liked a nice five-mile walk, and we were talking about movies and the conversation got around to *The Philadelphia Story*. Kate said, 'I slept with Hughes to get the film rights.'

"She enjoyed shocking people. She shocked me.

"I said to her, 'You mean you slept with Hughes *just* to get the rights to *The Philadelphia Story*?'

"She said, 'Yes, I did. Well, not *just* to get the rights. I had a very good time doing it, too.'

"'Were you thinking about *Philadelphia Story* when you were in bed with Hughes?'

"'Well, yes and no,' Kate said. 'Before and after, but not during.'

"George and Kate both were full of mischief, and they liked playing little jokes on each other. George would say Kate was 'full of beans.' He used that to mean she was full of life and peppy.

"Kate didn't ever like being recognized as Katharine Hepburn when she went out to the theater. She felt she should be able to have a private life and just be in the audience. She would wear a scarf over her hair and pull up her collar. She had a lot of big collars, especially in New York. She liked to enter at the last minute and slip into the seat just before the lights went down when the audience would be concentrating on the stage.

"I remember once we went to the theater in New York. Before we went in, Kate had been fussing about not wanting people to recognize her. George never enjoyed it when she went on like that, with a lot of complaining. I think it was because he felt he had seniority for fussing.

"The house lights went down, and we went in. Kate slid down in her seat. She was wearing her scarf and a big collar. She never liked to leave her seat during the intermission and be the focus of a lot of attention, which she always was, if she got up during the intermission.

"This one time, for intermission, George stood up and turned, and he faced the people behind us. We had the house seats, you know, and we were far up front. George said loudly and clearly, you know how he did it, so no one could miss him, pointing down at Kate:

" 'Would you like to meet Katharine Hepburn? This is Katharine Hepburn. Katharine Hepburn is sitting right here.'

"Everyone in the theater heard him and looked at her. She really slid way down, like little boys at a Saturday matinée. You couldn't see the top of her head. You could hear, 'Is it really Katharine Hepburn sitting there? Yes. It is.'

"When the lights went down for the start of the next act, Kate got up and quickly left. She didn't feel comfortable having everyone know she was there. Maybe she didn't like the play and was glad to escape. If she'd really liked it, I think she might have stayed. George may have done what he did because he was getting bored. Maybe she just wanted to *show* George, which she did when she left. Of course, he got up and followed her out.

"It didn't seem all that funny to me, but it was not unusual for George or Kate. They found each other incredibly funny.

"I'm naturally a morning person. I've always liked to get up early and get an early start to the day. That made me very popular with Kate. I don't think I was ever up ahead of her.

"I was also punctual, naturally. During the time I worked for George, he placed a high value on punctuality, not just other people's, but his own.

"I remember once when Ava Gardner came to one of those great dinners at George's, and she was a little late. You know how George hated anyone coming late. It ruined the dinner.

"He wouldn't have hesitated to scold her in front of everyone, but she spoke first. She was all out of breath, looking rumpled and very upset. She said her car had a flat tire about a block away, and she didn't know what to do.

"Kate was there, and she sprang into action. She went out and changed the tire.

"I knew Kate didn't like anyone being late to meet her. I was especially careful not to be late going by for her. But, one day when I went by to pick her up to ride our bikes, I got there too early. I thought about sitting in the car and waiting, but then I thought maybe we'd get an early start. The door was open. I knocked.

"Kate was standing there, in a robe with a lot of big towels, and her hair was covered with hair dye. It was an earth reddish-brown color. When she saw me she didn't look at all pleased. She was pretty angry because I caught her with her dye on.

"I went outside and waited for her. She took a long time. Maybe because she was angry. I wondered why she did her hair herself. She could have afforded the greatest salon, the best hairdresser."

I suggested that she liked to do things herself.

"And she didn't like to waste money," Woodruff added. "And maybe she didn't want anyone to know that she colored her hair. I was surprised that she cared that much about what *I* thought.

"I'll tell you something she was self-conscious about, and I think she'd always been self-conscious about it. Her teeth. She said, 'People think I have a beautiful smile, and that's because all they see is my top teeth.' She smiled for me. 'If they saw my crooked bottom teeth, they'd be appalled.' She showed me. She was right. It wasn't her imagination. She really did have terrible bottom teeth.

"Kate was very fussy about putting on her lipstick. She thought she had thin lips. In the thirties, when she began her career, a makeup person taught her how to draw her lips in a way to make them look fuller. She took great care with that, even when the lipstick was so light colored, you couldn't tell she was wearing any, and even though she said she didn't really care about makeup.

"Kate didn't care for shopping for clothes. She said she had all the clothes she needed. For people who didn't know her well, she seemed to always be wearing the same outfit. Kate saw the difference in her pants, her shirts and sweaters, her sneakers. She would say about one red cashmere cardigan, among several that looked just like the same sweater, 'This is my favorite.'

"She was very concerned about fit. She liked to order men's shirts from a catalog. She knew exactly what she wanted, and she didn't care much about variety, but she was very clean and wore her shirts always in perfect condition. I remember once she got a shirt that didn't fit just right, so she gave it to me. She bought shirts and pants and sweaters in duplicate and triplicate. The big thing was she always liked to feel comfortable.

"A lot of her clothes were men's clothes. Her sweaters were nice cashmere. She told me some of the clothes were Spencer's. This was years after Spencer died. I don't know if she wore his clothes because it made her feel close to him or because she didn't like to waste anything.

"When George and I came to New York for the Lincoln Center Film Society Gala, we were surprised to find Kate at the airport, standing there waiting to meet us. George was very pleased. She was sort of hiding behind a post and she stepped out. As we were walking with her down the long corridor to leave the airport, we heard people whispering, 'Katharine Hepburn, Katharine Hepburn.' It was a tremendous sound.

"George acted totally oblivious, but he was actually very pleased by the reaction and his part in it.

"During the time we were in New York, Kate got tickets for us to go to three plays, *Sweeney Todd, The Elephant Man*, and something by Noël Coward.

"Kate always had the house seats. You know what that means. The seats weren't free, and she had to pay full price. But the house seats are held back, so they can be had on short notice, and they're always the best seats in the theater, close, but not too close, maybe about row G or H.

"George and I stayed at the UN Plaza so we could be close to Kate's house in Turtle Bay.

"Right after we saw you in New York, Charlotte, when the three of us went to the drama classes at NYU [New York University], George and I left to visit Kate at Fenwick.

"That night there, after dinner, we were shown to our bedroom. Kate always liked to go to bed early and get up early. I was in bed, about to go to sleep, when I heard an unexpected sound, like the bedroom door being locked. I got up and tried the door. It didn't open. We had been locked in by someone.

"My first thought was, what if there's a fire? I could just climb out the window, but what about George? How would I get George out? Then, I thought about it. Who had locked us in? Why?

"George was already asleep. I knew he wouldn't like it if I woke him up. I was right.

"I woke him and I told him what had happened and asked him what to do.

" 'Go to sleep, Danny,' was the only answer I got. I guess he couldn't figure it out any better than I could. I didn't sleep all night, or practically all night. I finally fell asleep. In the morning the door was unlocked.

"Back in California, I asked George again, why and who? He didn't have any more idea than he'd had that night, or than I did.

'You'll have to ask Kate,' he said. But I never did. I've wondered about it ever since, and I'd welcome any theories."

When George Cukor was nominated as the 1978 honoree of the Film Society of Lincoln Center, he was extremely happy but grew nervous as the date drew closer. "Do you think anyone will come?" he asked me.

The person he most wanted to have appear for him at the ceremony was Katharine Hepburn. "Do you think she might do it?" he asked me.

"I think she might, but only if *you* ask her," I replied.

She might have been the only person in the world who hated speaking to a live audience as herself more than George did.

"I feel naked if I don't have my part to hide in," she would say.

As the date grew nearer, Cukor made the call. "They're having a retrospective of my films, as they do for all old gentlemen. I don't suppose you would care to appear at Lincoln Center the night I'm being honored?" He shaped the question to make a "no" easy. His voice trailed away at the end. It was clear that he was setting himself for the answer he expected: a negative response, polite but clearly negative.

Cukor had a very expressive face, "an open-book face," Kate said. The call was short. He was happily surprised.

"She said yes?" I guessed.

"I can't believe it," he said. "She said, 'Only for you, George.' The only thing she wanted was not to have her appearance promoted."

Kate knew a star had a public appeal beyond that of a director, and she didn't want to diminish Cukor's glory.

She told the audience that evening that she had spent sleepless nights over the idea of appearing. She told me afterward that she would have spent sleepless nights for the rest of her life if she *hadn't* been there. There were standing ovations for Cukor and for Kate.


Publicist Dale Olson told me about his experience working with Katharine Hepburn on one of her last films.

"A friend of mine who was a successful television director, Richard Colla, asked me if I would do the publicity for his first feature film, *Olly Olly Oxen Free*, starring Katharine Hepburn.

"A film publicist I knew had been assigned to a Katharine Hepburn film, and when he introduced himself, telling her his name and that he was the publicist for the film, she said, 'Hello. This will be our first and last conversation.' And it was."

Olson knew that getting a lot of really good publicity depended on having the cooperation of the star, Katharine Hepburn, and he wanted to avoid the experience of the earlier publicist.

Olson had worked with the National Theatre Company of Great Britain when they appeared at the Ahmanson Theatre in Los Angeles, and he had come to know Laurence Olivier. He called and told Olivier that he had it on good authority that Katharine Hepburn could be quite unpleasant if she chose to be. Olivier agreed. Olson asked his advice on how he should proceed.

Olivier said, "When you introduce yourself, say that you're a friend of mine, that I hope the two of you are going to be good friends, and that I've given you a message for her." Then Olivier told Olson what the message was.

About five days into shooting, Olson was on the set and saw Katharine Hepburn sitting alone in the corner. He approached her, introduced himself as "a friend of Laurence Olivier's," and said Olivier hoped they were going to be friends, and then, he told her that he had a message for her from Olivier.

"So what does the old goat have to say?" she asked.

"He said, 'You're a dotty old bat whose bark is worse than her bite.'"

Olson remembered she looked him up and down, and then she said, "Sit down."

"After that, she did everything I asked her to do," Olson told me.

"One day we were having lunch in a local place when a group of tourists rushed in with paper and pens, and came toward us.

" 'Oh, I'm going to be signing autographs,' she said, looking displeased.

"The people ran right by us to a table where an attractive young woman was sitting. Kate, who only knew her as the wife of the director, wondered why there was such desperation for her autograph. I explained that she was Denise Alexander, the star of the daytime television serial, *General Hospital*. People watched her in their homes every day, and they felt they knew her.

"We went on with our lunch. About half an hour later, another group of tourists rushed past us, never even looking at Katharine Hepburn, going straight toward Denise Alexander.

"Kate Hepburn." Olson paused. "I liked her a lot."

The title of this film is taken from a children's game, which is a variation of hide and seek.

## Olly Olly Oxen Free (1978)

Miss Pudd (Katharine Hepburn), an elderly spinster, owns a San Francisco antique shop. It does very little business, since she only sells to people she likes, and she likes hardly anyone. Generally, people regard her wares as junk.

She does like two little boys, Alby (Kevin McKenzie) and Chris (Dennis Dimster). Alby has a dream, to organize a birthday tribute to his grandfather, the Great Sandusky, who was once a famous Hollywood stuntman.

Miss Pudd rents a hot-air balloon and she, the boys, and a large sheepdog, float down to Los Angeles, where they land in the Hollywood Bowl, and Alby's dream is realized.

The theatrical release of *Olly Olly Oxen Free* was delayed for three years, and when released, limited to short runs, and ignored by critics. "I did it," Kate said, "because they let me ride a balloon. How many people can say they've done that at seventy?"

Jane Fonda was the driving force behind *On Golden Pond*. She liked the play, and she put it all together as the producer. She personally went to Katharine Hepburn in New York and persuaded her to accept a part. Kate had always admired Henry Fonda and "working with him seemed a wonderful idea," Kate said.

"It was Jane's idea that I do something to break the ice with her father. She believed he was a very cool person, and that I had to make the first move because it was essential that Hank and I have the right warmth on screen. She didn't tell me *what* to do."

Kate arrived on the set with Spencer's favorite hat, which she gave to Fonda. It was the perfect gift. At the end of the production, Fonda painted a picture of the hat, and he gave it to Kate.

At a luncheon honoring her, Jane Fonda explained what she really wanted to accomplish with the film, something more important to her even than commercial success. It was an extremely successful film, but what she had wanted most was to have a warmer relationship with her father. During the making of the film, she felt that had happened.

She considered *On Golden Pond* one of the proudest achievements of her life. "I think it's a wonderful film, and it was even more important in my personal life, because that time with my father allowed us to work out our past differences and to find out how much we liked each other."

There was a certain anxiety during the production because everyone knew about the precarious state of Henry Fonda's health. He accepted the part because his daughter had asked him. He liked the part, he liked working with Kate Hepburn, and he loved to work.

## On Golden Pond (1981)

Norman (Henry Fonda) and Ethel Thayer (Katharine Hepburn) arrive at their summer house on Golden Pond. He is a disagreeable old New England college professor with serious health problems, cared for by his wife. Even if he survives his other problems, he is showing signs of dementia. His daughter, Chelsea (Jane Fonda), and he are on uneasy terms. She feels she has never pleased him.

Chelsea arrives with her fiancé, Bill Ray (Dabney Coleman), and his son Billy (Doug McKeon). She wants to leave the boy with her parents while she and Bill have some time together. The boy hates Golden Pond.

Norman starts out irritably with the boy, but then they build a bond. A boating accident brings father and daughter together.

Kate also won her fourth Best Actress Oscar for *On Golden Pond*, more than any other actor or actress had ever received.

"I got on famously with Kate," cinematographer Billy Williams told me. "We used to have a lot of fun, and I can honestly say it was the most enjoyable picture I ever worked on.

"We were in an idyllic situation. The wonderful cast. They were all great to work with, and everybody knew what they had to do.

And the wonderful American crew. I got on famously with them. I think I was the only English person on the crew.

"I had a house on the lake, and my wife and four daughters all came out to stay. Kate was wonderful with the family.

"She was very generous. After we did *On Golden Pond*, she gave me two beautiful paintings on enamel, one a nativity scene, the other the three kings. They both had a religious significance, so I wondered if she was religious."

Kate's last Broadway appearance was in Ernest Thompson's play, *West Side Waltz*, for which she received a Tony nomination. Thompson wrote *On Golden Pond. West Side Waltz* opened at the Ethel Barrymore Theatre in November of 1981 and ran on Broadway for three months. A Lawrence and Lee play, in which Kate would be Rose Kennedy, was considered as her next Broadway vehicle.

Playwright Jerome "Jerry" Lawrence, who with Robert E. Lee, wrote many Broadway shows, had an up and down relationship with Kate. Will Willoughby, his friend and production manager, told me of one instance as described by Lawrence to him.

"Jerry first knew Miss Hepburn during the filming of his and Bob (Robert E.) Lee's play, *Inherit the Wind*. Spencer Tracy was playing Clarence Darrow.

"Whenever they were filming Tracy's scenes, Katharine Hepburn was there on the set, knitting. She wasn't working at the moment. She was there, encouraging and praising Tracy.

"Several years after Tracy died, Lawrence and Lee wrote a play about Rose Kennedy called *Matriarch*. They wrote it in 1983 specifically for Katharine Hepburn whom they thought would be perfect as Rose Kennedy. Jerry sent her the script, and he heard indirectly that she was quite interested.

"Jerry had asked her for a picture of herself for the wall in his Malibu house, and she said, 'No.'"

"Several weeks later, he received a small package from New

York. Inside was a self-portrait of Katharine Hepburn that she had painted for him. In the picture, Kate was holding a rose, indicating to him that there was a good chance she wanted to do *Matriarch*. It became one of Jerry's most treasured possessions, until it was lost in a fire that destroyed Jerry's house.

"Jerry and Miss Hepburn met at a California party, and she told him she was going back to New York. Jerry said he was on his way there, too, and would she like to go with him to see his musical, *Mame*, which was based on *Auntie Mame*, a hit play he'd written with Lee. It was being revived on Broadway, starring Angela Lansbury. Kate, who loved the theater, accepted.

"In New York, they entered the theater ten seconds before the lights went down. She explained that she always had to go to the Broadway theater that way. She hoped she could sneak in and no one would see her because they'd all be watching the stage. And if they *did* see her, they couldn't come up and speak with her and ask for autographs, because the play would be starting.

"With the intermission, Jerry started to get up, but Miss Hepburn didn't rise. She told him, 'I can't go out during the intermission. I can't make it to the ladies room before the lights flash, and it's time to go back to my seat because of autographs. If I make it all the way and go in, somebody always follows me in. They don't care if I miss the first few minutes and have to disturb everyone else and break the mood, but I do. I love that first moment when the curtain goes up at the beginning of the show or after intermission. It's when you get into the show and live it.'

"Jerry sat down. Though she didn't exactly say so, it was clear to Jerry that she didn't expect him to desert her. Just before the curtain was about to go up on the next act, a little boy came over, and he said, 'Miss Hepburn, may I please have your autograph?'

"She gave him her maximum spinster-principal look, and pointed her finger at him and said, 'No. You should have better manners. Go back to your parents and tell them they should know better than sending you here to disturb me in the theater.'

"I guess Jerry looked a little shocked. 'He probably doesn't even know who I am,' she said, 'but his parents do.'

"Kate really enjoyed *Mame*, and she especially enjoyed seeing it with its author. She invited him to come to her house in Turtle Bay to have lunch and talk about *Matriarch*. Jerry felt the relationship had grown much warmer, but he was still a little nervous about going to her house for lunch.

"The lunch was with her and Phyllis, her companion, and there was a cook in the kitchen. The first course was soup. Jerry finished his bowl of soup and put his spoon down. There was still some soup at the bottom of the bowl. Miss Hepburn said rather sharply, 'Pick up the bowl. 'Waste not, want not.'"

"Jerry hesitated, not sure exactly what he was supposed to do.

"Miss Hepburn made it clear. *'Pick up your bowl.'*

"Jerry picked it up and drank the rest of his soup.

"It was an enjoyable lunch with a lot of talk about the theater, and Jerry, feeling relaxed, told a joke. He had told this particular joke several times before, and it had always been well received.

"The joke began with, 'A young girl is walking through Shubert Alley when she is attacked by a stagehand.' Miss Hepburn stiffened a bit over that, but Jerry was so engrossed in telling his joke, he only remembered that later.

"The girl was molested right there in Shubert Alley, and the police came and asked if she knew who did it. She said she didn't know exactly, but she knew he was a stagehand. 'How do you know?'

"She replied, 'Because he wasn't very good at his job. He made me do all the work. He talked during the entire act. He left before it was really over. And it wasn't a very good performance.'

"Jerry's joke wasn't received with laughter, not even with polite smiles. There was a frosty chill which lasted through Jerry's departure, and beyond."

"Katharine Hepburn was never friendly to Jerry again, and *Matriarch* was never produced."

Instead of doing *Matriarch*, Kate did *The Ultimate Solution of Grace Quigley*.


"It was terrible," Kate said, "to lose old friends. But the most terrible was that for some of them death was a welcome release from suffering. I saw Luddy suffer, and it was terrible for dear Laura [Harding]. The most horrible was my father. He was in terrible pain, even though he was so stoic he didn't want us to know what he was enduring. We knew because my brother Bob, the doctor, who followed in Father's professional footsteps, knew all about how bad it really was and that there was no hope. Being a doctor, Father knew all about how to end it quickly and painlessly, but didn't believe in suicide, called it the easy way, but I can't imagine why it's called that. Even though he wasn't a religious man, he did not believe in suicide.

"When I heard about Grace Quigley," Kate said, "I could understand what the character was feeling."

In *The Ultimate Solution of Grace Quigley* (1985), Kate's character hires a hit man (Nick Nolte) to put old friends who are lonely and in pain, or suffering from incurable diseases, out of their misery. Kate could understand "the idea of bumping them off."

"Because of Nick Nolte and me," Kate said, "the picture got to the Cannes Film Festival. I heard later that someone had said there was a chance I'd go to the Cannes Festival. It was the kind of thing I never could abide. Crowds. If I went to Cannes, it would have been to make a film or in the off-season in disguise to visit little antique shops.

"The French appreciated the black humor more than Americans, but not many French or Americans ever had the chance to see the film. When they did have the opportunity, they declined. American critics disapproved of Grace's 'ultimate solution.' What was that phrase Alfred Hitchcock used to say? 'It's only a movie.'"

Elliott Gould suggested I speak with Patty Doherty, who had begun her film career as a craft person on the set of *The Ultimate Solution of Grace Quigley*. When I asked Doherty what she did on the film, she answered modestly, "I made the coffee."

"At the time I met Katharine Hepburn," Doherty told me, "I'd just moved to New York to embark on my career. I was a craft service person. I couldn't get arrested to do much else.

"The movie I worked on with Kate, *The Ultimate Solution of Grace Quigley*, her *only* forgettable film as far as I can tell, but *she* was unforgettable. I know I might be complimenting myself, but she really made the effort and sought me out to put me at ease. You know, I was afraid of her. I just tried to steer clear, because I thought, 'Better to leave a legend alone,' than to get a legend mad or something and get in her way. So I elected from the beginning to kind of serve her from a distance. And quite frankly, being a craft service person, making the coffee, does not exactly elevate you to a position of conversing with the actors, or the director, or anybody else. You just do your job and hope you get hired again.

"One of the first places we filmed was near Coney Island. It was September, and it was the first scene of her going into the ocean. The stunt people had gone out, and they said there was a really bad riptide. 'Miss Hepburn could not, absolutely *should not* go out in that water.' No equivocation.

"I remember the first day I saw her. I was running around on my own, putting things in the campers, like flowers and magazines and water. People in New York in those days didn't do a lot of fancy things for anybody, and I thought it would be nice. I had just left her camper a few minutes before, when I saw her open the door.

"She looked horrible. Her hair was going every which way, and she was in this kind of frumpy big sack top, and she looked kind of frazzled. She was shaking, as she did at the time. It was a little shocking, frankly, because I had *The Philadelphia Story* in my head. I was twenty-three years old. She said, 'Hello. Who are *you?*' And I said my name, and she said, 'What do you do?' I said I do craft services, and she said, 'Craft *what?*' Craft services were not there in the early part of her career, but it had become a position, certainly in L.A.

"About an hour later, when she got on her makeup, the transformation was absolutely incredible. I remember I felt guilty about feeling a little bit of disappointment when I first saw her.

"And then she came on like a house on fire, full hair and makeup, strong and powerful, and she strode out of that camper onto the beach, and caught wind of the fact that someone was not going to let her attempt to kill herself in the ocean. She would have none of that, and she promptly informed Anthony Harvey, the director, and the stunt coordinator that nobody would be her double. She would go out into that water. She said she was accustomed to swimming in November in the Long Island Sound, back of her home, and she's not having anybody else do it. They all stood with their mouths open. No one wanted to tell her she couldn't do it. The producer was beside himself thinking about, well, here goes the insurance claim. So, out she goes, against their wishes. Sure enough, I'm standing there just thinking, 'Oh, *now* what am I going to witness?'

"So, she marches out, and the wave just whacks her one. And I'm telling you it *clipped* her, because they were big, hard September waves. They were cold, and they just smacked her down, and everyone gasped. She disappeared for a second. Then she came up and swung her head, she had her hair in the up-do, this kind of bun thing, and she swung her head up. She flipped her head backward. She *threw* her right fist up in the air and started *swinging* it at the ocean and said, 'Do that again!' and we all cracked up, because she would take on the ocean in a heartbeat. She spoke directly to nature. If nature did something to her, she had something to say *back* to nature. And she did it take after take after take, three or four. They'd get her dry again, and out she'd go.

"I went home that night, and I was ashamed of myself. I thought, 'Wow! She's just a force of nature.'

"Then, I avoided her. I went the long way around. I thought I'd better not make eye contact because I was afraid of her. One day, I was at the food table. I still put things in her camper before she arrived in the morning, which I did for all the actors. She came up to me and said, 'I'm curious. What kind of flowers were those that you left for me today?' It happened to be they were Rubrum lilies, which are *really* common, the ones that are pink and white, and you can get in all the Korean markets. She said, 'Oh, the Rubrum lilies. They were very lovely.' I thought, 'She's telling me I don't have to run around and hide anymore.' It was her way of saying, 'We can be friends. You don't have to hide.' So, after that, we conversed quite a lot, talking about one thing or another.

"One time, I'd had a sort of romance that didn't work out too well, and I had been going through turbulent times one evening trying to break up with this person, who would not stop calling. I unplugged the phone, and I overslept.

"In my job, I would start at three o'clock in the morning, because I would make the coffee in my loft on timers. I'd put it on my crazy freight elevator, the kind with the ropes, and I would load this little van. I'd go up to Forty-second Street and get the bagels at, like, four, and by five, I was on the set, and by five-fifteen, I was setting everything up, *hours* before the actors got there.

"When I woke up the next day, it was daylight. I thought, 'I've done it. My career has started and ended.'

"I plugged the phone back in. I called the office and said, 'Oh, I'm very sick. I'm very, very sick, and I'm sorry.'

"About twenty minutes went by, and the phone rang. I thought 'It's probably my boss. He'll yell at me or fire me.' I picked it up, and I just hear this—I can still hear it, clear as day—'Get up! You're not sick. Get up!' I went bolt-upright. 'Do you want Phyllis and me to come over and make you some soup?' I said no, and Katharine Hepburn said, 'Get up and go to work right now!' I never dressed faster in my life. I drove straight to the set. When I got there, she gave me a hard look, and then one kind of milder, and said, 'That's better. Never do that again.' She knew exactly why I didn't show up. 'You're better than that. Don't you ever succumb to that sort of nonsense again.' Needless to say, I never did.

"I felt really honored. She cared enough to make that call and she saw something in me, so that she decided that she was going to right that ship. That was *my* embarrassing story I'll cherish forever. Even into my senior years, I'll remember, 'Get up!' As soon as I complain too much about arthritis, I'll hear her say, 'Get up!'


"There were old stages, called the Empire Stages, where we built the sets of her apartment. We were going to be there for quite a long time, and they used to haul around this crazy old mirror of hers. It was, like, two-hundred pounds, but she insisted on having it.

"She decided she wanted to ride her bicycle around Brooklyn. The producer said it was bad enough that she wanted to walk into the ocean, but now she wants to ride a bike around Brooklyn. They knew that they weren't going to be able to tell her no, so they decided I was expendable. They got me a bicycle and said, 'You are to keep your walkie-talkie on. Follow her everywhere. You are not to lose sight of her.' I was her body-guard-slash-biking-companion.

"So, the two of us would ride around, not very far, mind you, but we'd go around for a little fresh air. We'd discuss one thing or another, just small talk. She admitted to me, 'You know why I do this? They deserve it. I like to make them crazy.' She was just having fun with them, just to keep their attention, and hers, I guess. She was reminding herself, and reminding everybody else, that she's here, thank you.

"There was an *Esquire* issue, which would have been 1983, and had recently come out. It was about the world's fifty most eccentric people. She was one of them. I was so excited, working with her, and I read the article. As a ten-year-old kid, my favorite actor was Humphrey Bogart. I was reading this article with this whole section in there about *The African Queen* and their adventure there.

"I brought it in, and someone said, 'Well, you know, you'd better not let her see that. She'll be offended by an article about her being eccentric.' I thought, she knows people think she's eccentric. This isn't news. Maybe she'll be amused by it.

"Well, anyway, I went into her dressing room, and I said, 'You know there's this article about you, and they say you're eccentric.' She laughed.

"She was getting her makeup done, and I was sitting on the floor of her dressing room, and she was sitting in her chair with her big mirror in front of her, so I could see her reflection from where I was sitting on the floor.

"She said, 'Well, let me see it.'

"I gave it to her, and she started reading the article out loud. She got to the part about Humphrey Bogart. When she would say his name, when she said, 'Bogie,' it went through the marrow of my bones, and I almost started crying. Every time she said 'Bogie,' I realized that I came just as close as I could ever come to meeting

Humphrey Bogart. She had that six degrees of separation sort of thing. She knew him very well, and hearing her say his name and knowing how well she knew him, it was like meeting him.

"She said something like, 'Well, it was all good fun,' something she sort of tossed off. When she would read the rest of the text, it was fairly straightforward, but when she got to his name, it was tender. She softened. Something softened in her voice. I think that's why I welled up in tears. I guess I thought when her voice softened, he entered the room a little bit. She dropped her guard down. There was that intimacy between them as friends.

"Afterward, I would send her a postcard of where I was, and she would comment back.

"My stories are in my heart. You don't know when you're in your early twenties and you meet someone like that, you don't quite realize that they will have an effect on you for the rest of your life. It was right after she asked me about what kind of flowers I'd left that she asked me to call her Kate."


"I heard about a woman doctor in the Civil War" Kate told me, "who sounded like the perfect character for me to play. Mary Walker was one of the few women doctors in the country at that time, a doctor like my father, a person standing up for women's rights like my mother, and she wore pants like me. She had to compromise even on the battlefield and wear her pants with a skirt over them.

"She fought all kinds of prejudices, opposed easy amputation on the battlefield, and when the government wanted to take back her medal of honor, she refused to give it back because, she said, they couldn't take back what she had done. She wore it every day of her life. Just what I would have done. I wouldn't have worn it unless they tried to take it back. She was buried with it.

"During the Civil War, Dr. Mary Walker wanted to enlist, but the Union would accept her only as a civilian doctor with a contract. She didn't believe in amputation unless absolutely necessary. This was when, on the battlefield, amputation was referred to as the "easy" way. She knew it wasn't "easy" for the person who left a limb or two behind.

"When she was captured, they thought she was a spy. They didn't believe her story that she was a doctor, a surgeon. When she was released, she won that Medal of Honor, which was rescinded.

"I saw a picture of her once. No beauty, she, but her face had character. I couldn't tell for sure in the picture, but I think her hair had a reddish cast, like mine.

"If you want to know why I didn't do it, besides there being no script, producers would probably have said it would cost as much as the Civil War to stage. Most important, there was no David O. Selznick around, and I was too old for the part when I found the story. For an actress, it's easy to go old on the screen, but it's impossible to successfully play much younger than you are."

I was sitting in George Cukor's living room while he enthusiastically told me about a project he was considering that would star Katharine Hepburn.

"This lady of a certain age," he began, "who doesn't understand a thing about baseball, and never wanted to, inherits a baseball team . . ."

Just then Kate marched into the room.

"Don't talk away your luck, George!" she said sharply.

Then, as abruptly as she had appeared, she departed.

Cukor laughed. "She's my tenant, and she pays her rent regularly. She thinks that gives her certain rights. She's always been indomitable and funny—two wonderful qualities in a woman.

"She's afraid I'll get to be like the director who tells at great length, in infinite detail, all about the movie he's going to make, in such elaborate detail, that he no longer needs to make it. Kate has always believed that if you tell your project, it will go away, that you have dissipated the energy that should have been guarded for the creative experience. She won't talk about her projects. She thinks it will chase her luck away."

Kate returned.

"George, how do you feel about retiring?"

"I don't," Cukor said. "I'll never retire. But I expect I'll *be* retired, like an old horse. Nobody asks a horse to choose."

"But, George, you don't have to pull a wagon or run in the Kentucky Derby."

"No, but I have to get insurance. The time between films when I make one is growing longer, so I can't afford a failure. One failure and it probably finishes me off. And what is a failure? A failure now is something that isn't a big success."

After Cukor's death in 1983, Kate told me, "I believe I was the woman in his life George loved second-best. First in time and in his heart was Frances Howard. She was an aspiring actress who loved George.

"When Samuel Goldwyn proposed to her, she asked George what she should do. He told her being Mrs. Samuel Goldwyn was the best part she'd ever be offered. George and she were friends the rest of their lives. Frances Goldwyn invited George to be buried next to her with her husband on the other side. George told me he accepted."


"We were at the theater," Jackie Mavrovic, a famous New York hairstylist, told me, "and just before the curtain went up, Katharine Hepburn and a man came down the aisle, and they went to their seats down front.

"When the play ended, many people began to move down toward where she was sitting. They were very polite, but several of them were holding pens with their programs, hoping for autographs. We were standing in the back and just stood and watched.

"In a flash, she was out of her seat and leaping and running, really fast over the backs of the seats, like a young professional athlete. She was wearing dark pants and some running shoes, and she never missed her step, and she disappeared out the door. I don't think very many professional athletes could have done that.

"And she wasn't young."

## 8

# The Creature and Kathy

"In December of 1982, I had an accident which brought me face-to-face with my own mortality, or anyway, my foot had to face its mortality. Ever since that telephone pole and the car I was driving had their unfortunate close encounter, my life hasn't been quite the same as before. I had never been very aware before that of the parts of my body. It is much better to be oblivious to your body parts.

"Now my foot sends me regular messages. 'Hello. Remember me?' It has a limited vocabulary. Sometimes it says, 'I hurt.' Well, face it, Kate, it *always* says, 'I hurt.' Sometimes it says, 'I hurt a lot!' Sometimes it whispers, 'I don't hurt so much right now.' Even then, I am waiting for the next scream.

"But I am lucky. I'm lucky I have the foot at all. I came very close to losing it. Very close. And whatever the price in pain, oh, beloved foot! I am so happy to have you!

"It was a stupid accident. I was driving and talking. I should say I was talking and driving. It was *my* fault, obviously, because it wasn't the telephone pole that moved.

"It happened late in the morning. Phyllis and I were on our way from Fenwick to New York. We certainly hadn't had anything to drink, although I was told there were whispers.

"I was driving, and I can't blame anyone but myself. I'm always more talkative in the morning. I've always awakened very early, filled with energy, I was babbling about what a lovely day it was, until suddenly it wasn't.

"After we hit the pole, the first thing I did was to look over at Phyllis. I said, 'Are you all right?' She didn't answer because she couldn't. And I could see she *wasn't* all right.

"I was never a passive person. No matter what anyone might have said about me, I don't think anyone ever called me that. Very early, I decided that I was capable of making my own bad decisions. I guess I didn't make too many mistakes, or if I did, I didn't have to pay for them.

"But I know one I made, and that was not understanding how dangerous driving a car can be. I was always a very good driver and after all those years of driving, I took it for granted and didn't keep my eyes on the road. I was talking too much the way I have a tendency to do, and I turned my head to talk at Phyllis and be sure she heard some unimportant thing I had to tell her, something like what a beautiful sky it was. I no longer remember what it was. But I'll remember the price I paid for telling it all my life. I could have paid with my life. Worse, I could have paid with Phyllis's life.

"And dear Phyllis, who never said a word of reproach to me in our entire life together, I could have injured her even more than I did. I could have killed her. I never told her how sorry I was because Phyllis already knew."

Kate confided to her friend, columnist and author Liz Smith, that she remembered being furious when the hospital wanted to cut off her slacks.

" 'Those slacks cost me fifteen hundred dollars and were made to order by my tailor. I never change my measurements, and I know what I like, so those pants were as wonderful, if a bit worn, as when I bought them . . . '

"She stopped and laughed," Smith said, "as she remembered how long ago it was that she had purchased the slacks."

"All my life," Kate told me, "I was conscious of how lucky I was to be perfectly healthy. I didn't get sick and I didn't get injured. Intellectually, I thanked my lucky stars.

"I knew some people were not so lucky, and I sympathized. But when you have this perfect health, you can't help but take it for granted, and you can't really imagine what it's like to have to use your energy to carry or drag a burden like my life after my accident. My foot drains my energy, and sometimes it hurts like hell, but I don't want you to think I'm complaining just because I am.

"I was so lucky that they were able to sew my foot back on. It was only hanging by a thread. It's been a good foot, and it's served me well, and I would have missed it terribly. I knew it when.

"Constant pain is so tiring. You have to learn to coexist with it. After my accident, for a long time, I tried not to moan. There's something to the idea that you hear yourself moaning, and the more you moan, the more you reinforce the pain. But *not* moaning didn't make it hurt less. So, I have given up on the moan factor. But, 'Ouch!'

"I hope you won't tell anyone about my whining until I'm safely tucked away in my urn next to Tom's urn.

"After the accident, when I came to and realized I still had my foot, the next thing I thought was, 'Oh, I won't be able to run on my toes.'"

Kate, who had never liked doing interviews and certainly not for television, agreed to appear with Dick Cavett on his talk show. During the interviews, Cavett said that it was too bad that she and Laurence Olivier hadn't appeared together. She responded, "We're not dead yet!"

George Cukor liked the idea and called his good friend Larry Olivier, who also liked the idea.

*Love Among the Ruins*, done in an Edwardian setting, offered Kate the opportunity to wear wonderful costumes. She plays an aging great star who is being sued by a gigolo. She seeks the help of a distinguished barrister (Laurence Olivier), not remembering that long ago they had had a brief affair, which she has forgotten and he remembers well. He saves her from the potential embarrassment.

The television movie aired on ABC in March 1975. It was directed by Cukor, who received an Emmy, as did Olivier and Kate.

"When we finished *Love Among the Ruins*," Olivier told me, "George said to me, 'I have never worked with two sweeter kids.'"

In 1978, Cukor directed Kate once more, in *The Corn Is Green*, the Emlyn Williams play that Bette Davis had done for Warner Brothers in 1945. Warner Brothers was again the producer, this time for CBS Television. Cukor had directed both actresses at important moments early in their careers.

Kate was hesitant about taking on the role because she thought Bette Davis had done a wonderful job. "Of course, she did, and so will you," Cukor reassured her, and Kate *was* proud of the film.

\*　　　\*　　　\*

Warren Beatty was planning a film to be titled *Love Affair*, a remake of an earlier film, *An Affair to Remember*, starring Cary Grant and Deborah Kerr, which was a remake of a 1939 film, *Love Affair,* with Charles Boyer and Irene Dunn. His costar was to be his wife, Annette Bening, and he was determined to persuade Katharine Hepburn to appear in a small part, perfect for her. He had long admired her and wanted to do a film with her. He understood that this was likely to be his last opportunity to do so. She had retired, and it was necessary for him to use every means at his disposal to woo her out of that retirement.

Beatty called friends of hers he knew and asked them what he could do. Kate's friend Cynthia McFadden told him it was like any romance or courtship, "Candy, flowers, caviar. You know."

Long-distance charm wasn't Beatty's specialty, but he proved himself good at it, nonetheless, and he won Kate's agreement to accept the role. He never knew that he didn't have to be quite as persuasive as he was, because Kate was sitting in her home, pining for a part. She felt she'd like to go back to California for a visit. "The part was not taxing," she said.

Beatty was faithful to his word, and did everything he had promised. But the relationship did not end as everyone had hoped. "An extremely successful film," Kate said, "would have helped."

Kate believed that she always did her best work on the first take, and she didn't see why she should do more than a second one. "The second take was in order to give some insurance from sleepless nights to the director, who wanted to do a lot of takes," Kate said. They compromised, and Kate did more takes than she wanted to do. The director got enough to have choices, but not as many as he wanted. "Compromise," Kate said, "never leaves anyone satisfied."

Kate liked Beatty and his wife personally, and she thought her performance as Beatty's aunt was "satisfactory." What made her sad was her visit to Los Angeles, to which she had looked forward. Many of her friends were no longer there. "It made me feel lonely, very lonely," she said.

"After Spencer's death, and during the years that followed," she told me, "I learned what the difference was between solitude and loneliness. Solitude is by choice. Loneliness is not."

One of my most memorable visits to Kate was at her Turtle Bay house in New York City, shortly after George Cukor died. She was sitting in a chair in her living room as I entered.

"I used to be as tall as you," she said, "but I shrank. I'm only five feet five and a half now. I miss the part of me that got away."

We were about to have tea. She motioned toward a sofa.

"Sit down and be comfortable," she said. "And if I don't think you're comfortable, it'll make *me* uncomfortable."

I sat down on the sofa, right on a spring that was coming through the upholstery.

"You got the wrong spot," she said. "I've been meaning to have that thing repaired, but I never get around to it.

"There are people who say to me that I should get rid of some of my old stuff that has outlived its usefulness. Well, that always makes me angry. I identify with my old things, and if they can get thrown away because they've worn out and have lost their luster and need more care to keep them going, the same could be said of me. And I'm not ready yet to be thrown away.

"It's the way I feel about flowers. You can see how much I love flowers. I feel any room that doesn't have at least one vase of fresh flowers in it is a wasted space. What I quibble with is the interpretation of the word 'fresh.' It has been suggested by some that I keep my flowers too long."

I glanced in the direction of the flowers in a vase on the table.

"Pretty, aren't they," Kate said. It wasn't a question. "You should have seen them on their first day.

"I've never understood how it is people are so quick to call flowers *wilted*. I feel we have to give the poor things a chance.

"I think flowers should have every minute of life that is theirs. We enjoyed the flowers in their prime, so we owe them something. I don't believe in flower-i-cide. I suppose that's because I identify with flowers.

"I have to have flowers in every room. I don't like fancy flowers from florists. Sometimes people send me some or bring me some they got from florists, professional bouquets. Well, I'm a little prejudiced against a dozen or two of roses, unless someone has a rose garden. Florists' bouquets always seem unnatural, a little bit like going toward artificial flowers. But I did value the thought of those who had a florist send me flowers. They weren't people who knew me well. I'm very happy cutting sunflowers along the road from my country house and bringing them home in buckets of water."

On my first visit to her Turtle Bay home, she had asked me, "Would you like to see the house?"

I answered that of course I would.

"Then, go right on up," she said, motioning for me to go on my own and "explore."

"I hope the beds are made," she called after me.

"I won't mind if they aren't," I called back.

Every room had the ubiquitous fresh flowers in vases. Well, some of them were not *exactly* fresh.

She didn't have any photographs in her living room, but there were pictures of her parents, of Spencer Tracy, of her brothers and sisters, and of her nieces and nephews in her bedroom and bathroom.

In her bedroom, next to a small picture of Spencer Tracy, there was a single fresh flower in a vase. It was a very fresh flower.

On the walls were paintings Kate had collected and some she had painted. There were also some of Tracy's.

"I won't tell you which ones Spence did," she said when I returned. "He wouldn't like it. He didn't mind my having the pictures, but he didn't sign them. He hoped that only I would know, especially as long as he was alive.

"He considered his paintings so very personal and private. He said the paintings were more private than being naked. 'Naked only shows your outside,' he said, 'but the paintings show what's in your heart, your deepest feelings and how you see the world.'

"I can't tell you which are Spencer's, but they're the ones that aren't mine." Kate always signed hers.

"Did you look at the photographs?"

I said that I had, and I noticed there weren't any of her.

"I have the photographs of the people I love. I don't have any pictures of myself. I don't need pictures of me. I have me."


"George and I had one thing in common. Well, we had many things in common, but something we shared was the way we loved our homes. We loved them with a passion. They were part of us. We were part of our homes, and they were part of us. He loved his in Los Angeles, and I loved mine, my family home, Fenwick, and my house in New York City."

Through the years that Kate had lived in the cottage on George Cukor's property, Cukor had never been able to bring himself to raise her rent. It had remained the same as what Spencer Tracy had paid when he rented the cottage many years before. After Tracy's death, Kate had taken over the cottage.

"Spence and I could have saved money if we could have lived together, but Spencer could *never* have done that. He did not want to hurt his wife, Louise. And I think he believed it was wrong for a man and a woman who weren't married to live together."

Cukor never wished to appear concerned with money, and he wasn't. Nearly everyone, even those who knew him best, believed he never thought about money. In the years of his great success in Hollywood, he never did. He told me that was his idea of being rich, never having to waste any time thinking about the price of anything. "It's your time that's priceless," he said.

Property taxes and the cost of the upkeep of his home and the three cottages on his property had increased over the years. Near the end of his life, Cukor was forced to think about money in a way he had never had to do before.

"The only cost that was going down was my fee as a director as I got older," he said.

Kate told me that she couldn't understand why George sold the cottage she had rented, and which Tracy had rented before her. "Do you have any idea why he sold it?" she asked me.

"For the money," I answered. "It was that simple."

"But why would he do it for the money? George was so rich. He never cared about money. He never gave it a thought."

"He gave it quite a bit of thought near the end of his life, but only because he had to," I said. "George was a totally generous spirit, and he didn't like to think about money, and he certainly never wanted to talk about money, especially his, and especially his lack of it."

"But if he was having money problems, why didn't he say anything to me?" Kate look perplexed. "We were best friends, you know."

"I think it was exactly for that reason. You were such longtime friends, and he had his pride. He had a great deal of pride."

"I never knew George once to not be generous," she said. "Living in that grand mansion with everything beautiful, entertaining so many people every weekend. They were such perfect dinner parties he had, and the people were so interesting, and always everything in the grand style. I don't think anyone who was invited ever said no. I know when I was in California, I only said yes to George.

"I never understood it. Personally, I didn't want to give parties, but he loved doing it. He always had the most fascinating people, and he had those great servants. He bought the best of everything in food and wine and liquor. It all must have cost a fortune."

"At the end, when you weren't living there anymore," I said, "he was serving some meat loaf, but it was the best quality meat loaf, and delicious."

"Meat loaf is just about my favorite," she said. "But it's most delicious when you eat it from choice, not necessity. The most wonderful thing not to have to think about is money. That's great luxury.

"I'm sorry now I was angry, hurt, when George said he was selling my home in Los Angeles. Of course, it was really *his* property, but I'd come to think of it as mine because Spence had rented it for so long, and then I had it for so long, and because that was the way George had made me feel when I took it over, that it was *my* home in Los Angeles.

"George offered me the chance to buy the cottage because he said he was selling it. I thought he was asking too much for it, but I was a fool. Not the first time I've been a fool. I was thinking of prices twenty or thirty years before, and ignorant about how prices had gone up on Southern California real estate, especially in such a divine place as George's.

"I moved out in a huff and maybe George's feelings were hurt. I hope I didn't do it for that reason, but I was angry. I took it personally. I felt he wanted to throw me out. I was shocked.

"Do you remember, he was always introducing me and saying,

'She's my tenant, and she always pays her rent on time.' Well, I always did. But George's introducing me that way was his style and humor, and I found it funny enough.

"But when he told me he was selling *my* cottage, I temporarily lost my sense of humor. A girl should never lose her sense of humor.

"And George couldn't have needed money. George was so rich."

"That was what people said about you," I said.

"Maybe they should have left out the 'so' before 'rich,'" Kate said. "I should have bought the cottage. But if George had needed money, he should have told me. Oh, that goddamn male pride. But we girls have quite a bit of it sometimes, too."


"Funny things were always happening to George and me," Kate said. "Well, *I* thought they were funny. George had a wonderful sense of humor, very sophisticated. Mine was less sophisticated, but we laughed together a lot. Sometimes I think we forgot what we were laughing at. He was someone I could be silly with, which is very important. I knew he would never consider me silly, no matter how silly I was. That was because he had a streak of silliness of his own, which he hoped was concealed beneath his dashing attire. George had a wonderful flair for directorial fashion. He *looked* like a director. His clothes always felt good when I accidentally, or deliberately, brushed against them, cashmere, vicuña, that sort of thing. There's nothing like the feel of wonderful material.

"If I could have chosen anyone in the world to be my father except my own father, it would have been George. He was such a dear friend. He was the person in my life I was most comfortable with, besides Spencer.

"George was so permissive and always showed pleasure when I did something well. Life with my own father had some of the tension of walking on a high wire. I don't know if George would have been as good for my backbone. Maybe I would have grown up a softy.

"I'll tell you a funny story, but to really appreciate the moment, you had to see the look on George's face. I won't imitate it because I can't. I'm telling *you* because you knew George well enough to know those expressions. It was years ago, before I stayed in the cottage.

"George called me to say he'd like to drop by and see a house I'd rented. When he arrived, I took him around amidst oohs and aahs, saving the living room, the pièce de résistance. I'd lit a nice fire in the fireplace. It seemed to me very nice to combine the cozy warmth of the fire with the cool fresh breeze, fresh air mixed with the aroma of the nearby woods.

"I opened the living room door for George, who entered, but only briefly. He exited faster, nearly knocking me over. I'd never seen him move so fast.

" 'Don't go in there,' he warned me. Well, that was enough for me. I rushed in, but I didn't go very far.

"I saw him. I assume it was a him. Anyway, I don't think his gender mattered. I never found out, and I hoped he wouldn't stay long enough for me to name him. He was the largest rattler I've ever seen. The rattlesnake was curled up in front of the glowing fireplace. I've never seen *anyone* look more comfortable.

"I tiptoed across the room to open the terrace doors wider. Then I left the room, closing the door tightly behind me. I didn't venture back for hours.

"When I opened the door, I didn't exactly fling it open. I peeked in, gingerly. The spot in front of the fireplace was empty. It was so empty, it was hard to believe it hadn't always been empty.

"But George was my witness. It hadn't been my overactive imagination. It had been an overactive rattler drawn by the comfort of my drawing room. Who could blame him?

"But he was a wise rattler, and I suppose when he awakened, attracted by the cool breezes and the awaiting woods, he unwound and, wriggling, hightailed it."

That afternoon there in New York City, there was a fire in the fireplace. "Fireplaces are divine," Kate commented. "Don't you think so?" She didn't wait for my answer. "Most people enjoy them in the winter and at night. I enjoy a nice fire in the fireplace anytime— morning, afternoon, spring, or summer."

I never visited Kate in the morning, but what she said about her fire in the fireplace was always true when I was there in the afternoon, and even in summer.

Kate liked to go antiquing at flea markets and antique fairs. Her townhouse was filled with *objets d'art* and collectibles.

"I collect on impulse," she said. "I can't really say I'm a connoisseur of anything. I don't read books or study about anything. I just see what I like, and I don't let go. I'm more of a hunter than a shopper.

"I loved the pleasure of the hunt, and I can understand when our ancestors went out of the caves and brought back their prizes of food. These are the prizes of the food for my soul. I never considered it shopping. I considered it hunting.

"People can be disappointing, things can be reassuring. In my home, as you can see, my policy has been, there's always room for one thing more. These things all around us tell the story of my life. I remember when and where I acquired each one of them. But what I never remember is the price. Well, *almost* never.

"When acquiring, I don't like to think about practical matters, such as where can I put it. Having to be too practical spoils everything. It's enough to think about having the money to pay for it. But I must say I never fell in love with anything I couldn't afford. I think it must be the Scottish bargain hunter in me.

"Now, if I'd had a passion for jewelry, that would have been a totally different story. Howard [Hughes] loved to buy expensive jewelry. He told me he never asked the price, because he went to only the best places, and there, he said, you always get what you pay for. I remember those little reddish boxes from Cartier. The boxes were so beautiful I almost didn't need anything inside, but what was inside was always beautiful. Howard really had great taste, besides having the money to indulge it. Or maybe if you shopped where he shopped, you just couldn't go wrong.

"When I was young and just beginning my film career, I was more smitten with jewelry. I enjoyed seeing my chum Laura wear hers. But I think I was influenced by Father's attitude. He didn't feel I should accept expensive jewelry from Howard. He said the jewelry was a foolish investment of money! I don't know if part of his attitude was because he didn't like Howard flying in and out and landing at Fenwick, or if he thought it wasn't proper for me to accept anything that cost too much money.

"Whatever it was, Father had spoken on the subject, and Mother said nothing, but I did notice that when I showed her something, her eyes opened very wide, and while Father only glowered, she would have short Mona Lisa smiles.

"An advantage of jewelry is, it's small. I'm lucky to have two houses, and if things don't fit here, I can always send them off to Fenwick, where there's more room.

"I've decided on the next thing I'm going to collect. Thimbles.


"I miss George terribly," Kate said. "I keep wishing I'd called him. When was the last time you spoke with him?" she asked me.

"A few days before he died," I said. "I called him because he had told me he was going to the dentist, and that he was going to do everything he was told he needed, all at once. George was terrified of going to the dentist, and he told me he hadn't gone for a very long time because he hated going. When he had last gone, he was told there was a lot of work to do, and he wanted to get it all over with as fast as possible. He said he hadn't slept for several nights in anticipation of the dreaded dental work. I tried to persuade him not to do it all at once. I called again to try to persuade him not to make it such a torture by trying to get it all over with so fast. He listened, but I didn't think I was persuasive enough. I found out after his death that I hadn't been."

"Aren't you going to ask me," Kate said, "'To what do I most attribute my success?' Well, I've just saved you the trouble. And I can answer it for you in just one word. Luck!

"I was bloody lucky. I think I'm the bloody luckiest person who ever lived. I've loved what I do so much that I can't help but think it must be selfish and self-indulgent.

"One may become a relic or be forgotten. I seem to have become a landmark.

"I don't mean to say I didn't deserve my luck. I worked hard for it. But other people who worked just as hard weren't so lucky. The important thing is to keep going long enough for something good to happen to you. If you quit, you might quit the day before you get the part of your life.

"But not quitting takes confidence, believing that you deserve to be lucky; the ability to bear up under the slings of outrageous fortune without getting hurt feelings and slinking away for a long and unsatisfying sulk. Lady Luck isn't attracted to sulkers. Who is?

"Some people don't respect you as much if they think you've had to try too hard for your success. They think if you had to try too hard, it means you didn't have what it takes, the real thing—talent, that is. I've never understood that.

"Of course, it helps if you've got some kind of monetary support, an inheritance, a supportive family, savings. And don't forget good health. That's *real* luck!

"It's a terrible moment when anyone has to recognize that he or she isn't ever going to have his or her dream, the American Dream, here in America. Everyone, everywhere, has his or her dreams. It must be terrible that day when you know you have to settle.

"I was very lucky in life. I was born in the right cradle. Oh, that good old stork!

"Some people make it without all of the advantages, and my hat's off to them, figuratively speaking, since I don't wear hats anymore, only maybe a baseball cap. So, if you'll pardon the expression, I had a head start.

"If you're lucky, people make room for you, and you get the chance to be successful. Being an actor is functioning in a very crowded field, and there are many gifted people who never get their chance before they give up. You must get your moment. I came along at the right time for me."


"I've never kept a diary, so I have to look up dates or ask other people when something happened to me. I'm better on other people's lives than on my own. I've never been chronologically oriented, even though it seems the most obvious way to remember. I know people who remember my life better than I do. Facts, that is, not emotions.

"Through the years, I did write down some notes and impressions, but not dreary things. I feel if you have to live through something unpleasant, you certainly don't want to read about it years later and relive it. You wish you could forget about the downers, but usually you can't. I didn't want to bore my diary, and whenever I had the free time to write, it wasn't one of my most exciting moments.

"A friend gave me a gift of an Hermès leather agenda and then a refill each year for a few years. Wasn't that nice? Well, the first year, I didn't use it until the middle of the year, not because I was against writing in an agenda, but because that one seemed too pretty to write in, especially since I was always crossing out things and spoiling the look of a page. I usually didn't write comments, but it did allow me to date some of my life.

"It was never hard for me to look back and know all about my professional life, laid out there, a matter of record. But my personal life, I never remembered it in exact order, and certainly not with dates. It's all just part of me.

"Probably I should have kept a plot diary of my movies and plays. I think I remember the plots, or most of them, because I have quite a good memory, but at my age you have a lot to remember. One memory crowds out another as they fight for their place in my head. I'm often surprised at the funny little things I remember, and the more important things that I *don't* remember.

"I've never wanted to have a lot of photos either, certainly not of myself. I want a few people I love. In the end, I think the only pictures I care about are the ones in my head."


"I find teatime is a delicious time to invite people to my home for a good conversation and robust tea," Kate told me, her mouth full of a butter cookie. "Some people like a drink or two at that time, and we always have good Scotch available or a nice sherry. Personally, I prefer strong tea and homemade cookies and brownies made in my home by me, and I've never had any complaints. It was an inviolate tradition of my mother. Any afternoon she was home, which was nearly always, tea was served to all of us who were home, and to any guest we might have. People could set their watches and their appetites by it, and we frequently had drop-bys dropping in. Mother often wore a Japanese kimono when she served tea. My parents were bohemians, but not from the country of Bohemia.

"I like sweets. I find most people do, and it's nice to enjoy them when you're really hungry, as I am at five P.M., instead of at the end of a big meal, the time when dessert is served.

"Perfect happiness, I would say, is a really good, very pure vanilla ice cream. Vanilla ice cream isn't the only happiness. There's coconut ice cream, not to mention a butterscotch sundae, hot butterscotch over cold vanilla. Yum. Do you like butterscotch sundaes?"

"Doesn't everyone?" I said.

"I knew you must. We'll have some later. Or maybe some coffee ice cream . . . ? Ice cream tastes even better if you enjoy it with a friend. I always like high butter fat content. In the ice cream, that is, not the friend.

"The way I enjoy teatime most now is in my own home, served on a tray you can have in your lap. "I appreciated your invitation to the Palm Court at the Plaza, but I don't like to have to dress up for tea, and the worst part is the gawkers. I don't want to be on exhibition, studied, even discreetly, with every bite or sip I take.

"There's another wonderful thing about teatime. It has a beginning and an end. It's not rigid and fixed as to time, but you can stop filling the teapot. If tea is served punctually at five, did you ever hear of anyone staying until eight? Unheard of. And for people who get stuck in their chairs and aren't wearing watches, there's always the little white lie, 'I'm going to the theater tonight and I have to get dressed.' That always does it, and sometimes it's true.

"Did you ever see the film *I Know Where I'm Going!*?" she asked me. "Wendy Hiller. It's one of my favorite films."

"One of mine, too," I said. "You would have been great in that film as the heroine."

"I would have liked that part, but Wendy Hiller was perfect. I didn't play it in the film, but more important, I had that role in real life. I was the I-know-where-I'm-going girl.

"But I'll tell you what was even more important. I was the I-know-where-I'm-*not*-going girl.

"You can still make some choices pretty late, as long as you haven't made those choices that determine your whole life very early. You know, marriage, and especially children. You can leave a marriage, not as easily as people think, but it's possible. I did, but not without certain pangs. You can't walk away from a child.

"The story *I Know Where I'm Going!* didn't end the way the heroine had expected. She didn't go where she thought she was going. She did all the right things to take her to her goal, to a rich, urbane, social husband who would provide a secure place in society for her. Then, on the way to her wedding, romance found her, or she found romance, and she abandoned those plans for a more challenging and somewhat impoverished rural life with the titled Scottish hero she loves."

"I wondered if afterward she was happy with her choice," I said.

"Oh, she must have been," Kate said. "It's like what happened to me with Spencer. I met him, and I quivered like Jell-O if you gave it a slight shake. I was mush. Absolute mush.

"I could be downright silly. I'd never had the experience before of having to try to reshape myself like a pretzel to please a man. How foolish and unnecessary when I was perfect the way I was. Take me or leave me. That was my attitude. And there were all the takers I needed.

"With Spence, I didn't act like I did with the others who were naturally pleased by me, as pleased as I was with myself.

"When I first met Spence, I was wearing high heels, and I was almost as tall as he was then. I've been shrinking over the years.

Spence was much taller than he photographed. He had such broad shoulders and such a big chest, which made him look shorter than he was. There I was looking him in the eye. He *had* me, and I loved it!

"Just like the girl in the film, I was a sucker for romance, too. I didn't know it about myself until Spence stepped into my life. I think without romance, deeply felt, my life would have been incomplete. There would have been an emptiness in me if I'd never had that.

"Now, I miss Spence all the time. I look at his picture when I wake up in the morning. It's the first thing I see in the morning, and it's the last thing I see at night, his picture before I go to sleep. Of course, I don't really need a picture at all. I have all the pictures I need of him in my head.

"But I'm not sad for what I've lost. I'm glad for what I've had."


"I've always been asked about whether I miss having had children, and why I didn't have them," Kate told me. "It's very simple.

"When I determined I wanted to be an actress, I understood that all of my dedication and energy had to go into the achievement of that goal because though I was totally optimistic—I couldn't have tried if I hadn't been optimistic—I didn't think it was easy to attain what I wanted. Though I might not have articulated it for anyone but myself, I said to myself in my head, 'Kath, you have to keep your focus.'

"I had no interest in getting married. I don't think I would have said, 'No, never, I would never marry.' But it was not something I thought about. It was not for me in the foreseeable future.

"As for children, I felt I already had all the pleasures and none of the problems and responsibilities because of my siblings, who were all much younger than I, especially the two girls. I was sort of like a young aunt. Sometimes, I even felt like they were *my* children. I loved them very much, and they satisfied any need for children in my life. I could entertain them and spoil them.

"I was married very young to Luddy, my first and only husband. We were apart a lot of our marriage, and Luddy was very understanding, never mentioning children during those days. After our Mexican divorce, I never married again. When I met the love of my life, Spence, he was married, and he had two children.

"Hypothetically, who knows, even if Spence had been free when we met, and we'd married, maybe children wouldn't have happened. Sometimes they don't. Not everyone is as fertile as my mother. People who talk about family planning have in mind not having more babies than they can take care of, not those people who plan for a baby and don't have one."

One day in the 1980s when I mentioned to Douglas Fairbanks, Jr., that I was going to have tea that afternoon with Katharine Hepburn at her home, he said, "I'll call her, and I'll come with you. I haven't been there for a while, and I've been meaning to call her."

I was pleased because it gave me the opportunity to be with Kate and one of her oldest friends, one of her favorite people for more than half a century.

From the first moment, they were flirtatious with each other. I had not previously seen Kate coquettish. She had put more time into arranging her hair for her meeting with Fairbanks, which she didn't feel was necessary for me, and I was glad it wasn't. She was wearing black pants and a black turtleneck sweater, a small white scarf tucked into the sweater, and a pendant, which she said was a genuine witch doctor's good luck charm, a souvenir from her *African Queen* experience. She said, "It was good luck for me that I survived that shoot, all in one piece."

"Does it bring you luck now?" Fairbanks asked.

"I don't know," she responded. "I was lucky before I got it. I was lucky after I got it, so it's hard to tell if it's lucky. I wear it because I like it."

Fairbanks said, "It's very attractive, and it's certainly a conversation piece."

"Yes," Kate said, "but I don't see many people these days, so I'd have to have the conversation with myself, and I already talk to myself too much, just moving my lips or out loud. I find myself thinking about something, sitting here all by myself, and suddenly I hear my voice. I'm saying to myself what I was just thinking, and I've forgotten that I don't have to speak out loud when I'm the only audience. If anyone catches me doing it, I say, 'I'm rehearsing.' That does it, except they probably wonder for what part, since I'm not working much these days. Do you find yourself talking out loud to yourself these days?" she asked Douglas.

"I can't say that I have," he answered, "but it may mean that I haven't noticed."

Occasionally, as they spoke, Douglas would call her "Pete," and she would reply by calling him "Pete." It was a very private joke. Fairbanks later shared its origin.

"I never called my father 'Daddy' or 'Father,'" he said. "He would have murdered me if I'd called him 'Dad,' even when it was just the two of us, let alone if we were with other people. My father would have preferred to introduce me as his younger brother if he could have gotten away with it. Actually, he would have preferred to introduce me as his *older* brother, but that would have been a bit tricky.

"He didn't want me to call him 'Douglas,' either, because he didn't like the name. Personally, I'd always liked the name very much. So, usually, I didn't say anything, but one day I asked him what he would like me to call him.

"He said, 'Call me Pete.' I was a little surprised.

" 'Why Pete?' I asked.

" 'I always liked that name,' he said. So, that's what I called my father, 'Pete.'

"When I told Kate the story, she said, '*I'm* going to call *you* Pete.'

"That was fine with me," Douglas continued. "I asked her what she wanted me to call her. Without hesitating, she said, 'Call me Pete. We'll both be Pete, and nobody will understand, just us. Very private.' "

Douglas said, "Well, I don't know if 'us' understood. I wasn't certain *I* understood. But it made perfect sense if you thought of it as Katharine Hepburn sense, nonsense.

"Then, I got used to it. I'd write to her as 'Pete,' and she'd sign her notes to me 'Pete.'

"I thought it was interesting that the better she knew you, the more curt and abrupt the note she felt she could send you. One could expect a 'Call me,' signed, 'Pete.' That let you know your place in her private pantheon, that of a dear old friend with whom she could be herself."

"Are you working?" Kate suddenly asked him.

"Not really. I'd like to. Nobody's asked me. When I worked a lot, I always had other things I wanted to do, but now that I'm not working, I can't remember what all those things were, or when I do, they don't seem that interesting. They were in-between things, not meant to be full-time. Actors and actresses have the problem of having to wait for the phone to ring."

"It's strange," Kate said. "We worked together for seven days and we've been friends for almost ten years for every one of those days. You were smart to try producing so you didn't just have to wait for the phone to ring."

"I'm not certain that I was so smart."

"I guess, Douglas, we're both really performers, show-offs."

"Yes, indeed."

"I have a lot of trouble with my skin these days," Kate said. "You've probably noticed it. I always had sensitive skin, and I loved the sun and being outside in it.

"I was a sun worshipper myself," Fairbanks said, "and I've had problems, too. Cutting off some of the problems left some scars."

She was quiet for a moment, and then she said, "I've had a wonderful life, but it's strange, thinking that most of my life is behind me."

"One of the bad things about dying," Fairbanks said, "and there are quite a few, is that it gives writers the chance to say all the bad things about you that they were afraid to say when you were alive."

"The other bad thing, even worse," Kate said, "is if no one says *anything* about you, because you're forgotten. That's a risk you run by living a long time and outliving your fame."

"A risk well worth it," Fairbanks added.

When Phyllis Wilbourn died in March 1995, in accord with what Phyllis had wished, Kate arranged to have her ashes buried in Connecticut with the Hepburn family. Kate's longtime friend and devoted companion was five years older than Kate.

"It's a terrible shock when you start losing the people who shared your favorite memories. It makes you feel very lonely when you accept you won't ever be able to talk with them about your shared experiences, even though you never talked with them about those experiences when they were alive. You knew they had these memories in their heads, the same ones you did.

"It was like that with Phyllis before she died. She began to suffer from dementia, and I hoped it would go away, but it didn't. I was told it would only get worse, and it only did get worse. I could never say to her again, 'Do you remember when?' because I knew the answer was she didn't.

"Some of the people who have gone were older than I, and that was difficult enough to adjust to because I never thought of them by their ages. Then, when I lost people younger than I was, it made me conscious of mortality.

"Mother and Father didn't believe in spirits or guardian angels or any of that sort of thing. I sometimes wondered. I was so lucky, I thought I might have a guardian angel, and he was Tom."

Publicist Dale Olson, who worked tirelessly for the Motion Picture Home, serving on the board and contributing his services, told me about the day Katharine Hepburn arrived there with Phyllis.

"Katharine Hepburn's assistant and dear friend began to forget things. When it became clear that she would not be getting better and needed help, Miss Hepburn brought her to the Motion Picture Home and said that she needed a room. She was told that there were no empty rooms at the time and that they would have to wait.

"Kate sat down with Phyllis and said, 'We'll wait.'

"And they did.

"Miss Hepburn took a book out of her bag and began to read. Four hours later, the two ladies were still sitting there, patiently.

"Someone finally came and said, 'We've found a room for Miss Wilbourn.'

"Katharine Hepburn had contributed money over the years and had attended a benefit. She rarely made that kind of appearance, but she considered the cause extremely worthy because it helped not only actors, but anyone in the film business who experienced hard times because of age or illness, and who needed a place to live and receive care. For that reason, she made an exception and contributed her celebrity, as well as her money."


In her late years, Kate found a new friend, Liz Smith. Liz became a regular for dinner at Kate's home, along with television correspondent Cynthia McFadden, classical archaeologist Iris Love, and Barbara Walters. Kate chose McFadden as the co-executor of her estate. Often after dinner, the group would go to the theater with Kate.

"The theater was one of the few public activities that Kate couldn't resist." Smith said. "She loved the theater, as she had all her life."

In her private life, Smith found that Kate "had more of the personality of a director than of an actress. She liked to be in charge and in control of her environment. She liked to eat in her own home. The meal was just what she liked, just the way she wanted it, just exactly when. Kate said, "My cook, Nora, is always right on time with a delicious meal."

When Smith tried to return the favor, Kate made it clear she didn't want to be taken out to a grand restaurant, or to *any* restaurant. After eating the dinners prepared by Nora at the Turtle Bay townhouse, Smith understood. So she reciprocated with flowers and caviar. Chocolates had been my own choice. Kate loved to receive gifts, and I had found I couldn't go wrong with chocolates.

"The time for arrival was always six," Smith remembered. "Kate would stoke the fire in the fireplace, and dinner was always on time. Dessert was ice cream accompanied by cookies, or angel food cake. Everything baked was home-baked in Kate's own home.

"Kate sometimes would plan an evening at the theater for our group after we had dinner at her house," Smith said. "She insisted on getting our tickets, and she provided the limousine. She said she had chosen a white limousine, so it would be easy to find, and we could all make a quick exit. Then, we didn't make our escape but we went backstage. She wanted to say encouraging words to the actors, who, of course, were well aware she was in the theater.

"After she was pretty much retired, she even made some comments in support of worthy plays that needed a helping hand."

Kate told Smith that when she went to the theater or out to shop, or just for a walk, "the fans expected to see 'the Creature,' the

Katharine Hepburn of the screen especially, and of the stage. They always expect me to look like her. Instead, they just get me in my old clothes, and I see disappointment on their faces."

Smith did her best to reassure Kate that the fans were not disappointed. "They always observed her respectfully, politely, with relish," Smith recalled.

For many years, Kate had been thinking about the extraordinary experience she had during the filming of *The African Queen*, and she decided she wanted to write about that experience. In 1987, *The Making of The African Queen: Or How I Went to Africa with Bogart, Bacall, and Huston, and Almost Lost My Mind*, by Katharine Hepburn was published.

"It took me thirty years to get around to writing a thin book."

For photographs, Kate turned to the amazing Ben Carbonetto collection, considered the best on Katharine Hepburn. Carbonetto provided the photographs. When she wanted to return them, she invited him to her home, saying she had to be at the hospital to visit a sick friend, Greta Garbo, so would he be there at eleven and "be punctual."

Carbonetto sat with Miss Hepburn in her backyard, and he remembered her being extremely gracious. "She told me," he said, "that she enjoyed having her picture taken in the early days of her career. Then she got tired of it, but she did it anyway. She said, 'I would've been a damned fool not to.'"

When Carbonetto asked her how she handled fame, she told him, "There's Katharine Hepburn and there's me." He found her to be "herself, not full of herself."

After years of Kate's saying she would "never, never, never" write an autobiography or her memoirs, in 1991, Alfred Knopf published her *Me*, subtitled, *Stories of My Life*. Kate had told me, "I guess I'll explore how I happened to become me and pay tribute to my wonderful parents who made me what I am. I didn't have anything else to do, so I agreed, and it was nice to get some fresh money."

The last time I visited Kate, she said to me, "I've always understood about animals, like some apes and wolves, who slink away to die alone, so no one will see the shame of their old age, illness, and death. I can understand that, but I don't think I'd have that kind of courage. I have my lair reserved at Fenwick with only my near and dear family, who can't throw me out, and no strangers to stare and whisper, 'Poor Katharine Hepburn. Doesn't she look terrible?'

"I've never been *poor* in any sense, and I don't mean to start now. I don't want anyone's pity, ever. I've been too lucky to have pity from anyone, especially from myself."

On the afternoon of June 29, 2003, at the age of ninety-six, Katharine Hepburn died in her bed at Fenwick. From her bedroom there was a view of the water. There were vases of wildflowers in the room, and there was a fire crackling in the fireplace.

Her ashes were buried in Cedar Hill Cemetery in Hartford, next to those of her brother Tom, who had died more than eighty years before.

I remembered what she said the last time she had spoken with me about Tom.

"I had a perfect life, a wonderful life—until that day my brother died.

"After that, I've had a long and fine life, filled with accomplishments that made me feel worthwhile and gave me joy, a combination of work and frivolity. I feel grateful and lucky. But after Tom died, nothing was ever quite perfect again. Wonderful, but not perfect.

"It's the kind of thing that could have driven me crazy if I obsessed about the end of my brother's life and not the whole of his life, short though it was. I thought of him every day afterward, and that was fine. I wanted never to forget him, so he would live as long as I did. When my thoughts were filled with guilt over how I might have let him down, I could find no peace. And the worst was, I couldn't figure out *how* I let him down, even though I replayed it in my mind.

"I had dreams which weren't good dreams, but I couldn't remember them the next morning. Some thoughts, which my conscious self could not control and shut out and defeat during the day, found their way into my subconscious at night.

"I'll tell you something that happened not long ago. It was a dream I had. Or I *think* it was a dream.

"It was about my brother. He was almost sixteen when he died, and as I told you, I was the one who found him. I think I've been having dreams about it ever since, even though I never could remember what I dreamed.

"This time, it was different.

"I walked once again into that room where I had found Tom dead. It was that morning again. Nothing had changed. Tom was there with a twisted piece of material tied around his neck.

"It was not like a dream at all. It was like it was happening for the first time. The shock. The pain. I knew exactly what was going to happen.

"But then, something different happened.

"Tom turned and smiled at me. He was full of life and handsome as always. He loosened the noose and slipped it off.

" 'Look,' he said to me. 'I figured it out. The trick. I know how to do it. I know what I did wrong.

" 'I learned how to do it, but too late,' he said wistfully.

"I woke up and thought, 'It *was* an accident, after all.' Tom had come to tell me that.

"He had *wanted* to live! It was a prank gone wrong.

"This was his way of telling me it wasn't my fault, that I hadn't done anything wrong. After that dream, I was able to think about Tom and remember our good times, without the pain I'd always had because of how his life ended.

"I felt that somehow Tom had done this for me, come back in the dream to take away the pain and guilt. I thought that maybe Tom had tried to get through to me before, but that this was the first time he was able to do it. My first thought was I wished I could tell Father.

"I slept better after that. Once I understood what they were, I never had bad dreams again.

"I hope you won't think I'm crazy," Kate had said to me, "or on my way there, because I'm not. I've still got all my marbles, and my brains, too, for the moment, anyway. But sometimes when I'm at Fenwick, I look out at the tallest tree, and for just a moment, I think I see Kathy sitting up there at the very top of the tree. I know I shouldn't speak because I don't want to startle her.

"She might fall, and we might miss our wonderful life.

"Another time, I thought I saw young Kath go off the diving board. It was a perfect dive. I felt quite proud of myself.

"This has happened over the years. In the beginning, I wasn't sure I'd seen anything. It was like seeing a mouse. You wonder. Was it really there? And you persuade yourself it wasn't.

"But the strange thing is that now, as my vision is less good, my visions are getting clearer. The last time I saw Kath at Fenwick, she was so clear. I wonder what it means?"

Katharine Hepburn was totally aware of her public self, and she knew that it was not the same as her private self. She gave her public self a name. The Katharine Hepburn image was something she had created and perpetuated. It was her persona for the world, and she knew it was different from the real her, different from Kathy. She called it "the Creature," and she told me that it should be spelled with a capital C.

When I first visited Kate in her home, I hadn't seen any pictures of her from the days of her glamorous career. "I don't keep pictures here in my home of my professional self because those aren't pictures of me. Those are photographs of the Creature, and I don't bring her home. I don't allow her in my house."

In our conversations, she previously had touched on the subject of the Creature, but it was the last time I saw her that she offered her most extensive discussion on the subject. She said she could do this because she was dismantling the Creature, the Creature having held her in bondage for so long. Now, she had no more need for her, so the Creature no longer had any power over her.

"I was called Kathy when I was a little girl, and I guess I never grew up or outgrew that little girl. I feel very much the same inside. It's how I think of myself, which is quite often.

"I created the Creature, but I didn't completely understand her. Sometimes, she took off on her own. Ungrateful thing. She didn't remember I created her, and I was put in the position of being her psychiatrist or a personal assistant or even a white slave because she knew I was more dependent on her than she was on me.

"I believed if people knew the person I really am, they wouldn't have been very interested in me. They might have said, 'Boring.' So I had to always think first about the Creature before I thought of myself.

"I'll tell you someone I felt sorry for. That was Marilyn Monroe. You know why? She let her Creature take over.

"She was a participant in creating her mystique, because she went along with it, but others were really in charge, so I think she must have felt out of control of her own life and herself. Living at the whim of others always seemed unbearable to me.

"I think it must have been very difficult for her to face her middle thirties as a sex symbol. And she was also without the baby she wanted. She wasn't looking forward, and looking forward is a big part of happiness. For an actress, the chances are your career will end in middle age. It's like going into old age at the end of your thirties. The present was too difficult for her, and the past had gone by so very fast.

"The public me developed a mystique. I don't know exactly how it happens. I have a theory. I think you become all of the parts you have played. If you're lucky, it's palatable chow mein. If you're very lucky, it's scrumptious chop suey.

"It's true I always said I'd never retire, what I told you and George that night at his house. But I found I couldn't keep the Creature going.

"I'm not retiring because I have a fatal disease. Well, in a way it is a fatal disease, fatal to the Creature. I've lost a part of me, a very valuable part which I've grown accustomed to taking for granted. I expected it to always be a part of me. Then, one day, I had to accept it was gone.

"It wasn't that it disappeared in one day. It was that one day I noticed its absence. It was my energy.

"No one ever had more energy than I did. But not now. I understood immediately that I couldn't push the Creature out there anymore.

"Some people are good at being their public image and some people even enjoy it. I'm not one of those. When I'm playing a part, I know what to do. I get into my role. But if no one gives me a part, the worst thing you can say to me is 'Be yourself.'

"I've never known how to split myself and be two-faced. I can put my whole heart into the Creature, but that took a lot of effort, and if I could, afterward, I'd flee back to my home in New York City or the family house in Connecticut, where I could just be myself. I don't have anyone there I have to perform for and my family is used to me the way I am. Do you know the philosophy of how our family has always coexisted? 'Live and let live.'

"A really good script won't be coming my way anymore. I'm too old. There might be a bit part of quality for an old lady, but I don't want to do that. And if, by some miracle, a wonderful part turned up I truly liked, I would say no. I could no longer do justice to it."

I asked her, "How do you feel about the Creature? Do you like her?"

"Oh, yes. Very much. Very, very much.

"I'm not the Creature, but, after all, I did create her, only now I just don't have the energy to *be* her, too. So now, I'm only me, with a small m.

"I no longer have the energy to be Katharine Hepburn. I can't push the Creature out there anymore.

"If you have a place to hide, you don't have to be a celebrity all of the time. Fenwick was always my place to hide. My celebrity and I can be separate. Katharine Hepburn is safely frozen on the screen, so she is taken care of.

"I think I'll be Kathy again."

# Katharine Hepburn's Feature Films

### A Bill of Divorcement (1932)

Director: George Cukor. Cast: John Barrymore, Billie Burke, David Manners, Henry Stephenson. RKO.

### Christopher Strong (1933)

Director: Dorothy Arzner. Cast: Colin Clive, Billie Burke, Helen Chandler, Ralph Forbes. RKO.

### Morning Glory (1933)

Director: Lowell Sherman. Cast: Douglas Fairbanks, Jr., Adolphe Menjou, Mary Duncan, C. Aubrey Smith. RKO.

## Little Women (1933)

Director: George Cukor. Cast: Joan Bennett, Paul Lukas, Edna May Oliver, Jean Parker, Frances Dee, Spring Byington. RKO.

## Spitfire (1934)

Director: John Cromwell. Cast: Robert Young, Ralph Bellamy, Martha Sleeper, Louis Mason. RKO.

## The Little Minister (1934)

Director: Richard Wallace. Cast: John Beal, Alan Hale, Donald Crisp, Lumsden Hare. RKO.

## Break of Hearts (1935)

Director: Philip Moeller. Cast: Charles Boyer, John Beal, Jean Hersholt, Sam Hardy. RKO.

## Alice Adams (1935)

Director: George Stevens. Cast: Fred MacMurray, Fred Stone, Evelyn Venable, Frank Albertson. RKO.

## Sylvia Scarlett (1936)

Director: George Cukor. Cast: Cary Grant, Brian Aherne, Edmund Gwenn, Natalie Paley. RKO.

## Mary of Scotland (1936)

Director: John Ford. Cast: Fredric March, Florence Eldridge, Douglas Walton, John Carradine. RKO.

## A Woman Rebels (1936)

Director: Mark Sandrich. Cast: Herbert Marshall, Elizabeth Allan, Donald Crisp, David Manners. RKO.

## Quality Street (1937)

Director: George Stevens. Cast: Franchot Tone, Fay Bainter, Eric Blore, Cora Witherspoon. RKO.

## Stage Door (1937)

Director: Gregory La Cava. Cast: Ginger Rogers, Adolphe Menjou, Gail Patrick, Constance Collier. RKO.

## Bringing Up Baby (1938)

Director: Howard Hawks. Cast: Cary Grant, Charles Ruggles, May Robson, Walter Catlett, Virginia Walker. RKO.

## Holiday (1938)

Director: George Cukor. Cast: Cary Grant, Doris Nolan, Lew Ayres, Edward Everett Horton. Columbia.

## The Philadelphia Story (1940)

Director: George Cukor. Cast: Cary Grant, James Stewart, Ruth Hussey, John Howard. M-G-M.

## Woman of the Year (1942)

Director: George Stevens. Cast: Spencer Tracy, Fay Bainter, Reginald Owen, Minor Watson. M-G-M.

## Keeper of the Flame (1942)

Director: George Cukor. Cast: Spencer Tracy, Richard Whorf, Margaret Wycherly, Donald Meek. M-G-M.

## Stage Door Canteen (1943)

Director: Frank Borzage. Cast: Cheryl Walker, William Terry, Marjorie Riordan, Lon McCallister. United Artists.

## Dragon Seed (1944)

Directors: Jack Conway and Harold S. Bucquet. Cast: Walter Huston, Aline MacMahon, Akim Tamiroff, Turhan Bey. M-G-M.

## Without Love (1945)

Director: Harold S. Bucquet. Cast: Spencer Tracy, Lucille Ball, Keenan Wynn, Carl Esmond, Patricia Morison. M-G-M.

## Undercurrent (1946)

Director: Vincente Minnelli. Cast: Robert Taylor, Robert Mitchum, Edmund Gwenn, Marjorie Main. M-G-M.

## The Sea of Grass (1947)

Director: Elia Kazan. Cast: Spencer Tracy, Robert Walker, Melvyn Douglas, Phyllis Thaxter. M-G-M.

## Song of Love (1947)

Director: Clarence Brown. Cast: Paul Henreid, Robert Walker, Henry Daniell, Leo G. Carroll, Konstantin Shayne. M-G-M.

## State of the Union (1948)

Director: Frank Capra. Cast: Spencer Tracy, Van Johnson, Angela Lansbury, Adolphe Menjou. M-G-M.

## Adam's Rib (1949)

Director: George Cukor. Cast: Spencer Tracy, Judy Holliday, Tom Ewell, David Wayne. M-G-M.

## The African Queen (1951)

Director: John Huston. Cast: Humphrey Bogart, Robert Morley, Peter Bull, Theodore Bikel. United Artists.

## Pat and Mike (1952)

Director: George Cukor. Cast: Spencer Tracy, William Ching, Sammy White, Aldo Ray, George Mathews, Loring Smith, Charles Bronson (billed as Charles Buchinski). M-G-M.

## Summertime (1955)

Director: David Lean. Cast: Rossano Brazzi, Isa Miranda, Darren McGavin, Mari Aldon. United Artists.

## The Rainmaker (1956)

Director: Joseph Anthony. Cast: Burt Lancaster, Wendell Corey, Lloyd Bridges, Cameron Prud'homme, Earl Holliman. Paramount.

## The Iron Petticoat (1956)

Director: Ralph Thomas. Cast: Bob Hope, James Robertson Justice, Robert Helpmann, David Kossoff. M-G-M.

## Desk Set (1957)

Director: Walter Lang. Cast: Spencer Tracy, Gig Young, Joan Blondell, Dina Merrill. Twentieth Century-Fox.

## Suddenly, Last Summer (1959)

Director: Joseph L. Mankiewicz. Cast: Elizabeth Taylor, Montgomery Clift, Albert Dekker, Mercedes McCambridge. Columbia.

## Long Day's Journey into Night (1962)

Director: Sidney Lumet. Cast: Ralph Richardson, Jason Robards, Jr., Dean Stockwell, Jeanne Barr. Embassy.

## Guess Who's Coming to Dinner (1967)

Director: Stanley Kramer. Cast: Spencer Tracy, Sidney Poitier, Katharine Houghton, Cecil Kellaway. Columbia.

## The Lion in Winter (1968)

Director: Anthony Harvey. Cast: Peter O'Toole, Jane Merrow, Timothy Dalton, Anthony Hopkins. AVCO Embassy.

## The Madwoman of Chaillot (1969)

Director: Bryan Forbes. Cast: Giulietta Masina, Charles Boyer, Yul Brynner, Richard Chamberlain, Edith Evans, Danny Kaye. Warner Brothers/Seven Arts.

## The Trojan Women (1971)

Director: Michael Cacoyannis. Cast: Vanessa Redgrave, Geneviève Bujold, Irene Papas, Patrick Magee. Cinerama.

## A Delicate Balance (1973)

Director: Tony Richardson. Cast: Paul Scofield, Lee Remick, Kate Reid, Joseph Cotten, Betsy Blair. American Film Theatre.

## Rooster Cogburn (1975)

Director: Stuart Millar. Cast: John Wayne, Anthony Zerbe, Richard Jordan, John McIntire. Universal.

## Olly Olly Oxen Free (1978)

Director: Richard A. Colla. Cast: Kevin McKenzie, Dennis Dimster, Peter Kilman, Jayne Marie Mansfield. Sanrio Communications.

## On Golden Pond (1981)

Director: Mark Rydell. Cast: Henry Fonda, Jane Fonda, Doug McKeon, Dabney Coleman. Universal.

## The Ultimate Solution of Grace Quigley (1985)

Director: Anthony Harvey. Cast: Nick Nolte, Elizabeth Wilson, Chip Zien, William Duell. Cannon.

## Love Affair (1994)

Director: Glenn Gordon Caron. Cast: Warren Beatty, Annette Bening, Garry Shandling, Pierce Brosnan. Warner Brothers.

# Katharine Hepburn's Television Films

## The Glass Menagerie (1973)

Director: Anthony Harvey. Cast: Joanna Miles, Sam Waterston, Michael Moriarty. ABC.

## Love Among the Ruins (1975)

Director: George Cukor. Cast: Laurence Olivier, Colin Blakely, Richard Pearson, Joan Sims. ABC.

## The Corn Is Green (1979)

Director: George Cukor. Cast: Ian Saynor, Bill Fraser, Patricia Hayes, Anna Massey. CBS.

## Mrs. Delafield Wants to Marry (1986)

Director: George Schaefer. Cast: Harold Gould, Denholm Elliott, Brenda Forbes, David Ogden Stiers. CBS.

## Laura Lansing Slept Here (1988)

Director: George Schaefer. Cast: Lee Richardson, Joel Higgins, Karen Austin, Schuyler Grant. NBC.

## The Man Upstairs (1992)

Director: George Schaefer. Cast: Ryan O'Neal, Henry Beckman, Helena Carroll, Brenda Forbes. CBS.

## This Can't Be Love (1994)

Director: Anthony Harvey. Cast: Anthony Quinn, Jason Bateman, Jami Gertz, Maxine Miller. CBS.

## One Christmas (1994)

Director: Tony Bill. Cast: Henry Winkler, Swoosie Kurtz, T. J. Lowther, Tonea Stewart. NBC.

# Index

# INDEX

# INDEX

# INDEX

# INDEX